T0320559

MEMORY PERFORMANCE OF PROLOG ARCHITECTURES

THE KLUWER INTERNATIONAL SERIES
IN ENGINEERING AND COMPUTER SCIENCE

FRONTIERS IN LOGIC PROGRAMMING ARCHITECTURE
AND MACHINE DESIGN

Consulting Editor

Doug DeGroot

'FRONTIERS IN LOGIC PROGRAMMING ARCHITECTURE AND MACHINE DESIGN' is a unique collection of books describing closely related research subjects at the forefront of logic programming architecture and machine design. Initially, the collection will consist of the following books:

PARALLEL EXECUTION OF LOGIC PROGRAMS
by John Conery

A HIGH PERFORMANCE ARCHITECTURE FOR PROLOG
by T. P. Dobry

INDEPENDENT 'AND' - PARALLEL PROLOG
AND ITS ARCHITECTURE
by Manuel Hermenegildo

MEMORY PERFORMANCE OF PROLOG ARCHITECTURES
by Evan Tick

John Conery's seminal work at the University of California at Irvine presented the first model for the parallel interpretation of logic programs called the AND/OR Process Model. The same year Conery's work was published , John Warren wrote a landmark paper describing an abstract sequential architecture for Prolog. These two works spawned research efforts throughout the world. One of the largest of these was led by T. P. Dobry at the University of California at Berkeley whose efforts resulted in the design of the Programmed Logic Machine which was the first high-performance Prolog engine. At the same time, at the University of Texas at Austin, Manuel Hermenegildo designed a truly efficient parallel execution model and multiprocessor architecture for logic programming which was the first practical realization of Conery's framework. At Stanford University, Evan Tick designed and measured memory organizations suitable for both Warren's sequential and Hermenegildo's parallel architectures.

This collection of books is designed to provide up-to-date information on Logic Programming Architecture and Machine Design in a timely fashion to researchers and students in the most timely manner possible.

MEMORY PERFORMANCE OF PROLOG ARCHITECTURES

by

Evan Tick

Stanford University

KLUWER ACADEMIC PUBLISHERS
Boston/Dordrecht/Lancaster

Distributors for North America:
Kluwer Academic Publishers
101 Philip Drive
Assinippi Park
Norwell, Massachusetts 02061 USA

Distributors for the UK and Ireland:
Kluwer Academic Publishers
MTP Press Limited
Falcon House, Queen Square
Lancaster LAI IRN, UNITED KINGDOM

Distributors for all other countries:
Kluwer Academic Publishers Group
Distribution Centre
Post Office Box 322
3300 AH Dordrecht, THE NETHERLANDS

Library of Congress Cataloging-in-Publication Data

Tick, Evan, 1959–
    Memory performance of prolog architectures / by Evan Tick.
       p. cm. — (The Kluwer international series in engineering and
computer science ; SECS 40. Frontiers in logic programming
architecture and machine design)
  Bibliography: p.
  Includes index.
  ISBN 0-89838-254-8
  1. Prolog (Computer program language)   2. Computer architecture.
I. Title.   II. Series: Kluwer international series in engineering
and computer science ; SECS 40.   III. Series: Kluwer international
series in engineering and computer science.   Frontiers in logic
programming architecture and machine design.
QA76.73.P76T53   1987   87-26283
005.1—dc19   CIP

For R.K.

Contents

List of Figures

List of Tables

Preface

One suspects that the people who use computers for their livelihood are growing more "sophisticated" as the field of computer science evolves. This view might be defended by the expanding use of languages such as C and Lisp in contrast to the languages such as FORTRAN and COBOL. This hypothesis is false however — computer languages are not like natural languages where successive generations stick with the language of their ancestors. Computer programmers do *not* grow more sophisticated — programmers simply take the time to muddle through the increasingly complex language semantics in an attempt to write useful programs. Of course, these programmers are "sophisticated" in the same sense as are hackers of MockLisp, PostScript, and Tex — highly specialized and tedious languages. It is quite frustrating how this myth of sophistication is propagated by some industries, universities, and government agencies. When I was an undergraduate at MIT, I distinctly remember the convoluted questions on exams concerning dynamic scoping in Lisp — the emphasis was placed solely on a "hacker's" view of computation, i.e., the control and manipulation of storage cells. No consideration was given to the *logical* structure of programs. Within the past five years, Ada and Common Lisp have become programming language standards, despite their complexity (note that dynamic scoping was dropped even from Common Lisp). Of course, most industries' selection of programming languages are primarily driven by the requirement for compatibility (with previous software) and performance. To achieve performance, C and similar languages are based on the functionality of the underlying host machine. As a result, they have no *logical* structure corresponding to the application.

This socalled trend toward "sophistication" belies a deep-seated problem: computers are simply becoming more difficult to program (contrastingly, the "use" of computers, i.e., pressing buttons, is becoming *easier*, e.g., with the Macintosh). There is nothing wrong with expanding a language to make it more powerful, so long as the expansion is consistent with the basic structure of the language. A language can be extended in directions away from the fundamental basis, if it is ensured that the renegade extensions will very rarely be used, and so do not confuse the programmer. For example, Lisp has purposefully evolved contrary to this view, as a "ball of mud." In general, implementation issues are a mystery to most programmers (and some implementors), forcing the use of the dirtiest parts of a language in an attempt to gain performance. Often these attempts have no effect or backfire, but they always destroy the logic of a program. In addition, the parallelization of such languages, in an effort to increase performance on multiprocessors, often entails the creation of additional constructs, such as a Future (in Multi-Lisp) or Parallel-Let (in QLisp), with complex semantics which are difficult to use effectively and safely.

Computer programming can benefit from clean, logical program semantics because such semantics facilitate understanding, hence ease of debugging, program modification and high-performance implementation (further arguments can be given concerning program verification, etc.). Logic programming languages are a family of programming languages based on the first-order predicate logic, and manage to retain a semblance of declarative semantics. Although logic programming languages have not yet achieved the ideal plateau of *complete* declarativity, for the most part, the semantics, e.g., of NU-Prolog and CLP($\mathfrak{R}$), are so easy to understand that complex programs can be built with little effort. Recently Prolog has been successfully implemented on multiprocessors, with no need to change its logical semantics. Even within the logic programming community, however, the conflict between performance and clarity (logical interpretation) rages in the arena of parallel implementations. Languages such as GHC and CP sacrifice ease of programming to facilitate implementations on multiprocessors.

This book is concerned with the design and performance of computer architectures, i.e., instruction sets and storage models, for logic programming languages. This book is concerned with the Prolog language because it is commonly used and is representative of a large number of other logic programming languages. Few comments are given as to the relative merits of Prolog as compared to other logic programming languages, or functional languages — that will require an entire other book. Logic programming languages, although far from perfect, are more useable and offer more cost-efficient multiprocessor implementations than other symbolic programming paradigms. In the future, Prolog will no doubt be extended in many areas, e.g., to include efficient and logical definitions of arrays and modules. Because of the strong logical foundation, ease of programming will be retained and parallel implementations will abound.

Acknowledgements

Many people deserve acknowledgement for helping me to write this book. Professors Michael Flynn and Stephen Lundstrom of Stanford University have generously shared their knowledge and experience in supporting my research. I am also thankful for the encouragement and assistance of Susan Gere, Leslie Tick, and the colleagues with whom I have worked most closely: Fung Fung Lee, Bill Lynch, Hans Mulder, and Andrew Zimmerman.

At Quintas I have been fortunate to work in an challenging environment created by Lawrence Byrd, William Kornfeld and David H. D. Warren, where many fresh ideas were generated (and stale ones discarded). It has also been a rewarding experience and a great pleasure to work with David Bowen, Tim Lindholm, Brendan McCarthy, Richard O'Keefe, Fernando Pereira, and David Znidarsic.

The "WAM" and "PWAM" architectures discussed in this book are entirely the respective works of David H. D. Warren and Manuel Hermenegildo, to whom both I am greatly indebted. Bill Lynch helped write the WAM emulator described in Chapter 3. Hans Mulder supplied and helped analyze the Pascal data. Philip Bitar, of the University of California at Berkeley, patiently explained cache coherency to me. Manuel Hermenegildo and Richard Warren, of the Microelectronics and computer Technology Corporation (MCC), supplied and helped analyze the PWAM multiprocessor traces. This book was most strengthened by numerous discussions with Fung Fung, Manuel, and Tim.

MEMORY PERFORMANCE OF PROLOG ARCHITECTURES

1 Introduction

The main reason that current computer applications in symbolic processing fail to meet speed constraints on current machines is the gap between the applications and the languages and architectures in which they are implemented. Applications such as natural language understanding and symbolic equation solving, as compared with conventional applications such as numerical modeling and simulation, are further removed from conventional procedural/functional languages such as Pascal and Lisp and their corresponding numeric/scientific processor architectures. This is because these ambitious new applications must, in a sense, be written as *meta-level interpreters*. A meta-level interpreter is a program which performs additional levels of interpretation to implement features not present in the host language, e.g., nondeterminate execution for parsing or a reduction mechanism for theorem proving.

Any approach to improving program performance involves implementing these applications with appropriate languages and designing efficient architectures that either directly correspond to these languages or support interpretation of these features. Features which previously required meta-interpretation are now included in the instruction set and are implemented directly in the architecture.

This book presents a study of abstract machine architectures for Prolog, a well-known *logic programming language*. Logic programming is a programming paradigm constructed from the abstract model of first order logic. Prolog is representative of that class of languages with powerful enough functionality to facilitate the development of advanced applications. Prolog is used primarily for artificial intelligence and database applications, as well as general applications such as compiler writing. Prolog differs from procedural languages, such as Pascal and Lisp, in that it is applicative (variables can be bound at most once in an execution path), nondeterminate (alternate paths are executed in an attempt to create a consistent set of variable bindings), and uses unification (a type of pattern matching) as the primary operation. Thus, means to efficient Prolog execution will likely differ from those of conventional languages.

As the gap between language and architecture decreases, fewer instructions are executed within the program. These instructions do more work and may therefore be more difficult to implement. In most high-level-language-architecture machines, the complexity of the instruction set forces a microcoded implementation. An alternative is to implement the abstract machine interpretively on a lower-level host machine. The selection of the most cost-effective implementation strategy depends on many considerations — technology, instruction set compatibility, design effort, etc. Regardless of the relative weight of each consideration, any design approach requires an understanding of the dynamic Prolog program behavior, i.e., the characteristics of the abstract machine corresponding to Prolog. This book supplies this information.

The problem of increasing Prolog execution speed is approached from the vantage point of memory design. High-speed processors are ultimately limited by memory bandwidth and architectures that require less bandwidth have greater potential for high performance. The memory-referencing characteristics of well-designed abstract machines are minimal in the sense that a host which directly implements the abstract machine instructions as atomic actions will make fewer memory references than other types of hosts. No matter what the host, however, the memory-referencing characteristics measured in this book are, for the most part, applicable.

A family of *canonical* Prolog architectures with advantageous bandwidth requirements is defined in close correspondence to the semantics of Prolog. The Warren Abstract Machine (WAM) architecture [96], used for memory design throughout the book, is a member of this family. Measurements of the Prolog Canonical Interpretive Form (CIF) indicate upper memory-performance bounds afforded by "ideal" attributes (which go beyond the WAM).

High-speed uniprocessor performance is necessary, even within a multiprocessor, because not all types of parallelism exist or can be exploited in all applications. Within a shared memory multiprocessor, local processor memories are necessary to reduce bandwidth and allow undegraded execution of sequential code. The main portion of the book concerns modeling and analysis of two-level memory hierarchies for sequential and parallel Prolog architectures. A trace-driven simulator is used to measure local memories. Sequential Prolog programs are compiled into the WAM instruction set and emulated, producing a memory-address-trace file. Restricted AND-Parallel (RAP) Prolog programs [34] are compiled into the PWAM instruction set [35] and similarly emulated, assuming a shared memory multiprocessor with a small number of tightly-coupled high-performance processing elements. Main memories are evaluated with asymptotic queueing models.

This book synthesizes logic programming architecture design with the lessons learned from procedural programming architecture design and memory organization. The field of logic programming machine design is new. It is therefore not surprising that little has been published in the area of logic programming machine performance. The vast store of knowledge and folklore available about procedural language architectures and machines is absent for logic programming languages. This book helps fill this gap.

In this book, successive refinements of models of abstraction allow the measurement of the expected memory performance of both sequential and parallel logic programming languages on host processors. The initial level of abstraction is the Prolog source language, leading to canonical interpretive forms (CIFs) for Prolog. These canonical architectures are refined into realizable architectures (Direct Correspondence Architectures — DCAs), such as the WAM and PWAM. Simulations of these architectures executing on a two-level memory model produce memory bandwidth requirement statistics. Refinement of the simple two-level memory model into a queueing model allows the measurement of time dependent statistics, such as processor performance degradation.

At the various levels of abstraction, important results are uncovered. At the architecture level, it is shown that traditional CIF models can be constrained, at little cost in performance, to CIFs more suitable for current technology hosts. The WAM can be viewed as a DCA defined from such a constrained CIF. At the memory simulation level, shallow backtracking is shown to be the primary source of the WAM bandwidth requirement. The analysis of the efficiency of several memory organizations at reducing the bandwidth requirement indicates that caches offer the best memory performance — a result similar to that found for procedural language processors [2]. Less costly memory organizations also perform quite well, a result of the WAM's high locality. At the queueing analysis level, PWAM is shown to exploit parallelism, on a tightly-coupled shared memory multiprocessor, with little overhead with respect to the WAM. It is shown, however, that even for a limited number (eight) of high-performance processing elements, bus capacity is the critical performance bottleneck. This is not to say that shared memory multiprocessors are an inferior design — on the contrary, it is shown that with emerging bus technology and an interleaved shared memory, this type of limited multiprocessor organization can achieve significant speed-ups exploiting Restricted-AND Parallelism alone.

The primary contribution of this book is the successive refinement of architectures and performance models for logic programming languages, resulting in an accurate description of their dynamic memory-referencing behaviors. A summary of the detailed contributions of the book follows.

- A family of canonical architectures, called CIFs, closely corresponding to Prolog, are described. Measurements of the CIFs are presented, indicating the memory-performance bounds afforded by attributes such as tight instruction-encoding, split-stacks and ideal indexing.

- The memory-referencing characteristics of realistic Prolog programs are determined. Evidence is presented indicating that shallow backtracking is the primary memory-performance bottleneck of environment stacking Prolog architectures.

- Local memories which reduce performance bottlenecks, for various costs, are designed and analyzed. These memories include choice point buffers, stack buffers, copyback data caches, "smart" copyback data caches, instruction buffers, and instruction caches.

- Local memories which solve shared memory multiprocessor consistency problems, specifically for the Restricted AND-Parallel Prolog architecture PWAM, are designed and analyzed. These memories include broadcast, hybrid, and write-through coherent caches. The hybrid cache is a new combination of write-through and write-broadcast cache designs, that takes advantage of RAP-Prolog attributes to guarantee consistency with low overheads and inexpensive hardware.

- Interleaved main memories, for both sequential and parallel architectures, are analyzed with queueing model formulations of the local memories.

In the remainder of this chapter, Prolog is first introduced with examples. Arguments are then given for studying high-level Prolog architectures, as opposed to other alternatives. Lastly, previous work in the fields of architecture design, benchmarking, and memory organization of logic programming languages and machines is reviewed.

1.1. What is Prolog?

Prolog is the first practical logic programming language, designed by Colmerauer in 1973 [70], with its theoretical groundwork laid by Kowalski in 1974 [44]. Prolog is the primary representative of logic programming languages — most other logic programming languages are derivatives of the Prolog computation model. To the first order, results of Prolog execution measurements can be extended to Prolog-like languages and logic programming languages in general.

```
isotree(void,void).
isotree(tree(X,Left1,Right1),
        tree(X,Left2,Right2)) :-
     isotree(Left1,Left2),
     isotree(Right1,Right2).
isotree(tree(X,Left1,Right1),
        tree(X,Left2,Right2)) :-
     isotree(Left1,Right2),
     isotree(Right1,Left2).
```

Figure 1-1: Prolog Program Example: isotree/2

Prolog programs and data are composed of *terms*. A term is either a *simple term* or a *compound term* (also called a *complex term* or *structure*). A simple term is either a *constant* or a *variable*. A structure consists of a *functor* and *arguments*. The functor is composed of a *name* and *arity* (this is usually written as *name/arity*). The name is the symbolic identifier of the structure, the arity is the number of arguments, and the arguments themselves are terms. An example of a structure is `tree(1,void,Subtree)`, with functor `tree/3`. A constant is a structure with zero arity. This may be a number or an atomic identifier. Examples of constants are 1 and `void`. A (logical) variable is an object which can be bound (only once) to another term. Prolog uses a capitalized identifier to represent a variable, e.g., `Subtree`.

A Prolog *program* consists of collections of *clauses* known as *procedures*. A clause is a term consisting of a *head* and a *body*. The head contains the formal parameters of the procedure definition. The body consists of a (possibly empty) set of *goals*. A goal is a procedure invocation with its corresponding passed parameters. A procedure is uniquely specified by the name and arity of the head of each of its clauses. The arity of a procedure represents the (fixed) number of arguments it must be passed when invoked.

Figure 1-1 illustrates a program (from [78]) which determines if two trees are isomorphic. The program consists of a single recursive procedure, `isotree/2`, which has three clauses. The first clause has an empty body and is called a *unit clause* or *fact*. The second two clauses are called *conjunctive clauses*, *non-unit clauses*, or *rules* because they define relations between facts and/or other rules. A third necessary program construct is a *query*, e.g.,

```
?- isotree(tree(1,tree(2,void,void),
           tree(3,void,void)),X).
```

In its simplest form, a query is a procedure invocation with external input, i.e., a request to execute a program with given data.

Prolog semantics can be viewed declaratively or procedurally. The *declarative view* treats a procedure as a logical disjunction of its clauses and a clause as a logical conjunction of its goals. This view benefits programmers. Variables in queries are existentially quantified. For instance, the query given above is read: "Does there *exist* a tree **X** such that the tree represented pictorially below is isomorphic to it?"

Variables appearing in the head of a rule are universally quantified. Variables appearing only in the body of a rule are existentially quantified. For instance, the second clause of **isotree/2** has an informal declarative reading: "*Any* two trees are isomorphic if they both have the same value and the left subtree of one is isomorphic to the left subtree of the other and the right subtree of one is isomorphic to the right subtree of the other."

The *procedural view* treats a procedure as an ordered sequence of entry points (clauses) which must be executed until one succeeds. A clause is treated as an ordered sequence of procedure calls (goals), all of which must be executed for success. Upon failure of any goal, the computation is backed up to the entry of the most recently invoked procedure with unattempted clauses. That procedure is re-entered at its next clause and the computation continues. The main implementation distinction between Prolog and procedural languages is that Prolog programs *backtrack* in this manner.

The procedural semantics are derived from the observation that to solve an existential query Q with a universal fact P, one finds a *common instance C*, i.e., two *substitutions*, τ_1 and τ_2, such that $C = P\tau_1 = Q\tau_2$. There are two deduction rules in effect here: *generalization* — an existential query is a logical consequence of an instance of that query, and *instantiation* — an instance of a universally quantified fact is a logical consequence of that fact. The combination of these rules is called *resolution*.

Generalizing, the query Q is a logical consequence of program P with the universal rule $A :- B_1, B_2, ... B_n$, if A and Q have a common instance and B_1, B_2,... B_n are also logical consequences of P. This is called *Horn clause resolution*, developed by Robinson [66]. In other words, a goal is executed by attempting resolution with the heads of the clauses of the procedure of the same name and arity as the goal. Successful resolution involves successfully *unifying* each goal argument to each corresponding head argument. Unification finds a *most general* common instance of its input terms to avoid specializing the proof more than necessary.

If the goal cannot match (unify with) any clause of its associated procedure, the goal fails. When the goal matches a clause and it can be determined that no other clauses can match, it is called *determinate execution*. When the goal matches a clause and other (untried) clauses can possibly also match, it is called *nondeterminate execution*.

The *scope* of a variable is a clause; therefore the occurrences of **X** in the second and third clauses of isotree/2 in Figure 1-1 are unrelated. The goal isotree(tree(X,void),void) can successfully resolve with the heads of either the second or third clauses. Note again that the scopes of the **X** in the goal isotree(tree(X,void),void) and the **X** in the clause heads are independent, and therefore these two variables are unique and can be bound to distinct objects. The goal isotree(void,void) can match only the first clause and the goal isotree(X,Y) can match any clause.

For convenience and efficiency, Prolog has been given additional support for:

- **lists** — a list, which is a structure with functor ./2, is given a special syntax in Prolog. The list '.'(X,Y) can be written as [X|Y]. A list of two objects, '.'(1,'.'(2,[])) can be written as [1,2]. Note that [] is a special constant representing nil (end-of-list). In most tagged Prolog architectures, including the ones considered in this book, the list data type is given a unique tag.

- **built-ins** — many procedures are predefined in Prolog. The most frequently used of these include arithmetic, construction and destruction of terms, conditional tests for types of terms, and strict equality (wherein no unification is allowed to take place).

- **cut** — this is an extra-logical control feature, represented by "!", used to prevent undesired backtracking over the clauses in a procedure. As a goal in a clause of a procedure, cut always succeeds, causing a side effect of disallowing subsequent clauses of that procedure to be tried in the event of backtracking.

As another example, Figure 1-2 shows the most commonly executed Prolog procedure in the QC1 benchmark measured later in this book. The flattenCode/3 procedure flattens a binary tree structure into a list removing empty sequences represented by the atom void, e.g., the query

```
?- flattenCode((1,(2,3,void,(4,5))),X,[]).
```

instantiates **X** to the list [1,2,3,4,5]. Read procedurally, flattenCode/3 recursively processes the left and right branches of a subtree, using a *difference list* (see [78, p. 239]) to collect the resulting leaves. The second and third arguments of the procedure represent the difference list as an answer list and the tail of the answer list, facilitating efficient concatenation of the resulting sublists from the left and right branches. This method of concatenation is illustrated in the second clause, where the answer is composed by instantiating the tail of the first sequence's flattened list, Code1, to the second sequence's flattened list.

```
flattenCode(void,Code,Code)  :- !.
flattenCode((Seq1,Seq2),Code0,Code)  :- !,
    flattenCode(Seq1,Code0,Code1),
    flattenCode(Seq2,Code1,Code).
flattenCode(Instr,[Instr|Code],Code).
```

Figure 1-2: Prolog Program Example: flattenCode/3

Read declaratively, `flattenCode/3` specifies three rules concerning flattening. The result of flattening an empty sequence is an empty difference list. The result of flattening a binary tree, (`Seq1,Seq2`), is `Code0` (with tail `Code`), if flattening the left subtree, `Seq1`, results in `Code0` (with tail `Code1`) and flattening the right subtree, `Seq2`, results in `Code1` (with tail `Code`). The result of flattening anything else, `Instr`, is a list with head `Instr` and tail `Code`.

1.2. Why Prolog?

This book discusses how to make Prolog programs execute quickly. In this section the selection of Prolog as a target language, and a high-level Prolog architecture as a target instruction set, are justified. Three arguments are given: for designing complex instruction architectures over reduced instruction architectures, for analyzing Prolog instead of a committed-choice nondeterminism logic programming language, and for choosing Prolog over Lisp, a popular functional language.

1.2.1. Reduced Instruction Set Architectures

An alternative approach to increasing the execution speed of logic programs is to translate the high-level architecture into a lower-level target or *host* instruction set. For instance this host can be a *reduced instruction set computer* (RISC) [63, 61, 81]. The goal of reduced instruction set machines is to simplify the instruction set, allowing more effective compiler optimizations and streamlined hardware. For the most part, results of this book are applicable for *any* host. Exceptions are results concerning instruction referencing characteristics. In the case of instructions, a microcode implementation of a high-level architecture cannot be easily compared to a reduced instruction set architecture.

Reduced instruction set architectures were originally designed for current hardware technology, procedural languages and general purpose applications. It is argued here that such architectures are not necessarily as well-suited to advanced hardware technology and symbolic processing applications, as are high-level instruction set architectures. First instruction referencing, then data referencing characteristics are considered.

Given advanced (denser) hardware, the benefit of a reduced instruction set and a corresponding necessarily large instruction cache is not clearly superior to a complex instruction set and a corresponding necessarily large micro-store. Prolog code, when compiled into a reduced instruction set, expands to a size incompatible with current on-chip (reduced instruction set machine) instruction caches. Borriello et al. [8] report that to achieve similar miss ratios, SPUR, a reduced instruction set microprocessor [81], requires significantly larger caches than would the PLM, a microcoded complex instruction set machine [21].

General purpose applications and procedural languages have certain attributes, such as high locality, not shared by symbolic processing applications and applicative languages. For example, in this book (Section 4.2.6), it is found that for a 1024 word copyback data cache (with a four word line size), typical Prolog programs display four times the traffic ratios of typical Pascal programs. Most reduced instruction set machines rely on high locality to allow their pipelines to operate efficiently. The specialization of the architecture, to incorporate attributes such as tags (e.g., SPUR) and shadow registers (e.g., Pegasus [71]), is necessary to reduce the data bandwidth requirement.

The critical resource is the *available on/off chip bandwidth*. The gap between Prolog and conventional RISC architectures is so great as to make the available chip bandwidth intolerable. Complex instruction set architectures, specialized for Prolog, reduce the gap to a reasonable level, thereby reducing the bandwidth requirement.

These arguments aside, assume that a reduced instruction set host can be made to execute Prolog programs faster than a microcoded implementation of a high-level architecture. Raw speed of compiled, optimized programs does not in itself solve the *software crisis*. The software crisis refers to the growing complexity and cost of *developing* applications. High-level architectures allow the use of relatively simple (and therefore fast) compilers. In addition, decompilation for symbolic debugging is facilitated by high-level architectures. The application development cycle involves multiple recompilations, as well as debugging of code. Both of these activities are supported by a single high-level architecture host. Although two different machines can be used for the purposes of application development and delivery, this is not a reasonable solution except for the largest commercial applications.

1.2.2. Parallel Logic Programming Languages

Parallel logic programming languages are of considerable interest for attaining high performance on future multiprocessors. Gupta et al. [33] and others have shown, however, that unlimited parallelism does not exist in many application programs. Therefore, as with conventional multiprocessors, one performance bottleneck will be the speed of sequential execution of a single processing element.

Many parallel logic programming languages are based on *committed-choice nondeterminism*, wherein once a clause head (and an extension to the head, called the *guard*, consisting of simple goals) succeeds, the procedure commits to that clause and will not backtrack. This weakening of the logic programming paradigm once again increases the gap between the application and language. In addition, the storage models required by committed-choice languages cannot be implemented as efficiently on sequential processors as sequential languages, such as Prolog. Committed-choice-language architectures are based on the hypothesis that the *amount* of parallelism uncovered by the language will outweigh any inefficiencies incurred in single processor execution.

There is no doubt that multiprocessor execution is of the *utmost importance* in increasing logic programming performance. The view taken in this book is in agreement with Butler et al. [11], Hermenegildo [35], and others, who propose parallel architectures for Prolog built around an efficient *sequential* architecture, i.e., storage model. These architectures are based on the hypothesis that the efficiency of single processor execution outweighs the restricted amount of parallelism uncovered by the language. Local and shared memory design and modeling for one such parallel architecture are presented in this book.

1.2.3. Lisp

Lisp, a symbolic language based on function application [51, 77], is both more popular and more mature than Prolog. Studies of Lisp architecture performance have been conducted [29] and Lisp machines built (e.g., Symbolics 3600 [80], SPUR [81]). There are two primary deficiencies with Lisp as

program	Sun Common Lisp†	Quintus Prolog‡	Lisp:Prolog
Boyer	15.08 sec	25.50 sec	0.59
Deriv	4.24 sec	6.30 sec	0.67
Puzzle	8.44 sec	2.43 sec	3.47
Tak	0.47 sec	4.59 sec	0.10

† native code
‡ emulated byte-code

Table 1-1: Lisp vs. Prolog: Sun-3/160 Comparison

compared with Prolog — both stemming from the evolution of Lisp (e.g., to Common Lisp). Lisp programs, as written by most programmers (see, for instance, the benchmarks presented in Gabriel [29]), have no declarative reading, and are not applicative. The first deficiency reduces the reliability, readability and extensibility of Lisp programs. The second deficiency reduces the ability to parallelize a Lisp program, either automatically or by the programmer. Although these arguments are common in the literature, here a third argument is introduced.

It is argued below, with evidence presented in Tick [83], that as a result of increased functionality (over Lisp), Prolog holds more promise than Lisp for *future* high-speed processors. Studies of Prolog performance as compared with Lisp [59, 92] have been favorable to Prolog. In Tick [83] evidence is given that Prolog has greater *semantic content* than Lisp. Two results are given based on the assumption that memory bandwidth is the ultimate performance measure.

The first result is that Lisp is better mapped onto current machines than Prolog. This is tenuously supported by comparisons between commercially available Lisp and Prolog systems, executing a subset of the Gabriel benchmarks as shown in Table 1-1. Although "apples vs. oranges," comparing these implementations serve to indicate that Lisp runs faster than Prolog on hardware with a limited number of state registers. Whether Prolog can reach Lisp performance on conventional machines is primarily dependent on how much of the Prolog state can be contained in available state registers, and if Prolog compilers of the same level of sophistication as those used for Lisp can be built.

The second result is that Prolog has a greater potential to exploit the additional state and state transfers advanced hardware can offer. The high semantic content or *potency* of a language is indicated, for a given program, by a high mean number of memory references per instruction executed and a low total number of instructions executed. From the statistics shown in Table 1-2, Prolog

	Tak			Boyer		
	Lisp	Prolog	L/P	Lisp	Prolog	L/P
instructions	683792	811008		9093949	4011264	
data ref	667891	508865	1.31	8200807	5752632	1.43
instr ref	747401	938226	0.80	12078345	4555707	2.65
data ref/instr	0.97	0.63		0.90	1.43	
instr ref/instr	1.09	1.16		1.33	1.14	

	Deriv			Puzzle		
	Lisp	Prolog	L/P	Lisp	Prolog	L/P
instructions	598	277		12172280	525650	
data ref	515	537	0.96	3711662	842468	4.41
instr ref	708	366	1.93	15759345	617679	25.5
data ref/instr	0.87	1.94		0.30	1.60	
instr ref/instr	1.19	1.32		1.29	1.18	

Table 1-2:   Lisp vs. Prolog: Abstract Machine Comparison

displays greater potency than Lisp because the functionality of backtracking and unification are integrated into Prolog and its architecture.

In summary, to reduce the execution time of a given application, one wishes to both

- reduce the gap between the architecture and the language.
- increase the semantic content of the language, increasing its performance potential.

As shown, available hardware and compiler technology constrains these criteria, currently favoring Lisp. Future technology may well favor Prolog.

1.3. Previous Work

1.3.1. Architectures

Flynn and Hoevel [27, 26] derived the theory of ideal language machines for FORTRAN. Wakefield [91] implemented this theory by designing and measuring ADEPT, a direct correspondence architecture (DCA) for Pascal. This book extends these concepts from procedural languages to applicative, logic programming languages, specifically Prolog. The step to Prolog is much larger than from FORTRAN to Pascal, because of attributes such as single-assignment, nondeterminism, pointers, and unification. The singular contribution of the ideal Prolog architecture is the inclusion of a two-level name space (registers and memory), displaying superior memory-referencing characteristics under assumptions of a less costly host.

Sequential Prolog architectures designed by D.H.D. Warren [93, 96], Byrd [9], and Bowen [10] are called *environment-stacking* architectures. These models utilize a stack holding local procedure variables in frames called *environments*. These architectures have been designed in the traditional manner, as evolutionary improvements from interpreter to compiler to abstract machine model. A contribution of this book is to show how the theory of ideal language machines is another equally valid design methodology, resulting in the same high-performance Prolog architectures.

PWAM, designed by Hermenegildo [35], is an AND-parallel Prolog extension of the WAM. The PWAM model extends the initial work in Restricted AND-Parallelism by DeGroot [18], by developing an efficient architecture with a viable backtracking semantics. A contribution of this book is the measurement of the memory-referencing characteristics of PWAM executing on a shared memory multiprocessor. It is shown that PWAM's memory efficiency compares well with the WAM for sequential code and that PWAM has low communication overheads for parallel code.

1.3.2. Benchmarking

Many studies of both the static and dynamic characteristics of Prolog programs have been undertaken. Warren [93] measured the execution time of small Prolog programs to compare the performance of DEC-10 Prolog with the performance of various other programming languages. This was one of the first sets of Prolog benchmarks published with performance measurements. Wilk [98] measured the execution time of small, synthetic Prolog programs to compare different systems. He discusses the important attributes of a Prolog system, ranging from garbage collection to debugging capabilities.

Ross [68, 69] measured the memory-referencing behavior of small sequential Prolog programs. In contrast to this book, he studied the Prolog working set, i.e., page referencing characteristics, between main memory and backing store. Prolog was found to have a larger working set than typical C programs. A Prolog paging strategy was designed which avoids transferring pages not belonging to the current valid storage areas (as defined by stack pointers, etc.). For compiled programs, this reduced page traffic by a factor of two over a conventional paging strategy.

Matsumoto [50], Ratcliffe [64], and Onai [60] performed static analysis of large Prolog programs (including versions of the CHAT and PLM benchmarks used in this book). They measured several attributes such as the number of cuts per clause, and the number and type of built-in goals per clause. These high-level statistics were aimed at evaluating compiler techniques, but not at directly analyzing the performance of the programs. Since static code was measured, these statistics don't necessarily reflect runtime behavior. Nor were these high-level analyses based on architecture models, as is done in this book.

Ratcliffe measured parallelism metrics from static benchmarks to determine the amount of potential concurrency. Onai also measured parallelism metrics from two dynamic benchmarks. These high-level analyses were also not based on architecture models. Dobry [21], however, measured the execution time and simple memory-referencing characteristics of small Prolog programs, to illustrate the effectiveness of the PLM architecture. This work was extended by Touati [86] to include several larger benchmarks, including versions of the CHAT and ILI benchmarks used in this book. Touati's study presents measurements of detailed high-level characteristics of the PLM, such as cdr-coding efficiency, with the aim of evaluating compiler optimization strategies. Many of the results presented confirm those in this book. Note that although the PLM was built, the studies cited above used simulation for their measurements.

Hermenegildo [35] measured the performance characteristics of small, synthetic benchmarks to illustrate the effectiveness of the PWAM architecture. His analysis assumed an idealized shared memory organization and emphasized high-level-architecture characterization. This book extends this work by analyzing PWAM memory-referencing characteristics assuming a realistic shared memory multiprocessor organization.

1.3.3. Memory Organization

A few comparative sequential Prolog hardware studies have been conducted [8, 54, 31] and several Prolog machines built [41, 57, 58, 56, 21, 71]. The Kobe University PEK machine [41] compiles Prolog into horizontal microcode that is executed from a writable control store (WCS). The PEK architecture is similar to that of DEC-10 Prolog [93]. In addition to a 16K (by 96 bit) WCS, the PEK also incorporates a 4K (by 34 bit) stack buffer, 16K (by 34 bit) heap buffer, and 16K (by 14 bit) trail buffer.

The ICOT High-speed Prolog Machine (HPM or Chi) instruction set is a derivative of the WAM [57]. The HPM incorporates an 8K (by 36 bit), 4-way set associative write-through I/D cache. Two ICOT Personal Sequential Inference

(PSI) machines have been designed. The PSI-I [58] is a microcoded interpreter for KL0, a simple compiled form of Prolog. PSI-I is equipped with an 8K (by 40 bit), 2-way set associative copyback I/D (combined instruction, data) cache. The PSI-II [56] instruction set is a derivative of the WAM. It incorporates a 4K (by 40 bit), directly mapped copyback I/D cache. The PSI-II incorporates a "write stack" operation which avoids fetching the next (invalid) word at the top of stack. This is a limited example of the more general "smart cache" described and analyzed in this book.

The UC Berkeley Programmed Logic Machine (PLM) is a pipelined, microcoded Prolog machine [21, 20]. The machine instruction set is a derivative of the WAM. The PLM incorporates a fixed-size single choice point buffer, a look-ahead instruction buffer, and a write buffer (to queue outstanding write requests). The X1 [22], a version of the PLM built by Xenologic Inc., includes two directly mapped 64K (32 bit) word caches (separating instructions and data) without the choice point buffer. The local memories simulated in this book are smaller (up to 1024 32-bit words) than those in the machines previously described. The intention is to model local memories that can be integrated with the CPU.

The Mitsubishi Pegasus is a pipelined, RISC microprocessor for Prolog [71]. The tagged, load/store architecture incorporates a *shadow register set*, similar to that suggested in this book. Measurements made of small benchmarks running on Pegasus indicated that the shadow registers can improve program performance by up to 17% [71].

The Hitachi IPP [1] is a pipelined, microcoded Prolog machine. The instruction set is a derivative of the WAM. The IPP incorporates a four word instruction prefetch buffer, write-through cache, and write buffer. Processor performance has been simulated for small programs, indicating that advanced indexing techniques and global register allocation can give speedups of up to 3.4 times that of unoptimized code. Optimizations similar to these are discussed in Chapter 2.

Borriello et al. [8] described and measured the execution of Prolog on SPUR, a microprocessor with a tagged RISC architecture. 14 small Prolog benchmarks were executed on the SPUR and PLM simulators, allowing comparison of execution cycles. The results indicated that number of SPUR cycles executed was 2.3 times that of the PLM. The number of SPUR instructions executed was 16 times greater than the PLM. Borriello concludes that assuming similar memory configurations for PLM and SPUR, the SPUR can achieve 66% of PLM performance, if minor tag modifications and compiler improvements are made to SPUR.

Mulder and Tick [54] described and measured the execution of Prolog on an

MC68020 microprocessor. Approximation methods were used to compare PLM and MC68020 execution cycles for three large benchmarks (the instruction frequencies presented in Appendix B of this book were used to estimate the number of execution cycles). The results indicated that assuming equivalent main memory speeds, the number of MC68020 cycles executed was 2.5 to 3.5 times that of the PLM.

Gee, et al. [31] microcoded a VAX 8600 general-purpose computer to directly emulate WAM instructions. They found that 85% of the PLM execution performance could be obtained for simple benchmarks. Because a general-purpose host was used, high-performance numeric computation was also achieved.

Studies in memory organizations for high-level procedural language architectures include the works of Alpert [2] and Mitchell [53]. Alpert described and measured the data memory performance of *contour buffers* and copyback data caches for Pascal architectures. The contour buffer is similar in function to the stack buffer presented in this book. Alpert's cache simulator is used here to make uniprocessor copyback cache measurements, and has been extended to model write-through caches. Mitchell described and measured instruction cache performance for a wide range of architectures. Pascal benchmarks were simulated, providing performance metrics with which to compare architectures.

Cache studies for traditional architectures are numerous. Most heavily referenced in this book are works by Smith [75], Bitar [6], Archibald [3], and Hill [38]. Smith and Hill present detailed studies of uniprocessor cache design and performance. Bitar and Archibald present detailed studies of multiprocessor (coherent) cache design and performance. This book extends these studies by analyzing cache performance for logic programming language architectures.

1.4. Book Outline

This book assumes familiarity with Prolog (refer to [78] for instance). Detailed knowledge of the WAM and PWAM instruction sets are *not* necessary. These architectures are reviewed in the Chapter 2, although the interested reader is referred to Warren [96] and Hermenegildo [35], respectively, for complete details.

The body of this book contains four parts. The first part, Chapter 2, describes a family of Prolog architectures defined from the principles of canonical high-level language architectures. Prolog Canonical Interpretive

Forms (CIFs) are introduced which have attributes with certain "ideal" qualities not present in the WAM. The WAM is introduced from a historical perspective of DEC-10 Prolog and its variants. PWAM, chosen for later multiprocessor performance measurements, is also reviewed.

Chapter 3 presents the tools and benchmarks used to make empirical measurements of memory models introduced in Chapter 4. The WAM, Prolog CIFs, and PWAM memory-referencing characteristics are presented and compared.

Chapter 4 presents two-level memory hierarchies well-suited for sequential Prolog architectures. Local memory models are described and measurements are presented. The local memory designs are generalized into parameterized queueing models for main memory design. These models are evaluated, giving the *bandwidth efficiency* of both the main memory and the memory bus, and the expected processor *performance degradation* due to the local memory miss penalties, aggravated by main memory contention.

Chapter 5 presents memory hierarchies well-suited for parallel Prolog architectures, specifically PWAM. Shared memory multiprocessor consistency problems for PWAM are outlined and local memory models are presented which solve these problems. The queueing models previously introduced are extended to describe shared memory multiprocessors.

Finally, Chapter 6 presents conclusions drawn from the research and points to directions for future research.

2 Prolog Architectures

This chapter describes a family of high-level instruction set architectures for the Prolog language. The Prolog architecture family is *canonical*, i.e., it is defined from the semantics of Prolog in the tradition of Flynn and Hoevel's work on canonical architectures for procedural languages [27]. The most notable member of the Prolog architecture family is the Warren Abstract Machine (WAM) architecture [96], currently implemented on general purpose hosts via native-code (e.g., Tricia [14]), interpretation (e.g., Quintus Prolog [62]), microcoded interpretation (e.g., on the VAX 8600 [31]), and on dedicated hosts (e.g., the UC Berkeley Programmed Logic Machine (PLM) [21] and the ICOT PSI-II [56]).

The canonical Prolog architecture family includes attributes such as *ideal indexing* (a model for directly selecting the correct procedure entry point in a nondeterministic procedure invocation) and tight instruction encoding. Although not all of these attributes are realizable, they indicate upper bounds on sequential execution performance. In addition, they can be used *constructively* to aid in the design of realizable architectures on current hosts. It is shown that the WAM is such an architecture, i.e., the WAM instruction set closely corresponds to the Prolog source language. Results are presented indicating the extent to which the WAM achieves the canonical measures.

An alternative introduction to the WAM architecture is also presented by means of its historical ancestor, the DEC-10 Prolog abstract machine (Prolog-10) [93]. These two architectures are compared in the area of memory performance. Evidence is presented suggesting that the WAM achieves its goal of optimizing the execution of determinate code (with respect to Prolog-10), at the cost of slower nondeterminate execution. The performance difference (in terms of memory references made) is greatest for shallow backtracking programs.

Finally, an overview of the Restricted AND-Parallel Prolog architecture (PWAM) [35] is given. In the next chapter, memory-referencing characteristics of these architectures are presented and the relative merits of their attributes are compared.

2.1. Canonical Prolog Architectures

In this section, terminology is introduced with which canonical Prolog architectures are defined. These architectures are informally called Prolog *canonical interpretive forms* (CIFs). The importance of studying these architectures is then given. Metrics for measuring the characteristics of CIFs are introduced. Detailed definitions of the CIF architectures and metrics are given in subsequent parts of this section.

A (sequential) *machine*, used to execute a program (i.e., a set of instructions), is defined as the combination of an *interpretive mechanism* and a *store*. The machine is called the *image machine* or *abstract machine model*. The store or *image store* is often called the *storage model*. The interpretive mechanism is often called the *execution model* and can be implemented with another machine, called the *host machine*. *Architecture*, as defined in this book, is the *image machine instruction set semantics*, i.e., how the interpretive mechanism updates the image store during program execution.

The *name space* of the architecture is the set of (data and instruction) objects that can be referenced by the instruction set. Prolog data objects are described in Section 1.1. Each data object is given a name or *identifier* in the source program. Recall that in a Prolog program, variable names are capitalized, and thus easily distinguishable from constants. The (lexical) *scope* of an identifier is the largest program segment over which the identifier has a consistent definition. The scope of a constant identifier is the entire program. The scope of a variable identifier is only a single clause. In a *one-level* name space, as defined in this book, instructions can only reference identifiers whose scope is visible from the currently executing clause. In a *two-level* name space, instructions can also reference identifiers from a register set.

A Prolog canonical interpretive form (CIF) is the measure of Prolog program events which limit a machine architecture. Alternatively, a Prolog CIF is a high-level architecture directly corresponding to Prolog. Flynn and Hoevel [26] developed the theory of canonical architectures and applied it to procedural languages such as FORTRAN and Pascal (CIFs developed for these languages are referred to as *procedural CIFs* in this book). The CIF models assume Von Neumann hosts where the memory bandwidth between the processor and memory is the primary performance bottleneck. Other types of hosts, e.g., dataflow machines, are not considered.

A two-phase evaluation model is assumed here, as in Flynn and Hoevel [27]. In the first phase, the Prolog source program is *translated* into an intermediate form, the Prolog CIF, with a compiler. In the second phase, the Prolog CIF is *interpreted* by the host. The purpose of defining a Prolog CIF is three-fold.

- The CIF execution performance gives the best case program performance because memory referencing is minimal and stability (lack of disruption of sequential interpretation, e.g., taken branches) is maximal. The CIF is ideal only in the sense that the CIF corresponds closely to the source program, so that the CIF does not *limit* the source program performance. Given a direct correspondence, source-to-source compiler optimizations (not investigated here) can improve upon the CIF performance.

- The CIF attributes, although not totally realizable, can be used constructively to implement high-performance architectures. Flynn and Hoevel have termed these architectures *direct correspondence architectures* (DCAs).

- The description of the Prolog CIF can be viewed as an exposition and justification of the WAM model [96].[1] The WAM is considered a Prolog DCA.

Flynn and Hoevel [26] define five design criteria for a canonical architecture:

1. **transparency (1:1 rule)** — the source and CIF correspond closely to one another.

2. **size** — the CIF data and instruction objects are as concise as possible.

3. **referencing** — a minimal number of objects are interpreted.

4. **stability** — there is minimal disruption of sequential interpretation.

5. **distance** — a minimal number of unique objects are interpreted.

Each criteria defines a measure that must be optimized to attain the CIF. The optimality of these measures cannot be guaranteed for all programs written in the source language. For instance, given knowledge of a program, an object encoding may be developed requiring less space than the CIF (which is designed without specific knowledge of the program). The variance in CIF attribute optimality is greater for Prolog than for procedural CIFs because the use of dynamic data structures and nondeterminate execution is highly program dependent in Prolog.

The first two criteria comprise the static measures of an architecture. The last three criteria comprise the dynamic activity measures of an architecture. The

---

[1]For another method of justifying the WAM, see Kursawe [46].

dynamic measures are meant to reflect execution performance on three classes of machine: low-end, high-end, and confluent (unlimited hardware). Distance is not discussed here.

In the following sections three CIF models are described in terms of the CIF metrics above. Measurements of the memory-referencing characteristics of these models are presented in the next chapter. The first two CIFs, which are identical in construction, are called the *naive* and *traditional* CIFs. They are informally derived in a manner similar to the formal derivations of Flynn [27] and correspond closely to Prolog. The naive model is inefficient because a memory reference is required for each identifier referenced in the program. The traditional CIF's data traffic is analyzed assuming a more sophisticated host. In this case, a memory reference is no longer required for a reference to an identifier in the current scope. With the new analysis, the traditional model performs significantly better than the naive model, reducing data references by about 79%, but the underlying assumptions are shown to be costly to implement for Prolog. A *register-based* CIF is then described, incorporating a two-level name space. Under the assumptions of a less costly host, the register-based CIF performs reasonably well, reducing the naive CIF data bandwidth by about 14%.

2.1.1. CIF Data Encoding

In this section, the encoding of data objects used in the CIF architectures is described. The data objects manipulated by the Prolog CIF correspond directly to the objects manipulated by a Prolog source program. CIF data objects are encoded to correspond to the requirements of large Prolog applications programs executing on typical hosts. These programs reference many unique atoms, and a large number of data objects. Data objects or terms are composed of *words*, the indivisible unit of image storage. A word has a *tag* and a *value*, i.e., the CIF is a *tagged architecture*. Tags are necessary to dynamically distinguish between different types of data objects in order to implement unification, the fundamental Prolog operation.

A simple term (constant or variable) occupies a single word. An *indirect reference* or *pointer* to a term also occupies a single word. The indirect reference type is necessary to implement shared Prolog variables (see Section 2.1.2). An unbound variable is defined as *an indirect reference to itself*. This allows creation of a reference to an unbound variable by simply copying (verbatim) that value to another location. Although the CIF definition does not constrain the word size, the measurements made in this book assume a 32 bit word to facilitate comparison between the CIF and the WAM. The 32 bit words permit a large number of unique atoms and a large number data objects in the Prolog image store.

Compound terms (structures and lists) cannot be encoded in a single word. As a result, when binding a variable to a complex term, an indirect reference is required, pointing from the variable to the term. To speed up unification of compound terms, indirect references to compound terms are given tags indicating the type of the compound term. Specifically, a structure is encoded as an *indirect structure reference* to a functor word, followed by a single word for each argument (lists are described below). Note that a single word is allocated for each structure argument. For a simple structure (with simple terms as arguments), this is sufficient. A structure which is composed of structures uses indirect references to link complex arguments to encompassing structures. Note that indirect references to simple terms and to other indirect references do not indicate the type of the dereferenced value. This facilitates binding a variable because pointers to the variable do not have to be updated to indicate the variable's new value type.

A *list* is a special type of structure with two arguments. Lists are encoded as an *indirect list reference* directly to the head of the list. The subsequent location is the tail of the list. In a legal list, the tail is either another list reference or the constant *nil* signifying the end of list. Lists are not cdr-coded in the Prolog CIF to reduce the complexity of the architecture. Preliminary measurements indicated that cdr-coding saved an insignificant number of memory references for the benchmarks studied in this book. This has also been confirmed for the PLM architecture by Touati [86].

2.1.2. Naive and Traditional Prolog CIFs

In this section, a traditional Prolog CIF is defined from the semantics of Prolog. The CIF is called "traditional" because it is largely based on the procedural language CIFs of Flynn, in contrast to the "register-based" CIF introduced in Section 2.1.3. The naive CIF is identical to the traditional CIF with the exception of the underlying host assumptions. These differences are discussed later in this Section. A Prolog CIF consists of an instruction set and its corresponding semantics with respect to a storage model. The following sections define the traditional CIF storage model and the instruction set. The traditional model is instructive because it corresponds closely to Prolog and clarifies the later description of the register-based CIF.

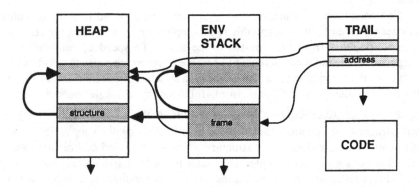

Figure 2-1: Traditional Prolog CIF Storage Model

CIF Storage Model

In this section, the traditional Prolog CIF storage model is defined. The storage model corresponds directly to the storage constraints imposed by Prolog semantics. It is argued that the storage model is "ideal" in the sense that it does not constrain reasonable host implementations. An overview of the CIF storage model is illustrated in Figure 2-1. The model is a variant of the *three-stack model* introduced in DEC-10 Prolog [93]. The *code space* is a static area holding the CIF program. The *heap, stack,* and *trail* are dynamic areas managed in stack-like manners. The thick arrows in Figure 2-1 represent typical indirect data references. The thin arrows represent typical management pointers. Only the most important connections from one area to another are shown. These connections and the individual areas are described below.

The storage model is centered around the *frame* (this notation is retained from the DEC-10 Prolog architecture) which holds all identifiers referenced within a scope. The frame is similar to a *contour* in procedural CIFs. A Pascal contour, for instance, contains labels, constants, local variables, pointers to non-local variables, pointers to global variables, and arguments passed to the procedure [91]. A single-level name space is used, wherein the instruction set references all objects via contour indices. This minimizes operand size, thereby minimizing instruction size. Unlike procedural languages, there are no non-local or global objects in Prolog, so these are not present in the frame. In addition,

Prolog does not reference labels and constants in a clause multiple times, mainly because recursion is used instead of iteration. These objects are directly encoded in the instruction stream as immediate operands. The remaining objects in a frame, collectively referred to as *frame variables*, are local variables, and arguments passed to the procedure. In addition, the traditional Prolog CIF frame also contains state information necessary to implement nondeterminate procedure execution.

Nondeterminate control flow or backtracking in Prolog is the action of selecting the most recent entry point with alternatives for a procedure invocation, restoring the state of the computation at that point and resuming execution there. Abstractly, the alternatives are called *branch points* because they represent OR-branches in the AND-OR tree representing the Prolog proof.[2] A unique frame is created for each procedure invocation. If a branch point is reached, the frame is loaded with additional state values necessary for nondeterminate program execution. A possible optimization avoids allocating space for these values in the frame until it is known if the procedure invocation is a branch point. This optimization is not of concern in the traditional CIF, because CIF memory characteristics are measured in numbers of references, not locality.

Since clauses may be nested, multiple clauses may be active during program execution, and therefore multiple frames must be managed. A *frame stack* is utilized, similar to a *contour stack* in a procedural CIF. Thus the traditional Prolog CIF is similar to the DEC-10 Prolog abstract machine. Unlike a procedural CIF, a *heap* is also utilized, as described below.

A frame variable is allocated only a single word. Binding a frame variable to a new structure (or list) is implemented by creating the structure on the heap and indirectly referencing the structure from the frame. On the heap, objects live until removed by failure.[3] Splitting the allocation of simple and complex objects onto the stack and heap is necessary because the space required by a scope for complex objects cannot be determined at translation time. Consider a variable in a clause which may be passed through arbitrary levels of procedure calls until it is bound to a structure. *Which* structure cannot be determined statically, so the variable's frame size cannot be calculated. Instead, these "excess" objects are dynamically allocated on the heap.

The two essential control functions of nondeterminate execution in Prolog are *fail* and *cut*. Therefore the CIF storage model must permit their efficient

---

[2]See Kowalski [45] for a discussion of the AND-OR tree.

[3]This is a simple view of the heap that avoids the issue of garbage collection but is sufficient for the purposes of this book.

implementation, i.e., minimal memory referencing, maximum storage reclamation (maximum locality), and fast execution. With this motivation, the Prolog CIF nondeterminate execution mechanism is now described and its corresponding storage model is shown to facilitate efficient fail and cut. Restoring the original state of the computation in general involves the following:

- restoring the frames active at the most recent branch point.
- unbinding the values of variables bound since the most recent branch point.
- restoring state variables active at the most recent branch point (e.g., stack pointers, etc.).

All frames in the stack corresponding to threads of execution leading to an active branch point must be saved until that procedure fails or succeeds unconditionally, i.e., until no alternative clauses exist for that procedure. Viewed as an AND-OR tree, all frames on a path leading from the root to an active OR-node must be saved. The most efficient method of implementing this is to freeze the stack (and heap) at each branch point, i.e., disallow deallocation of these frames. Failure is permitted to unfreeze the stack, discarding the portions of the stack and heap more recent than the last branch point. To implement this efficiently, the frames corresponding to branch points (called *branch point frames*) are connected in a chain.

To efficiently implement the task of unbinding variables during failure, the address (called the *trail address*) of each variable bound since the branch point must be saved. Since the number of such bindings is unknown at translation time, the trail addresses cannot be allocated within the frame. Alternatively, the trail addresses could be allocated on the stack as linked objects, independent of the frames. However, it is far more efficient to store trail addresses on a separate last-in/first-out (LIFO) stack, called the *trail stack*. The action of saving an address on the trail stack is called *trailing a binding*. The trail stack also permits efficient implementation of cut. Cut, like failure, manages the AND-OR tree. Cut removes zero or more active branch point frames, allowing subsequent backtracking to avoid executing OR branches that do not produce useful solutions. Cut can also have the side-effect of deallocating stack frames. Cut, however, cannot deallocate trailed addresses, which must be saved and *detrailed* (the locations to which the addresses point must be unbound, i.e., set to unbound variables) during the next failure.

CIF Instruction Encoding

This section describes the traditional Prolog CIF instruction set and encoding methods. CIF instruction and operand names are borrowed from the WAM [96] to avoid obscuring the similarities between the two. A mapping for algorithmic/scientific languages involves arithmetic operators and variables within an assignment statement. *In Prolog, the basic semantic operation is unification of a source level argument with simple terms as operands.*

For example, consider `append/3`, which can be used to append two lists:

```
append([],X,X).
append([X|L1],L2,[X|L3]) :-
       append(L1,L2,L3).
```

The first clause means that the result of concatenating a list, **X**, to the constant nil, [], is list **X**. The first clause is a simple example that introduces many of the correspondence subtleties. Since there are three source level arguments, three unification operators are expected. Each operator is a specialized form of *general unification.*[4] For example, to match the first argument, the specialized unification operator simply checks that the incoming argument is either unbound or nil. If unbound, it is bound to nil. Other types of incoming arguments cause the operation to fail. The second operator is specialized to match an unbound local variable, so it cannot fail. In fact, matching the second argument, in this case, requires no work (which is understood at the higher level of the declarative semantics).

Matching the third argument translates into a single operator; however, the operation entails an unknown (at translation time) amount of work, i.e., operand fetches. **X** (the second and third arguments) is a *shared variable* because it occurs multiple times within a scope. Shared variables can possibly cause additional operands to be referenced from memory when the variables are dynamically bound to compound terms and require general unification for matching. Thus an accurate operand count cannot be ascertained from the static code (c.f., procedural CIFs, where operator and operand counts can be statically determined). The following query exhibits this type of behavior — the third operator matches the first four elements of the lists before failure:

```
?- append([],[1,2,3,4],[1,2,3,4,5]).
```

The Prolog CIF translates the unification of simple terms and one-level structures into one instruction. Unifying a nested structure always requires one or more additional instructions. A clause head is matched using **get** instructions and the body goals are set up using **put** instructions. In the next paragraphs the syntactic structures of **get** and **put** instructions are described and the informal semantics are then given.

---

[4]See Lloyd [48] or Robinson [67] for general unification algorithms. See Tick [84] for the unification algorithm used for the measurements presented in this book.

The **get** instructions are composed of a source operand followed by at least one destination operand. The **put** instructions are composed of a destination operand followed by at least one source operand. Both sources and destinations are frame variables, encoded as indices into the *current* frame.

The **get** destinations and **put** sources are tagged. These tags indicate the format of the operand. In the case of **get** instructions with a single destination (**put**: single source), the format can be incorporated into the opcode (as in the WAM). In the case of multiple destinations (**put**: multiple sources), the formats are separated from the opcode because each operand can have a different format. The operands must be processed sequentially, from left to right, for correctness because the compiler may introduce dependencies between the operands.

In general, **get** instructions match their source operand to their destination operand(s). Destination operands may be tagged as **var**, **val**, or **const**. A **get** instruction first checks the destination format. If **var**, it assigns the source to the destination. If **const**, the source is compared to the destination. If **val**, the source is unified with the destination.[5] If the comparison or unification fails, the instruction fails, i.e., the failure routine is invoked.

In addition to the **get** instructions is **get_stct** (**get_list** is simply an optimized instance of **get_stct**). Unlike the previously discussed **get** instructions, **get_stct** takes a variable number of static operands. If the source is unbound, the operands are interpreted in *write mode*. If the source is a structure, the operands are interpreted in *read mode*. Otherwise the instruction fails. The source is matched to the first destination operand, which is a functor. Then arguments of the source structure are matched to the succeeding destination operands. Matching in write mode involves assignment to the heap. Matching in read mode involves comparison of terms.

In general, **put** instructions assign their source operand(s) to their destination operand. Source operands may be tagged as **var**, **val**, **const**, or **unsafe**. The **val** and **const** operands are assigned to the destination. An **unsafe** source operand must be moved onto the heap before assignment to the destination, to allow last call optimization (described below). A **var** source operand must first be initialized to an unbound variable in the frame before assignment to the destination. This allows an optimization wherein the frame is not initialized when allocated.

Some examples of CIF code are given in Figure 2-2. Y_i and Z_i represent caller and callee frame variables, respectively, at index i. It is assumed that Z_i

---

[5]Prolog unification does not perform an "occurs check," thus a circular term (i.e., a term that references itself) can cause an instruction to make an unlimited number of operand requests.

```
append([],X,X).
            get        Y0,const([])
       % get           Y1,var(Y1)
            get        Y2,val(Y1)
            proceed

append([X|L1],L2,[X|L3])  :- append(L1,L2,L3).
            get_list Y0,var(Y3),var(Y0)
       % get           Y1,var(Y1)
            get_list Y2,val(Y3),var(Y2)
       % put           Y0,val(Y0)
       % put           Y1,val(Y1)
       % put           Y2,val(Y2)
            execute    append/3

foo(f(a,b,g(X)),X)  :- bingo(f(a,X,Y,g(Y))).
       % get           Y1,var(Y1)
            get_stct Y0,f/3,const(a),const(b),var(Y2)
            get_stct Y2,g/1,val(Y1)
            put_stct Y0,f/4,const(a),val(Y1),var(Y1),var(Y2)
            put_stct Y2,g/1,val(Y1)
            execute    bingo/1

qsort([X|L],R0,R)  :- split(L,X,L1,L2),
       qsort(L1,R0,[X|R1]),qsort(L2,R1,R).
            get_list Y0,var(Y6),var(Z0)
            put        Z1,val(Y6)
            put        Z2,var(Y5)
            put        Z3,var(Y3)
            call       split/4
            put        Z0,unsafe(Y5)
            put        Z1,val(Y1)
            put_list Z2,val(Y6),var(Y4)
            call       qsort/3
            put        Y0,unsafe(Y3)
            put        Y1,val(Y4)
            put        Y2,val(Y2)
            execute    qsort/3
```

Figure 2-2: Traditional Prolog CIF Clause Examples

can be referenced with an offset from the top of stack. In contrast to a procedural CIF, the Prolog CIF relies heavily on the optimization of removing no-operations (e.g., **get Y1,var(Y1)** and **put Y0,val(Y0)** — these are marked in Figure 2-2 with "**%**").

Various control instructions are present in Figure 2-2. The **call** instruction is used to invoke a procedure, after the caller loads the passed arguments on the top of stack. Note that the top of stack is defined as the more recent of the current frame and the current branch point frame. The callee allocates a frame over the arguments passed from the caller. A large enough frame is allocated to contain the maximum number of frame variables in all clauses possibly matching a nondeterminate procedure invocation. Figure 2-2 shows only clause code, and therefore frame allocation instructions are not given. Note that a nondeterminate callee loads state information into the frame during allocation. As previously stated, these branch point frames are linked to efficiently implement fail and cut.

The **proceed** instruction causes simple procedure return. The **execute** instruction returns through a procedure call. A nondeterminate procedure resets its branch point frame to a standard frame when its last alternative clause is entered. This facilitates frame deallocation. The **proceed** deallocates the procedure's frame if it is a standard frame on the top of stack. This deallocation is performed by resetting the current frame to be that of the immediate ancestor of the procedure (its caller). Because the **execute** first invokes another procedure before it returns, the current frame is *reused*, not deallocated, as is explained below.

Last call optimization, also known as *tail recursion optimization* (TRO), reuses the current frame (if it is at the top of stack) for the last goal of a clause. The first use of TRO for Prolog was in DEC-10 Prolog [94] and is considered essential for the CIF because of Prolog's reliance on recursion instead of iteration. Procedural CIFs do not implement TRO because the languages do not rely on recursion. Huck [39] reports that typical FORTRAN programs execute on average 290 VAX-11/780 instructions between procedure calls. In this book it is found that on average, Prolog executes 15.3 (WAM) instructions between procedure calls (Section 3.2). TRO is necessary to increase frame referencing (spatial) locality. Spatial locality is a measure of the locus of memory references within the storage model. High locality implies that the storage areas do not grow and shrink rapidly. This type of behavior can be exploited by small (inexpensive) hardware buffers that capture a large percentage of all memory references. Such buffers reduce the effective memory access time thereby improving processor performance. The greater the locality, the greater the buffer cost-efficiency.

TRO is implemented in the CIF by passing arguments directly over the caller's arguments via **Y** operands if the caller's frame is at the top of stack. Abstractly, this amounts to deallocating the frame of the current scope just before invoking the last goal of that procedure. To avoid leaving references pointing into the old frame, frame variables thus referenced (i.e., **unsafe** operands) are copied onto the heap before deallocation.

Procedural CIFs as defined by Flynn and Hoevel [27], require that objects and actions at the architecture level correspond to objects and actions at the language level. This requirement ensures that the CIF uses no more storage space or interpretation time than described by the source program. The languages to which this concept was originally applied are much lower-level languages than Prolog. Attributes of these languages are closely related to host machine functionality, e.g., the FORTRAN addition operator and its correspondence to an ALU add function.

This view of translation requires *transparency* between source and object, where the only optimizations allowed are at the source level. For a simple language, such as FORTRAN, this view is logical — transparency can reduce computation complexity and increase reliability. A complex language such as Prolog, however, does not have the same strong notion of sequentiality of instructions as does FORTRAN. During resolution, head arguments can be matched in any order, and when matching an argument which is a complex term, subterms can be matched in any order. Thus the traditional view of transparency, a direct map between source-level and host-level state transitions, is unmotivated and restrictive for Prolog. It is for this reason that the order of the Prolog CIF instructions in Figure 2-2 does not always correspond directly to the source programs.

For the Prolog CIF, a tight instruction encoding is assumed. This includes variable length instructions on bit boundaries. Local branch targets are encoded into either one or two bytes, assuming a sophisticated linker capable of determining minimal offsets. Frame variable specifiers are $\log_2$ encoded (these attributes are further described and measurements are presented in Sections 3.3.2 and 3.4). Figure 2-3 gives an example of CIF encoding for the inner-loop of **append/3**, in bits. A WAM byte-encoding, using similar offset sizes, requires 15 bytes, an 88% increase in size.

CIF Data Referencing

In this section the CIF data referencing metrics are discussed. The interpretation of these metrics is dependent on the underlying host assumed. Two hosts are illustrated here — a simple host which holds the image store entirely in memory (the naive model), and a complex host which holds the frame

| | opcode | operands | | | |
		reg	tag	offset	total
get_list Y0,var(Y3),var(Y0)	8	6	6		26
get_list Y2,val(Y3),var(Y2)	8	6	6		26
execute append/3	8			16	24
	24	12	12	16	64 bits

Figure 2-3:   CIF Instruction Encoding (bits): append/3 Clause 2

stack in fast memory and the remainder of the image store in memory (the traditional model). Additional CIF metrics, not dependent on host, are discussed in Section 2.1.4.

Prolog data references fall into the following main categories: dereferencing terms, unifying terms, (un)binding (i.e., binding and unbinding) variables, (de)trailing (i.e., trailing and detrailing) bindings, and (preparing for) backtracking. Except for binding a variable, analogous to assignment, none of these are common in traditional procedural languages. Dereferencing, backtracking, and its preparation are discussed in the next section. The remaining types of references are discussed in this section. These represent the core Prolog operations of passing arguments and binding results.

Using the translation method described in the last section, references made while unifying terms correspond closely to the source language specification. In contrast to a procedural language, however, the Prolog specification is incomplete, thus minimality of referencing cannot be guaranteed. The nature of dynamic structure creation prevents determination (at translation time) of a minimal referencing method. For instance, using *structure copying* (as in the WAM and adopted in the CIF), new structures are created by copying pre-existing structures verbatim. Using *structure sharing* (as in DEC-10 Prolog), new structures are created by reusing the skeleton of pre-existing structures, copying only variable data. The efficiency of each scheme is dependent on the amount and type of structure creation and access in the program, because although structure sharing saves copying static parts of a structure, it requires indirection in accessing variable parts of a structure (see Mellish [52] for discussion).

One method of analyzing the CIF is to *simply count a memory reference for each identifier reference in the current scope*. This is called the *naive CIF*. Manipulation of structures or lists involves extra references, as described below. This metric specifies precisely the memory traffic implied by the source program making no assumptions about the underlying host. An example of this

```
                                                read    write
append(
        [X|L1],                                   3       2
                L2,
                        [X|L3]) :-                 3       4
        append(
              L1,
                 L2,
                    L3).
```

Figure 2-4:   Traditional CIF Data Referencing (words): append/3

referencing metric for one pass through the inner-loop of determinate execution of append/3 is shown in Figure 2-4, assuming a query such as

        ? - append([1,2,3,4],[5,6],X).

Simple operators, e.g., unification of L2, do not require instructions, because the no-operations are removed by the translator. During determinate execution the first argument is instantiated and the third argument is uninstantiated. One memory read is needed to access the first argument from the frame and check if it is a list. Two memory transfers, each consisting of a read and write, are needed to load the head and tail from the heap into the frame variables for X and L1. Two reads are needed to access the third argument from the frame and dereference it. A write is needed to bind the third argument to a list. A memory transfer is needed to load X into the head of the list. Two writes are needed to load the tail of the list and a pointer to the tail into the frame variable for L3.

This example shows that referencing requirements are directly specified by the program, *given knowledge of the argument modes.*   An argument mode indicates whether the passed argument is always bound, unbound, or possibly either.   Complete knowledge of the argument structure is needed to calculate referencing in a procedure clause containing shared variables. Recall that in the case of append/3 in Figure 2-4, X is a shared variable. The modes assumed for determinate execution indicate that the variable is being *copied* from the first argument to the third argument, therefore complete knowledge of the structure of X is not needed to determine the number of references. If however, the modes indicate that the first and third arguments are both bound, knowledge of the structure of X (i.e., is it a tree, an integer, etc.?) is necessary.

Note that the binding of the third argument in append/3 is not trailed because append/3 is clearly a determinate program. In general, the amount of trailing is impossible to determine statically from the source program at translation time. One could trail all bindings, but this is rarely necessary. The problem of determining the minimum amount of necessary trailing is addressed in the next section.

An alternative memory-referencing metric, more in keeping with procedural CIFs, counts a memory reference for each *initial* reference to a unique identifier in the current scope. This is called the *traditional CIF*. This metric assumes an underlying host that can capture subsequent references, e.g., a frame stack buffer of unlimited size. An unlimited heap buffer is not considered because the heap exhibits significantly less locality than the stack, making such an assumption less appropriate. An unlimited trail buffer is not considered, although it could be, because trailing does not significantly contribute to memory referencing. Recall that a CIF frame holds arguments passed to the procedure and local variables. Since neither of these objects requires initialization (e.g., from a *skeletal contour* [91, 2]), the alternative referencing metric results in *no* memory references for accessing the stack. Note however that the Prolog storage model also consists of a heap and trail. References to these areas (about 25% of all data references in typical programs) must be counted.

The **append/3** example is re-analyzed in Figure 2-5. Here the alternative metric is calculated, resulting in six memory references as compared to 12 references in Figure 2-4. Figure 2-5 simply discounts all references to frame variables in Figure 2-4. Measurements of both the naive CIF and traditional CIF data referencing metrics for large Prolog benchmarks are presented in Section 3.4.

---

	read	write
append(		
[X|L1],	0	2
L2,		
[X|L3]) :-	1	3
append(		
L1,		
L2,		
L3).		

Figure 2-5: Alternative CIF Data Referencing (words): append/3

2.1.3. Register-Based CIF

A register-based Prolog CIF is defined in this section. This CIF differs from the traditional model in that it has a two-level name space, leading to the separation of frames into *environments* and *choice points*. In this section, justifications for constraining the traditional CIF in this manner are given. In subsequent sections, the two-level name space, register allocation scheme, storage model, and instruction set are described.

The traditional Prolog CIF previously defined makes no memory references when referencing the stack. This measurement assumes a host with a stack buffer of unlimited size. Measurements presented in Chapter 4 indicate that for typical Prolog programs on the WAM architecture, which has excellent stack locality, a 256 word stack buffer reduces memory traffic by about 75%. Almost all of the remaining traffic is due to heap and trail references not captured in the buffer. In fact, the traditional Prolog CIF will almost certainly have inferior locality compared to the WAM, as is discussed in detail in the remainder of this section. These results indicate that a costly host (i.e., a host with a fast local memory of substantial size) is necessary to achieve the traditional CIF. For instance, a real host might use a non-architected cache (i.e., a local memory below the level of the architecture).

Recall that the Prolog CIF is an architecture that does not limit the execution of Prolog programs on *sufficiently powerful hosts*. Consider three types of host. In the first host a small register set is implemented, but no stack buffer or cache. In this case, the traditional CIF cannot be achieved and a register-based architecture will perform better. In the second host, a stack buffer is implemented, so that the traditional CIF can be achieved. In this case, the traditional CIF is the best architecture if the buffer is large enough. In the third host, a general cache is implemented, so that the traditional CIF is achieved, but at significant cost. At comparatively little *extra* cost, a small, *relatively faster* register set can also be implemented. Again, a register-based architecture will be advantageous.

Note that the first and third hosts have identical architectures because the cache is not explicitly referenced in the instruction set. Considering architectures for these hosts, it is beneficial to *constrain* the traditional CIF. The register-based Prolog CIF is such a model, assuming a host with only a small register set.

Two-level Name Space

A two-level name space is used in the register-based Prolog CIF. The first level is composed of *registers*; the second level is composed of *environments*.

Informally, an environment holds local variables of a clause, similar to a frame in the traditional CIF model. A more precise definition is given later in this section.

The register set as defined in this model is a group of words, one per register, that is addressed with an index. The major premise is that a host can offer faster access to an object stored in a register than to an object stored in an environment. In other words, the register-based Prolog CIF restricts the traditional CIF from assuming a host with a stack buffer of significant size to the more modest assumption of a single, small register set. When calculating the memory traffic for the register-based CIF, memory references are counted for all stack references, but not for register references.

Each unique variable in a clause (scope) is allocated either to the register space or environment space. These are called *temporary* and *permanent* variables respectively in order to retain the accepted nomenclature as introduced by Warren [96]. A temporary variable is defined informally as a variable which occurs in at most one *chunk*, where the head is considered part of the first chunk [17]. A chunk is a possibly empty sequence of *safe* goals followed by an *unsafe* goal. A safe goal is a built-in goal that does not modify the registers. An unsafe goal is a goal which is not safe. A permanent variable is a variable which is not temporary.

Although it is desirable to place all variables in registers, the definition of a temporary variable has been restricted. A simple compiler cannot determine whether a temporary variable will survive through a user-defined goal invocation (procedure call), i.e., whether a given register will be modified by the callee. Inexpensive and therefore simple register allocators are assumed here. Thus a variable whose lifetime extends beyond one chunk is categorized as permanent.

The single register set is shared by all clauses in the program. For each procedure call, arguments are passed through the registers (also called the *argument registers*). For very tight call loops (e.g., **append/3**) TRO operates entirely from the register set and no environments need be allocated. There are also disadvantages to using registers. For instance, a caller may pass some arguments to a callee through the registers. The callee allocates a subset of the arguments as permanent variables and must subsequently move them into its environment. If this register-to-memory transfer is verbatim, i.e., no useful unification is performed, then it is purely an artifact of the register-based architecture. This overhead is avoided in the traditional Prolog CIF.

The new storage model, illustrated in Figure 2-6, is similar to that of the traditional Prolog CIF (Figure 2-1). The thick arrows in Figure 2-6 represent typical indirect data references. The thin arrows represent typical management pointers. Only the most important connections from one area to another are shown. These connections and the individual areas are described below. The

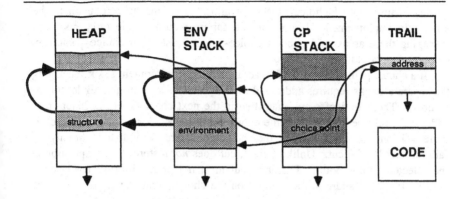

Figure 2-6: Register-based Prolog CIF Storage Model

major difference between the traditional and register-based storage models is that the latter splits a frame into an *environment* and *choice point*, allowing separate stacks for these objects. Figure 2-6 illustrates such a model.

Since arguments are passed through registers, there is no need to allocate arguments in an environment belonging to a determinate procedure. Instead, choice points and environments can be defined as independent objects. A choice point holds the arguments passed to a nondeterminate procedure and the state register values (so that these values can be restored upon failure). In addition, clauses composed of a single chunk do not have any permanent variables, and therefore do not require an environment.

In the traditional Prolog CIF, a frame is created for each procedure invocation. In the register-based CIF, an environment is created for each *clause* invocation, when necessary. A choice point is created for each nondeterminate procedure invocation. Since there may be multiple branch points active at any one time during program execution, multiple choice points must be managed. The most efficient manner of managing the choice points is in a LIFO stack. Informally, failure *restores the current (top) choice point.*

Choice points can be allocated either on the environment stack (as in the WAM), or on a separate *choice point stack.* In either case, a choice point must freeze all previously allocated environments to allow failure to properly restore them.   If choice points are allocated on the environment stack, cut can be implemented with relative efficiency, but because environments must not be removed by cut, cut is less effective in pruning the stack and thereby improving locality. Similarly, if choice points are allocated on the heap, cut cannot be efficiently implemented. If not for cut, failure would be the only operation managing these areas, and either a choice-point/trail-stack or choice-point/heap combination would be advantageous.

If a choice point stack is used in addition to the environment stack, managing the separate stacks requires additional memory references, but greater locality is attained. These tradeoffs are quantified in the next chapters. In addition, trail addresses could be allocated on the choice point stack. A separate trail stack is more efficient, however, because the choice points are manipulated not only for failure, but also for cut. Unlike failure, cut does *not* restore the computation at the selected choice point. Therefore cut must not prune the trail (or heap or stack). If trailed addresses are stored on the choice point stack, cut cannot be implemented to reclaim the maximum amount of stack space.

Instruction Encoding

This section describes the register-based Prolog CIF instruction set and encoding methods. The register-based instruction set is similar to that of the traditional Prolog CIF. The major difference is the pervasive use of register operands.

As previously described (for the traditional Prolog CIF) the CIF translates the unification of simple terms and one-level structures into one instruction. A clause head is matched with **get** instructions and the body goals are set up with **put** instructions. In the case of the register-based CIF, the **get** sources and **put** destinations are temporary variables (registers), whereas the **get** destination(s) and **put** source(s) can be both temporary and permanent variables.

The **get** and **put** instruction semantics are the same as specified in Section 2.1.2, with the exception of **put** with a **var** source operand. Recall that **put** instructions assign their source operand(s) to their destination operand. A **var** source operand must first be initialized to an unbound variable before assignment to the destination. For temporary variables, the unbound variable is created on the heap because an unbound variable cannot reside in a register (an unbound variable resides in either the heap or stack — it cannot exist solely in a register, which has no associated address). For permanent variables, the unbound variable is created in the environment.

Some examples of register-based CIF code are given in Figure 2-7. On careful examination, this CIF is similar to the WAM (described in Section 2.2.2), with **get/put_list/structure** encoded in a variable length instruction. Comparing this approach with a procedural CIF, the fundamental difference is

```
append([],X,X).
        get        X0,const([])
    %   get        X1,var(X1)
        get        X2,val(X1)
        proceed

append([X|L1],L2,[X|L3]) :- append(L1,L2,L3).
        get_list  X0,var(X3),var(X0)
    %   get        X1,var(X1)
        get_list  X2,val(X3),var(X2)
    %   put        X0,val(X0)
    %   put        X1,val(X1)
    %   put        X2,val(X2)
        execute   append/3

foo(f(a,b,g(X)),X) :- bingo(f(a,X,Y,g(Y))).
    %   get        X1,var(X1)
        get_stct  X0,f/3,const(a),const(b),var(X2)
        get_stct  X2,g/1,val(X1)
        put_stct  X0,f/4,const(a),val(X1),var(X1),var(X2)
        put_stct  X2,g/1,val(X1)
        execute   bingo/1

qsort([X|L],R0,R) :- split(L,X,L1,L2),
    qsort(L1,R0,[X|R1]),qsort(L2,R1,R).
        allocate
        get_list  X0,var(Y5),var(X0)
        get        X1,var(Y4)
        get        X2,var(Y2)
    %   put        X0,val(X0)
        put        X1,val(Y5)
        put        X2,var(Y3)
        put        X3,var(Y0)
        call       split/4
        put        X0,unsafe(Y3)
        put        X1,val(Y4)
        put_list  X2,val(Y5),var(Y1)
        call       qsort/3
        put        X0,unsafe(Y0)
        put        X1,val(Y1)
        put        X2,val(Y2)
        deallocate
        execute   qsort/3
```

Figure 2-7: Register-based Prolog CIF Program Examples

the use of registers and subsequent requirement of register allocation. This is not significant in the measurements presented in this book, where an unlimited number of registers are assumed, so that reasonable allocation is possible (although not perfect, in the sense that inter-procedural allocation is not done). For the benchmarks measured in subsequent chapters, rarely are more than eight registers used by this simple type of allocation.

The `call` and `proceed` instructions in the register-based CIF are similar to those of the traditional CIF. Specific `allocate` and `deallocate` instructions manage environments for each individual clause. TRO is therefore implemented with an explicit `deallocate` followed by an `execute`. Note that TRO is as efficient as in the traditional CIF — instead of overwriting the current frame, the temporary registers are overwritten.

The register-based CIF incurs frequent (de)allocation of environments during the execution of nondeterminate code because each clause is managed independently. The traditional CIF (de)allocates a frame only once per procedure invocation. Recall that the traditional CIF, however, must allocate frames with space enough for the maximum number of frame variables among the possibly matching clauses. Therefore the register-based CIF reduces environment size by incurring management overheads. In the emulator described in this book, the cost of allocating and deallocating an environment in the register-based CIF is six memory references, so this overhead is significant.

The `qsort/3` code in Figure 2-7 illustrates another overhead of the register-based CIF — the register transfer overhead. The `get X1,var(Y4)` and `get X2,var(Y2)` instructions in `qsort/3` are not necessary in the traditional CIF. They are present here because these arguments (R0 and R) are permanent variables and so they must be loaded into the environment. For the benchmarks studied in this book, 6.1% of the WAM instructions executed are of this type, generating 3.6% of the total memory traffic (see Table B-2 in Appendix B). Because the register-based CIF instruction set is more tightly encoded than the WAM, these register transfer instructions represent greater overhead, by percentage, in the CIF.

The register-based Prolog CIF is encoded in a manner similar to the traditional Prolog CIF. The only difference is that temporary register operands cannot be $\log_2$ encoded, resulting in slightly larger code. Figure 2-8 gives an example of CIF encoding for the determinate execution of the second clause of `append/3`, in bits. In this example, four bit register specifiers give a total of 76 bits, compared to 64 bits for the traditional CIF, a 19% increase in size. Register-based CIF data referencing for `append/3` is identical to the traditional CIF count given in Figure 2-5 because in this case, the register-based CIF operates solely from registers without accessing the stack.

		operands			
	opcode	reg	tag	offset	total
`get_list X0,var(X3),var(X0)`	8	12	6		26
`get_list X2,val(X3),var(X2)`	8	12	6		26
`execute append/3`	8			16	24
	24	24	12	16	76 bits

Figure 2-8: CIF Instruction Encoding (bits): append/3 Clause 2

2.1.4. Other CIF Metrics: Stability

In the previous sections, Prolog CIF metrics for transparency, program size, and memory referencing are introduced. Examples of these metrics are given for the traditional and register-based CIFs. In this section, another important metric, stability, is described. Stability measures the (potential) disruption to sequential interpretation of a program. Stability measures include:

- the number of state transitions within a scope (indexing)
- the number of state transitions between scopes (call/return)
- the number of state transitions between a scope and a trap handler (failure)
- the number of identifiers requiring a computation to map a name into a value (dereferencing)
- the number of binding operations potentially requiring unbinding operations upon failure (trailing)

Call/return instructions, similar to those of conventional architectures, will not be discussed further. Statistical results gathered in this study indicate that dereferencing is minimized with the rule introduced in the WAM: *dereference only when necessary*. One explanation of this is that Prolog programs produce very short pointer chains (almost always one or no indirections). Therefore, pre-dereferencing or saving of dereferenced values has little advantage. The following sections define the stability measures for trailing and indexing in detail. The discussion centers around the traditional CIF, however, the comments hold equally well for the register-based CIF.

Trailing

A trail function is sought with which each binding is tested to determine if the binding needs trailing. Two criteria must be met. The function must cost less than the memory write needed to trail the binding and must filter out a large percentage of the bindings, i.e., must reject trailing for a large percentage of bindings.

Note that all bindings reside either in the heap or in frame variables in the stack. Recall that failure deallocates portions of the stack and heap created after the most recent or *current* branch point. Thus bindings in these now deallocated areas did not need to be trailed. The trail function is an address comparison between the location to be bound and the locations in the stack and heap to be backtracked to in case of failure. The WAM performs a trail test of this type.

Recall that detrailing is the operation, during failure, of reading entries from the trail and resetting the corresponding locations to unbound, i.e., *unbinding* them. The writes can be filtered with an "inverse trail test," to check whether the locations are still in the machine state. An object may have been trailed, yet is no longer in the valid heap or stack, because a cut may have reset these areas. In fact, the trail function and inverse trail function are identical.

Another implementation of this optimization is to garbage collect the trail, using the inverse trail test, during a cut. This also increases the locality of the trail. Trail entries rejected by the test must be either marked invalid, or removed from the trail. If they are simply marked, detrailing must be prepared to interpret them. If they are removed, each entry in the trail must be read and rewritten during garbage collection. Thus the only advantage of garbage collecting the trail is to minimize its size.

Consider the following optimization. If successful execution can be guaranteed over some segment of the program ending in a cut, then the trail test over that segment can use a restricted trail test, i.e., using the branch point frame to be cut to. A restricted trail test reduces the number of trailed objects. The problem with implementing this optimization is determining that a given program segment succeeds. If success cannot be guaranteed then the restricted trail test does not work.

Another way to view this idea is as follows. It has been observed herein that in certain programs the trail writes exceed trail reads by a significant ratio (as high as 3:1 for the WAM). This indicates that determinancy in the program is not being detected by the architecture, which is doing extra work trailing bindings that are never undone. An example of this phenomenon is the procedure **integers/3**, shown in Figure 2-9, which creates a list of sequential integers.

The first clause repeatedly succeeds while building the list. Finally, the first clause fails into the second clause which closes the list. For each recursive call of the first clause, the callee matches the third argument, a variable in the caller's

```
integers(N, Max, [N|Rest]) :-
        N < Max,
        !,
        N1 is N+1,
        integers(N1, Max, Rest).
integers(_, _, []).
```

Figure 2-9: Prolog Program Example: Max-N+1 Trails

```
integers(N, Max, L) :-
        N < Max,
        !,
        L = [N|Rest],
        N1 is N+1,
        integers(N1, Max, Rest).
integers(_, _, []).
```

Figure 2-10: Prolog Program Example: No Trails

```
integers(N, Max, L) :-
        N < Max,
        L = [N|Rest],
        !,
        N1 is N+1,
        integers(N1, Max, Rest).
integers(_, _, []).
```

Figure 2-11: Prolog Program Example: Moving Comparison Into "Head"

frame, against a list. This structure creation requires trailing the argument in case the first clause fails. In practice however, the first clause succeeds **Max-N** times and fails only once. Therefore the ratio of trail writes to reads is **Max-N+1:1**.

An alternative encoding of this procedure is shown in Figure 2-10. By moving the binding of the third argument after the cut, no trailing is done because the cut resets the current branch point frame to before the caller's frame. This modification presupposes that binding the third argument can be placed after the cut, i.e., that the passed parameter is unbound. If the procedure is to be used to check the sequentiality of a list of integers, then this modification is erroneous because the base case (second clause) would not be reached. The modification could be done by a compiler given the *mode declaration* `integers(+,+,-).`[6]

Notice that the optimization given in Figure 2-10 is different than moving the arithmetic comparison as shown in Figure 2-11. This can be done independently of modes and simply moves the comparison, which binds no variables, before matching the third argument. A compiler should be readily able to do this also. In the Prolog CIF, these compiler optimizations are not assumed. Both trailing and detrailing functions are included however, and measurements of their efficiency are presented in the next chapter.

Indexing

In Prolog, invocation of a procedure causes the selection of a clause of that procedure to execute. Alternative clauses satisfying a nondeterminate procedure must be attempted in their textual order. A trivial selection strategy is to sequentially attempt to match each and every clause of the procedure. *Indexing* methods are selection strategies which improve upon the trivial strategy. In this section, motivations for designing efficient indexing methods are given. Indexing in the WAM and the Prolog CIF are then described. Measurements of indexing efficiency are presented in Section 3.4.

Failures occur within **get** instructions and built-in predicates. Consider an instruction failing in the currently executing procedure. There are two types of failure: either an alternative clause exists and is entered as a result of the failure, or the failure immediately causes the entire procedure to fail because no alternative clauses exist. Occurrences of the latter type of failure cannot be minimized in the CIF because they are representative of nondeterministic program execution (recall that the translation from Prolog source to CIF is quite simple and cannot analyze these occurrences statically). The former type of failure, called *head failure* or *shallow backtracking*, is indicative of a non-optimal clause selection strategy. This type of failure can be minimized with better indexing.

Indexing, as introduced for the WAM, hashes the first passed argument into a table of possible clauses [96]. The resulting selection may be a single clause if there are no collisions, or a group of clauses. This method significantly improves upon the trivial selection strategy, if programs properly utilize the first argument. *Ideal indexing* is a selection method introduced for the Prolog CIF. Ideal indexing chooses the correct clause, expending no extra work (i.e., instructions

---

[6]Mode annotation was first introduced in DEC-10 Prolog [12]. "+" specifies that the corresponding argument is bound. "-" specifies that the corresponding argument is unbound.

executed and memory references made), unless one the following conditions exists:

1. The head of a clause matches, but the body fails — this requires work to match the head.

2. Shared variables in the head of a clause fail to unify — this requires work to partially match the head.

For two or more of these occurrences, work is also required to initially load the state values into the branch point frame, and restore these values for each failure.

Ideal indexing is a CIF attribute introduced to maximize the stability of state transfers. Indexing reduces clause-to-clause transfers and failures. It also reduces overall memory referencing because work matching clause heads, and the loading and restoring of branch point frames, is avoided. The previous definition specifies that an ideal index *expends no extra work* when selecting a clause. In other words, the work required to match a head successfully is meant to approximate the work required to select the clause, the assumption being that the head variables are bound during the indexing.

Ideal indexing is simulated (using the tools described in Section 3.1) because it cannot be analyzed statically. The simulator discounts work expended in matching clause heads which fail because of mismatched ground variables. For example, trying to unify $f(a,b,c)$ with $f(X,b,z)$ fails, and is discounted. Trying to unify $f(a,b,c)$ with $f(X,b,X)$, however, fails but is counted because indexing cannot test shared variables. Consider the following procedure, for the query "?- p(3,b)."

```
p(1,a).
p(X,b)  :- X = 2.
p(X,b)  :- X = 3.
```

Ideal indexing discounts any work attempted to match the first clause. The work required to execute the second and third clauses is counted. Loading state values into the branch point frame in the second clause and the failure sequence restoring those state values for the third clause are counted. For the query p(2,b), however, loading the branch point frame in the second clause should be counted for ideal indexing because although the last clause is not executed, this cannot be determined *a priori*. The simulated model is not sophisticated enough to catch this subtlety and as a result, does not account for this overhead.

2.1.5. Summary

In this section, Prolog canonical interpretive forms (CIFs) are defined from the semantics of Prolog with some ideas borrowed from existing Prolog architectures. The CIFs define the measures that limit the execution performance of Prolog (measurements of the characteristics of the Prolog CIFs are presented in Section 3.4). Initially *naive* and *traditional Prolog CIFs* are described — they are based on the procedural CIFs given by Flynn and Hoevel [27]. The naive model assumes a simple host with no fast memory. The traditional model assumes a host implementing a stack buffer of unlimited size. It is argued that such an assumption is ill-directed for Prolog, where only 75% of the data references are to the stack. To achieve canonical performance somewhat costly hosts must be assumed. A real host might use a non-architected cache, for instance, to attempt to achieve the traditional CIF's performance. Other hosts may choose not to incur the expense, and therefore cannot achieve even a fraction of the traditional CIF's performance. In anticipation of this, it is beneficial to *constrain* the CIF so that the CIF does not rely on the assumption of a stack buffer of significant size. A *register-based Prolog CIF* is defined which assumes a host with only a single, small register set. Inexpensive hosts (with only registers) achieve greater performance with this constrained CIF than with the traditional CIF. Expensive hosts (with caches) have the opportunity, by implementing fast registers at a possibly small cost increase, to also achieve greater performance with the constrained CIF.

The register-based CIF naturally leads to direct correspondence architectures (DCAs) for Prolog, i.e., architectures that can be implemented on realistic hosts. The WAM architecture, defined in Section 2.2.2, can be viewed as such a DCA. DCAs based on the traditional Prolog CIF, such as the DEC-10 Prolog model described in the next section, may offer better performance than the WAM on a host with a large stack buffer or register window set. Even on these powerful hosts, however, the performance differential between the traditional and register-based DCAs is not anticipated to be large. On conventional hosts, the register-based DCAs are superior to the traditional DCAs. For this reason, the WAM architecture is chosen throughout the remainder of this book as the compiler target for the Prolog benchmarks studied.

2.2. Environment Stacking Architectures

The Prolog architecture family presented in Section 2.1 is an *environment stacking* model. The first environment stacking architecture was introduced in DEC-10 Prolog [93].[7] Historically, the WAM was derived from DEC-10 Prolog. It should be noted that the environment stacking model is not the only successful model used to implement Prolog. The original version of Symbolics-3600 Prolog uses a *goal stacking* model [97]. This architecture was chosen for the Symbolics implementation because it maps well onto the Lisp computational model and the 3600 organization [80]. The goal stacking model was not chosen as the basis of the Prolog CIF, nor will it be discussed in detail this book, because the environment stacking model has superior memory referencing characteristics.

In the goal stacking model, upon successful unification of a clause head, stack frames are created for each goal of the body. The stack therefore exactly mimics the resolvent of a proof as calculated with paper and pencil. This decreases the stability and compactness of the stack, reducing locality, as compared to the environment stacking model. In addition, because resolution *replaces* the top goal of the stack by the body of a matching clause, variables resident *only* in that goal must be transferred to the heap to prevent them from being overwritten. The check necessary to determine if a variable needs to be transferred must be performed at runtime. Although the environment stacking model also requires this safety operation, its frequency can be reduced by static analysis.

In the remainder of this section, both the DEC-10 Prolog and the WAM implementations of the environment stacking model are described and compared. This constitutes a more conventional explanation of the WAM than that of the previous section.

2.2.1. DEC-10 Prolog Abstract Machine

The DEC-10 Prolog architecture developed by D.H.D. Warren, as described in [94], is called the Prolog-10 model in this book. The stack (called the *local stack*) corresponds roughly to a conventional language's procedure invocation stack. A Prolog-10 *frame* is a variable-length stack frame holding the procedure's local variables, the arguments passed to the procedure, bookkeeping

---

[7]The phrase "environment stacking" was not coined until the WAM [96], but it is used informally here.

information, and, if the procedure is nondeterminate, information needed to retry the procedure at its next clause. Thus the frame is similar to the traditional Prolog CIF frame introduced earlier.

The Prolog-10 model is built around several state registers. The registers related to the local stack and necessary for the purposes of this discussion are L, the current local stack frame, and BL, the current backtrack frame. The top of the stack is defined as the greater of BL and L. The current frame pointed to by L heads a *continuation chain* of frames corresponding to the resolvent of the proof. An additional *backtrack chain* of possibly interspersed frames is headed by BL. These frames belong to nondeterminate procedures and are called *backtrack frames*.

The Prolog-10 calling convention is as follows. The caller loads arguments into dedicated argument registers and control is passed to the callee. The callee loads these registers into its empty frame. Indexing instructions select a callee clause to try. A nondeterminate callee also loads backtracking information from the state registers into its frame. Specialized unification instructions in the head of the selected clause attempt unification against the arguments. If the match succeeds, an **enter** instruction is executed which saves certain bookkeeping information in the frame, completing the frame. The goals are then called sequentially.

Failure occurs when a goal cannot be satisfied; i.e., when the caller's arguments fail to unify with a callee's head. Failure restores the current backtrack frame by assigning L=BL. Note that if the current backtrack frame is *already* on the top of the stack, the state registers have not changed — this is called *shallow backtracking*. If this is *not* the case then the bookkeeping information in the new current frame must be restored (*deep backtracking*). In either case, any bindings made by the unsuccessful goal are undone and execution proceeds with an alternative clause. The Prolog-10 model handles shallow backtracking efficiently. The price for efficient backtracking is the calling convention having the callee always load the argument registers into its newly formed frame and the overhead of always referencing variables from the frame to avoid refreshing the argument registers upon backtracking.

Cut is implemented in the Prolog-10 model by traveling down the backtrack chain until a frame is found predating the current frame. BL is assigned to point to this backtrack frame, trimming the stack.

ZIP and NIP, developed by Byrd [9] and Bowen [10] respectively, are environment-stacking models that form an architectural midpoint between Prolog-10 and the WAM. NIP, an improved version of ZIP, has a storage model with frames similar to those of Prolog-10. The NIP abstract machine is an improved (cleaned-up) version of the Prolog-10 abstract machine, similar in

E	current environment
B	current choice point
H	heap pointer
HB	heap backtrack pointer
TR	trail pointer
P	current instruction pointer
CP	continuation instruction pointer
S	heap structure pointer
X0...X15	argument registers

Table 2-1: WAM Model State Registers

many respects to the WAM. The NIP compiler moves certain primitive goals (e.g., `var/1`, `cut/0`, etc.) appearing immediately after the neck of a clause to before the neck. This further optimizes shallow backtracking by allowing failure to occur earlier, before work is expended completing the frame. Note that NIP differs most significantly with the WAM in that it does not have indexing.

2.2.2. Warren Abstract Machine

The WAM is a more recent environment-stacking model developed by D.H.D. Warren [96], based on the Prolog-10 and NIP models and first implemented for the VAX. The WAM model defines a stack with two types of variable-length frames: *environments* and *choice points*. An environment holds only local variables and bookkeeping information. A choice point holds arguments passed to a nondeterminate procedure and backtracking information. A continuation chain links environments and a backtrack chain links choice points. This separation permits compiler optimization of choice point allocation *only where necessary*.

The WAM model has state and argument registers, summarized in Table 2-1, which are similar in function to those of the Prolog-10 model. The stack is also managed similarly — the top of stack is the more recent of E and B. The backtracking information in a choice point includes a pointer to the environment active when the choice point was created.

The WAM model calling conventions are as follows. The caller loads arguments into dedicated argument registers and control is passed to the callee. Indexing instructions select a callee clause to try. If the callee is nondeterminate, i.e., if indexing cannot narrow down the field of possibly matching clauses to one, a choice point is created and loaded with the argument registers and backtracking information (**E**, **B**, **H**, **CP**, **P**, **TR**). Specialized unification instructions in the head of the selected clause attempt unification against the arguments. If the match succeeds, the goals of the clause are called sequentially.

Failure restores the machine state from the current choice point, which is left in place (a subsequent instruction will remove the choice point if no alternatives remain). **TR**, **CP**, **P**, **E**, and the argument registers are reloaded with values from the choice point. **H** is reloaded from **HB**, a state register which mirrors the **H** value saved in the choice point. Shallow backtracking occurs when the current choice point is the most recent frame on the stack. Otherwise deep backtracking occurs and resetting **B** trims the stack.

In the case of shallow backtracking, restoration of **E** and **CP** is unnecessary · because head unification cannot modify these registers. As mentioned, the Prolog-10 model avoids saving and restoring these registers with the **enter** instruction. It is also possible that the argument registers have not been modified before head failure. This cannot be guaranteed by compilers that overwrite registers during head unification. If this optimization is removed, saving and restoring argument registers is unnecessary until *after* the clause body is entered. With these two modifications, the WAM model approaches the Prolog-10 model's shallow backtracking efficiency.

One method by which cut can be implemented in the WAM model is by assigning **B** to the choice point immediately preceding the current environment. If the current environment is nondeterminate, **B** is reassigned to point to the choice point *before* this choice point. The action of resetting **B** may trim the stack. This implementation of cut is adopted here.

2.2.3. Comparison Between Prolog-10 and WAM

To compare the WAM and Prolog-10, consider the program in Figure 2-12. As described in the previous section, the WAM model [96], and the Prolog-10 model [94], do not correspond precisely to either the WAM variant measured in this book (introduced in the next section), nor to actual DEC-10 Prolog. For the purposes of comparison, however, the models described here are sufficient to approximate the performance of the actual architectures.

Table 2-2 shows the correspondence between the Prolog-10 frame and the WAM choice point and environment. For instance, **P(B)** represents the instruction pointer, **P**, saved in the current WAM choice point, pointed to by **B**. Thus **P(B)** indicates which instruction to execute next on backtracking. **BP(L)** corresponds to the same Prolog-10 information. Note that because the WAM splits the Prolog-10 frame into a choice point and environment, sometimes

---

```
a(a,X)  :- b(X).
a(b,X)  :- b(X),c(X),d(X).
a(c,1).

z(a,X)  :- b(X).
z(b,X)  :- b(X),c(X),d(X).
z(c,1).
z(_,_).

b(1).
c(1).
d(1).
```

Figure 2-12: Program Example: WAM/Prolog-10 Comparison

---

redundant information is saved, as $E(B) \equiv E(E)$ and $CP(B) \equiv CP(E)$. This happens whenever a choice point followed by an environment is created for the same clause.

To determine the differences in execution between the WAM and Prolog-10 models, various queries of the program in Figure 2-12 are considered. The queries are described in Table 2-3. The machine code and traces used to calculate these statistics are listed in Tick [85]. Table 2-3 lists the query, the success or failure of the query, the number of memory references made by each model, and the difference between memory reference counts. Also listed are whether the WAM model builds a choice point and an environment. The Prolog-10 model builds a frame for all queries and saves backtracking information only for the z/2 queries, i.e., the nondeterminate traces.

A hypothesis is that the WAM will do better (i.e., make fewer memory references) for determinate traces, Prolog-10 will do better for shallow nondeterminate traces and both will be equal for deep nondeterminate traces. Table 2-3 supports this hypothesis. Determinate execution of a/2 favors WAM by four to eight memory references. Deep backtracking (z(a,2) and z(b,2)) marginally favors Prolog-10 by one to three memory references. Shallow backtracking, z(c,2), favors Prolog-10 by six memory references.

One place where the shallow backtracking savings occur is the Prolog-10 **enter** instruction which separates the head and body of a clause. The **enter** instruction saves G, CL and CP (equivalently, H, E and CP for the WAM), which are later restored in the optimized last call by the **depart** instruction. If the head is not completed, i.e., it fails, the **enter** is never executed. The **fail** operation does not restore G, CL or CP because they are not modified in the head.

WAM	Prolog-10	contents
B(B)	BL(L)	pointer to previous choice point
H(B)	G(L)	pointer to heap frame for choice point
E(B)	CL(L)	pointer to environment
CP(B)	CP(L)	continuation pointer
TR(B)	TR(L)	pointer to trail
P(B)	BP(L)	pointer to instruction to try next
A1..Am(B)	A1..Am(L)	arguments
E(E)	CL(L)	pointer to previous environment
CP(E)	CP(L)	continuation pointer
Y1..Yn(E)	Y1..Yn(L)	variables

Table 2-2: WAM and Prolog-10 Stack Correspondence

				memory references		
query	cp	env	status	Prolog-10	WAM	diff
a(a,1)	no	no	succeeds	5	0	+5
a(b,1)	no	yes	succeeds	14	6	+8
a(c,2)	no	no	fails in head	4	0	+4
a(a,2)	no	no	fails in first goal	5	0	+5
a(b,2)	no	yes	fails in first goal	8	4	+4
z(a,1)	yes	no	succeeds	11	8	+3
z(b,1)	yes	yes	succeeds	11	16	-5
z(c,2)	yes	no	fails in head	11	17	-6
z(a,2)	yes	no	fails in first goal	16	17	-1
z(b,2)	yes	yes	fails in first goal	18	21	-3

Table 2-3: WAM and Prolog-10 Memory Referencing

Familiarity with the WAM will no doubt cause confusion as to why G, the heap pointer, cannot be modified in the head. This is because Prolog-10 uses *structure sharing* to represent terms in the heap. Since the WAM uses *structure copying*, H may be modified in the head, but E and CP are not.

If the WAM is modified to save E and CP in an instruction similar to **enter**, this would save four memory references (two writes and two reads) during shallow backtracking. Assuming that fetching the new **enter** instruction itself requires a one byte memory reference, the savings is reduced to 3.75 references. This savings can be attained only if shallow failure is distinguished from deep failure, to avoid restoring E and CP from the choice point in the former case. The conclusion here is that the WAM can be modified to

	Prolog-10	WAM
advantage	saves args once per procedure	references args from registers
disadvantage	references args from environment	restores args once per clause

Table 2-4: Prolog-10 - WAM Tradeoffs

incorporate Prolog-10 optimizations, although the savings may not outweigh the implementation overheads.

Another area where savings might occur is the method of saving arguments. In the Prolog-10 model, arguments are saved in an **arrive** instruction and then referenced from the environment by subsequent body instructions. The WAM model also saves the arguments (in a choice point by the **try_me_else** instruction) but references them from the register set (possibly modifying them). Thus failing clauses require the register set to be refreshed from the choice point. The trade-off here is summarized in Table 2-4.

A possible hardware solution to this problem is to flag modified argument registers in the WAM. If none are dirty, restoration may be skipped on failure. Although shallow backtracking may still entail modification of argument registers (while setting them up for a body which is never entered), most unit clauses can be compiled to avoid modification. Turk has also suggested this solution [87].

Register window sets are another idea to solve the register modification problem. In the simple case of shallow backtracking, the register window scheme is as follows. A clause matches its head from one window and places arguments to its first goal in an alternative window. Recovery from head failure is automatic. For more complex execution scenarios, however, register windows are more appropriate for the Prolog-10 architecture than for the WAM. A Prolog-10 frame maps well onto a window, whereas the WAM requires splitting windows between environment and/or choice point objects. Borriello et. al. [8] suggest using the SPUR processor's register windows for choice points only. Measurements presented in Chapter 3 suggest, however, that shallow backtracking is the predominant form of nondeterminate execution in Prolog programs. This implies that a single choice-point buffer, like that of the PLM or Pegasus, is sufficient to capture most choice point traffic. Therefore allocating an entire set of register windows for the choice point stack is not cost-effective.

On the SPUR, environments cannot be allocated in register windows because registers are not mapped onto memory addresses. Therefore an unbound variable (which points to itself) cannot reside solely in a register. Stack memory addresses can be aliased onto the register windows at the cost of additional hardware [42]. Simple aliasing hardware has the disadvantage of requiring that contiguous windows correspond to contiguous memory addresses. This implies that the advantage of overlapping windows can be gained only if the caller's environment is at the top of stack.

2.2.4. Lcode Architecture

The instruction set used in this study, called Lcode, derives from both the WAM model and the Berkeley PLM architecture [24]. About 90% of these instruction sets are identical. Differences between the models are detailed in the remainder of this section.

Lcode Instruction Set

Lcode is introduced by means of the flattenCode/3 example presented earlier in Section 1.1. The flattenCode/3 Lcode, annotated with the Prolog source program, is shown in Figure 2-13. Recall that flattenCode/3 flattens a structure into a list. Choice points created for the first two clauses of flattenCode/3 are immediately cut by their first goals. Choice points are created to allow the third clause, the "catchall," to be attempted should the others fail. The compiler could avoid creating these choice points by optimizing across clause boundaries within a procedure. However, this code is being used as a simple example of a more pervasive problem which cannot always be recognized and removed by the compiler.

When flattening a deeply nested structure, flattenCode/3 recurses around the second clause. The switch_term selects label 70 because the first argument, X0, is a structure. The try_me_else instruction at 70 creates a choice point and attempts the second clause. The choice point is created in anticipation of failing through to the following clause, beginning with a trust_me_else instruction. The second clause at label 75 first matches the head and then executes a cut. The cut removes the last choice point created (by the try_me_else at label 70). Subsequent recursive goals follow. The final goal uses TRO by deallocating the second clause's environment before the recursive call (the execute instruction).

Failing to match the head is an example of shallow backtracking. Figure

```
flattenCode/3:
    switch_term  71,69,70
    try  3,73
    retry  75
    trust  69

71: try_me_else  3,72          % flattenCode(
73: get_constant  X0,void/0    %     void,
    get_value  X1,X2           %     Code,Code) :-
    cut_strong                 % !.
    proceed

72: trust  69

70: try_me_else  74            % flattenCode(
75: get_structure  X0,',/2'    %     , (
    unify_variable  X0         %         Seq1,
    allocate  3
    unify_variable  Y2         %                Seq2),
    get_variable  Y0,X2        %     Code,
                               %     Code0) :-
    cut                        % !,
                               % flattenCode(Seq1,Code0,
    put_variable  Y1,X2        %     Code1
    call  flattenCode/3        %     ),
    put_value  Y2,X0           % flattenCode(Seq2,
    put_unsafe_value  Y1,X1    %     Code1,
    put_value  Y0,X2           %     Code
    deallocate
    execute  flattenCode/3     %     ).

74: trust_me_else  fail        % flattenCode(Instr,
69: get_list  X1               %     [
    unify_local_value  X0      %         Instr|
    unify_local_value  X2      %            Code],Code).
    proceed
```

Figure 2-13: Lcode Program Example: flattenCode/3

```
70:        try_me_else   74
75:        get_structure  X0,',/2'    % fails...
           trust_me_else  fail
```

Figure 2-14: Instruction Trace of Head Failure: flattenCode/3

```
70:        try_me_else   74
75:        get_structure  X0,',/2'
           .
           .
           .
           get_variable   Y0,X2
           cut
```

Figure 2-15: Instruction Trace of Head Success: flattenCode/3

2-14 shows the instruction sequence comprising choice point creation and removal for head failure. Figure 2-15 shows a similar sequence for head success. The importance of these two traces is that they both create and remove a choice point. The failure sequence restores the state held in the choice point giving it a larger penalty than the successful sequence. Both, however, contribute equally to choice point write bandwidth — an overhead contributing only indirectly to program execution.

Table 2-5 summarizes the Lcode instruction set. There are in addition several arithmetic instructions, not shown in the table. The operands are denoted as C - atom, integer or functor (constant), Xi - temporary variable (register specifier), Yi - permanent variable (offset in current environment), Vi - argument register or permanent variable, L - instruction address, and n - integer. The head and goal matching instructions are previously introduced as the get and put instructions in the Prolog CIF. The tag of a single get destination operand (or a single put source operand) is incorporated into the WAM opcode. In addition, all instructions are fixed length. get/put_list/structure instruction operands are allocated individual unify instructions. The arithmetic, cut, branch, comparison, and escape Lcode instructions are not present in the WAM. Refer to Tick [84] for the complete Lcode semantics. Refer to Warren [96], Gabriel [30], or Fagin [24] for the WAM instruction semantics.

goal matching	head matching	structure matching
put_variable Vi,Xi	get_variable Vi,Xi	unify_variable Vi
put_constant Xi,C	get_constant Xi,C	unify_constant C
put_nil Xi	get_nil Xi	unify_nil
put_list Xi	get_list Xi	
put_structure Xi,C	get_structure Xi,C	
put_value Vi,Xi	get_value Vi,Xi	unify_value Vi
put_unsafe_value Yi,Xi		unify_local_value Vi
		unify_void n

clause control	indexing	procedure control
allocate n	branch n,Xi,L	try n,L
deallocate	comp n,Vi,Vj	retry L
call L	cond n,Vi	trust L
execute L	hash C,L	try_me_else n,L
proceed	jump L	retry_me_else L
escape n	switch_term Lc,Ll,Ls	trust_me_else_fail
	switch_constant n	cut
	switch_structure n	cut_strong
		cutd L
		fail

Table 2-5: Lcode Instruction Set

Lcode Storage Management

Throughout the Lcode system, design decisions were made with speed and simplicity as the most important considerations. The emulator is only used to analyze program execution and therefore user interface, error recovery, and ease of program development were minor or nonexistent considerations. Note that the specifics of Lcode data types, tags, storage areas and storage management, as defined below, do not accurately resemble a realistic Prolog implementation. Many details, necessary for such an implementation (e.g., garbage collection), are purposely missing to facilitate analysis of the features which *are* included. The Lcode system is used to emulate a number of alternative architecture attributes and therefore is representative of a range of Prolog architectures, e.g., the PLM and the WAM.

The Lcode emulator manages six memory areas: code space, symbol table, heap, trail, stack and push down list (pdl). The code space contains the Lcode program object image. Assert and retract are not implemented, so this area is fixed. The symbol table holds the print-names of atoms, functors, procedures and top-level variables (i.e., variables in the query). The heap holds structures

```
               |<--              4 bytes                -->|
  integer      |          2s-complement value           011|
  nil          |00000000|00000000|00000000|00000111|
  atom         |00000000|   identifier    |    111|
  functor      | arity  |   identifier    |    111|
  ref          |            long address           00|
  unbound      |            self address           00|
  list         |            long address           01|
  structure    |            long address           10|
```

Table 2-6: Lcode Data Object Formats

and unsafe values and is dynamically managed as a stack. The stack holds environments and choice points. The pdl is used by general unification and ==/2, both of which are implemented as recursive functions. The emulator does not check for memory area overflows. No facilities for data area shifting, trimming or garbage collection are implemented. In addition, cut does *not* garbage-collect the trail. Maximum data area sizes may be specified as emulator input, and stay fixed during execution.

A data object is a word (32 bits) composed of a variable length *tag* and a *value*. Lcode data objects are defined in Table 2-6. An *identifier* is an offset into the emulator's symbol table. Unification of atoms, for instance, is done by comparing identifiers. An Lcode linker has not been implemented, so that entire Lcode programs must be assembled together to allow proper identifier assignment. A *long address* is a full 30 bit address pointing to another data object. An unbound variable points to itself (a *self address*) to differentiate it from an indirect reference.

Note that the Lcode architecture (like the WAM) is *structure copying*, i.e., unifying an unbound variable with a structure involves copying the entire structure in the heap. In addition, the Lcode emulator uses standard list coding, requiring two heap words per list cell.

Lcode instructions are either one, two or three words long. Minimal encoding is de-emphasized to allow fast emulation. The first halfword of each instruction is an opcode. An opcode is the address of the C code emulating that instruction. This allows fast instruction dispatch but requires that the emulator kernel fit in the first 64 Kbytes of virtual memory.

Arbitrarily large programs can be compiled and executed. This is implemented with both absolute and instruction relative addressing. To avoid a linkage phase, absolute addressing is actually implemented as base relative, where the base is the first location of the program. Base relative addresses are a full 32 bits long and are used only by inter-procedural branches, i.e., `call` and `execute`. Instruction relative addresses are 16 bits and are used by all other branches, i.e., all intra-procedural branches. This distinction required the introduction of the `jump` instruction to implement disjunction, rather than with the `execute` instruction, as is done in the PLM compiler. Note that intra-procedural branch offsets for the PLM are only eight bits.

Lcode choice points are composed of a fixed size bookkeeping area (seven words) and a variable size argument area (c.f., the PLM choice points which are fixed size of 15 words). Lcode environments are composed of a fixed size bookkeeping area (four words — c.f., the WAM with two words) and a variable size permanent variable area. Both choice points and environments remain statically fixed in size once they are created (c.f., the WAM, which trims environments).

Lcode Instruction Encoding

As is previously mentioned, the Lcode instruction set is loosely encoded to make emulation efficient. It is of interest, however, to measure the instruction bandwidth of more tightly encoded versions of the instruction set. The Lcode emulator calculates the bandwidth of several encodings. All instruction bandwidth measurements presented in this book are calculated independently of the actual Lcode encoding by first tallying instruction counts, and then scaling the counts by appropriate instruction sizes.

In this section two simple encodings are briefly described: word and byte boundary encodings. In Section 3.3.2, bit boundary encodings are introduced and instruction bandwidth measurements are presented for all the encodings. Word (byte) boundary encodings force each instruction to occupy an integral number of words (bytes). The Lcode instruction operand types are listed below. The operand sizes given are valid for word and byte boundary encodings only.

1. **immediate constant** — four bytes encode all Prolog data objects: integers, atoms and functors. In addition, several instructions use small (one byte) immediate constants, e.g., the `allocate` operand specifying the number of permanent variables in the environment.

2. **temporary register specifier** — four bits encodes 16 registers (c.f., PLM with eight registers). Extra procedure arguments can be collected by the compiler into the last argument. If more temporaries are needed during an arithmetic calculation, for instance, they can be allocated as permanent registers.

3. **permanent register specifier** — eight bits encode 256 registers. This should be sufficient for most applications (note that Quintus Prolog [62] and PLM also have this restriction).

4. **local (inter-procedure) branch target** — both one and two byte offsets (from the program counter) are measured. PLM, for instance, uses one byte offsets. Warren suggests using two byte offsets [96].

5. **global (procedure call) branch target** — a two byte offset from a segment register is assumed.

The Lcode formats are summarized in Table B-1 in Appendix B.

Split-Stack Architecture

The split-stack model is a modification of the WAM model wherein environments and choice points are stored separately in an environment stack (E-stack) and choice point stack (B-stack). The Lcode emulator can optionally execute Prolog programs with the split-stack model. The main advantage of this model is an increase in the spatial locality of environment and choice point references.

In Chapter 3, it is shown that after choice point references, environment references are the next largest contributor to the Prolog data bandwidth requirement. In Chapter 4, an E-stack buffer is investigated to reduce this bandwidth requirement, preferably a buffer which can hold the multiple environments at the top of the continuation chain. The buffer must hold only environments to avoid aliasing the choice point buffer. The split-stack model facilitates a directly addressable, wrap-around E-stack buffer much like the stack buffer previously described. As will be shown, an E-stack buffer of one half the size of a corresponding WAM model stack buffer will give similar reductions of environment traffic and effective memory access time.

The split-stack model must retain information implicit in the single stack model, i.e., the position of the choice points with respect to environments. The key is to expand the B register into a register pair {B,C} [13]. B serves the function of the old B, linking the choice point chain together within the B-stack. C points into the E-stack to where the choice point "would have been" (in the single-stack model). More precisely, C is the address of the top of E-stack when the choice point was created. The top of E-stack is defined as the topmost valid entry (in the topmost valid environment) in the E-stack.

The B pointer and choice point size entries in a choice point are now redundant because the B-stack is a true stack. Thus the size location can be reused to hold C. Note that the E pointer and environment size in an environment are *not* redundant because the E-stack is *not* a true stack, i.e., the current environment may not be at the top of stack.

The current instruction semantics work for the split-stack model with minor modifications for {B,C}. B represents not only the current choice point but also the top of the B-stack. Thus cuts naturally deallocate choice points from the B-stack and no "deep" choice points occur. E still points to the current environment, not the top of E-stack. The top of E-stack is defined as

```
if (C > E) TOS = C; else TOS = E;
```

When creating a new choice point, the state is pushed onto the B-stack and then C and B are updated:

```
if (E ≥ C) C = E;
B = B + sizeof(choice point);
```

A consequence of a true choice point stack is that cutting a choice point is permanent (this is not so with the single stack model, where an environment can "protect" a deep choice point). Thus, cuts in a nondeterminate clause cannot be permitted to cut out the clause's choice point if subsequent cuts in the clause are to work. There are two solutions to this problem: a *lazy cut*, described in Tick [82], or a compiler source-to-source transformation converting predicates with multiple cuts into a sequence of single cut predicates. For example,

```
p :- b1,!,b2,!,b3.
```

becomes

```
p :- b1,!,p'.
p':- b2,!,b3.
```

Recall that the WAM trail test is

```
trail(A,HB,B) :- A < HB ; A < B.
```

The split-stack trail test is similar:

```
trail(A,HB,B) :- A < HB ; A≤C.
```

2.3. Restricted AND-Parallel Prolog Architecture

Exploitation of parallelism in logic programming languages is of great interest because sequential performance is limited. The two main approaches to exploiting parallelism in logic programming are *committed-choice nondeterministic* and *don't-know nondeterministic* languages. Committed-choice nondeterministic languages sacrifice backtracking to reduce the complexity of the abstract execution model and efficiently exploit parallelism. The three most prominent members of this language family are Concurrent Prolog [72], Parlog [16], and Guarded Horn Clauses [88]. Don't-know nondeterministic languages, e.g., Prolog, retain full backtracking capabilities. Many implementations use an extended version of Prolog, exploiting both AND and OR parallelism. Examples are ANLWAM — an OR-Parallel Prolog architecture [11], and PWAM — a Restricted AND-Parallel (RAP) Prolog architecture [35].

As stressed in the previous derivation of the Prolog CIF, good memory referencing characteristics (e.g., high locality) are essential in a high performance architecture. In the next chapter, the Prolog CIF and the WAM are shown to have excellent memory referencing characteristics. In other words, the primary advantage of these architectures is their storage model. One would hypothesize that a parallel architecture based on this sequential architecture family would perform well *if it exploited a large enough grain of parallelism to remain within the sequential storage model most of the time while executing*. This is the seminal idea behind various parallel Prolog architectures such as ANLWAM and PWAM.

The key notion in RAP-Prolog is the annotation of a program with *conditional graph expressions* (CGEs). A CGE consists of a condition followed by a conjunction of goals. CGEs can appear anywhere a conventional goal can appear in a clause, including nested within another CGE. The condition is a logical combination of *checks* on any of the variables appearing *to the left of the CGE*. The checks test *independence* and (stronger) *groundness* of sets of variables. These checks can be expensive operations. A full check in general requires traversal of all terms associated with the variables being tested; however, much cheaper checks can be used in return for a certain loss of parallelism. In addition, mode and type analysis performed by the compiler with the aid of user annotation can reduce (or eliminate altogether) the number of required checks.

Figure 2-16 shows the `isotree/2` example of Section 1.1 written in RAP-Prolog. Note that if subtrees are left uninstantiated, `isotree/2` attempts to ensure isomorphism by binding. Suppose the user knows *a priori* that the first tree is always ground, but the second tree may have uninstantiated, possibly shared, subtrees. This information is indicated by the mode declaration `isotree(g,?)`, similar to a DEC-10 Prolog mode declaration. `indep/2` is the check of the CGE containing both AND-parallel recursive goals. The checks ensure that the second argument shares no variables, allowing the goals to be executed in parallel. If the second argument was known to be ground (`isotree(g,g)`) or contain no shared unbound variables (`isotree(g,i)`) then no checks would be needed.

At runtime, the conditions are evaluated to either *true* or *false*. During the execution of a CGE, if the conditions evaluate to *true*, the goals can be executed in parallel and are known as a *parallel call*. Otherwise the goals must be executed sequentially. A *parallel goal* is a goal invoked by a parallel call. Failure of a parallel goal cannot be affected by alternative executions of other

```
:- mode isotree(g, ?).

isotree(void,void).
isotree(tree(X,Left1,Right1),
        tree(X,Left2,Right2)) :-
    (indep(Left2,Right2) |
     isotree(Left1,Left2) &
     isotree(Right1,Right2)
    ).
isotree(tree(X,Left1,Right1),
        tree(X,Left2,Right2)) :-
    (indep(Left2,Right2) |
     isotree(Left1,Right2) &
     isotree(Right1,Left2)
    ).
```

Figure 2-16: RAP-Prolog Program Example: isotree/2

parallel goals (because they are all independent), and so the entire CGE fails. Failure *back into* a parallel call, from subsequent sequential goals *outside* the CGE, causes all parallel goals to the *right* of the rightmost goal with remaining alternatives to be *unwound* and restarted. This allows generation of tuples of results *in the same order as in a sequential execution*. This policy is more complex to implement than others which don't guarantee sequential backtracking order; however, *intelligent backtracking* may be purposefully indicated by the user's goal ordering and so order must be preserved. Other optimizations exist for a determinate CGE which is followed by a cut.

Note that the design of the PWAM architecture and memory hierarchy must account for the case when a parallel call spawns processes for all its conjunctive goals, and these goals are passed arguments from the parent. In addition, these arguments can be arbitrarily complex and contain hidden logical variables through which results will be bound by the child and passed back to the parent.

PWAM is an extension of the WAM architecture. A fundamental design criterion of PWAM is fast sequential execution for cases where there is no available (AND) parallelism. To this end, CGE semantics are integrated into the WAM storage model. PWAM extends the WAM storage areas as summarized in Table 2-7 [36]. PWAM adds Parcall Frames and Markers to the WAM stack. These can be allocated on a choice point stack in a split PWAM architecture. PWAM also adds Goal Frames and Messages, in their own separate storage areas. Each PWAM process references it own stack, heap, trail and pdl. The

Frame Type	Location	In WAM?	Races?	Locality
Env/Bookkeeping	Stack	Yes	No	Local
Env/Permanents	Stack	Yes	No[1]	Global
Choice Points	Stack	Yes	No	Local
Heap	Heap	Yes	No[1]	Global
Trail entries	Trail	Yes	No	Local
PDL entries	PDL	Yes	No	Local
Parcall/local	Stack	No	No	Local[2]
Parcall/global	Stack	No	No[4]	Global[3]
Markers[5]	Stack	No	No	Local
Goal Frames	Goal Stack	No	Yes[6]	Global
Messages	Mess. Buf.	No	Yes[7]	Global

Table 2-7:   PWAM Storage Model (notes 1-7 in text)

Goal Stack and Message Buffer are shared by all processes executing on a single processor (in the following chapters, references to the Goal Stack and Message Buffer are called the *communication* references of the PWAM model). For a complete discussion of the PWAM storage areas, see Hermenegildo [35, 36, 37]. Table 2-7 is annotated with the following notes.

1. The model guarantees that only one process can write each of these variables (goal independence parallelism). Several (child) processes can read them, but the parent process will not read them until *all* children have succeeded. Child processes cannot read the variables until these processes are scheduled.

2. The local part of the Parcall Frame contains bookkeeping information for parallel processes.

3. The global part of the Parcall Frame includes the number of goals still to schedule, the number of goals to wait on, and the process slots (one per goal in the CGE).

4. Although the process slots are global, they don't need to be locked — only a child process can write them and the only time the slots may be read by the parent is after the child has completely succeeded. Thus the situation in the Parcall frame is similar to that in environments:

   local part of Parcall Frame ≡ bookkeeping part of environment
   process slots ≡ permanent variables

   The other two global entries (the number of parallel goals to wait on and the number of parallel goals still to schedule) are semaphores and therefore require an atomic read-modify-write operation to avoid races.

5. For the purposes of memory referencing, the Input Markers, Wait Markers, and Local Goal Markers are identical. They are also similar to choice points, except that they do not save the argument registers.

6. There can be races while stealing a goal from the Goal Stack (several processes may simultaneously try to do so and the action entails several memory references). Thus, a lock is needed for controlling access to each processor's Goal Stack.

7. Several processes may simultaneously attempt to write into the Message Buffer, so this needs to be locked; however, messages represent a small percentage of references, since they are used only during deep and "intelligent" backtracking across processors.

2.4. Summary

Several instruction set architectures for Prolog are introduced in this chapter. Initially, a family of Prolog canonical interpretive forms (CIFs) is defined from the semantics of Prolog with some ideas borrowed from existing Prolog architectures. The CIFs define metrics that limit the execution performance of Prolog — measurements of these metrics are presented in the next chapter. Three CIFs are described: naive, traditional, and register-based. The naive and traditional models are based on procedural language CIFs. Whereas the naive model assumes a simple host, the traditional model assumes a host with a stack buffer of unlimited size. The register-based CIF constrains the traditional CIF, assuming a host with only a small register set.

The progression from one Prolog CIF to the next represents a refinement of the ideas of canonical architectures developed by Flynn and Hoevel [27]. The naive architecture directly corresponds to the Prolog language, to the extreme degree that the entire name space is mapped into a single memory space. The observation is made that references to local identifiers and arguments within a scope can be captured for reuse by a hardware buffer. The traditional architecture maps stack references into such a hardware stack buffer (of unlimited size) in the underlying host. Such a model is "traditional" in the sense that procedural CIFs make a similar host assumption. This assumption is possibly more warranted for procedural languages, which make frequent procedure stack references, than for Prolog, where only 75% of the data references are to the stack. Prolog makes frequent use of the heap also, for dynamic creation and unification of data structures. The register-based CIF is a further refinement of the traditional model, wherein the assumption of an underlying stack buffer is removed and replaced with a register set. These changes represent a relaxation of the correspondence between the CIF and Prolog, and a divergence from the traditional view of canonical architectures. The constraints imposed, however, offer higher performance for direct correspondence architectures (DCAs), i.e., Prolog architectures that can be implemented on realistic hosts. A DCA based on the traditional CIF is the Prolog-10 abstract machine. A DCA based on the register-based CIF is the Warren Abstract Machine (WAM). These two architectures, in addition to PWAM, a Restricted AND-Parallel Prolog extension of the WAM, are described in this chapter.

The presentation given here of the Prolog-10 and WAM models constitute a conventional or evolutionary approach to Prolog architecture design. These environment stacking architectures represent the two most popular Prolog implementations.   A comparison of the high-level memory-referencing characteristics of the two is given. The results suggest that the WAM makes fewer memory references in determinate programs, Prolog-10 makes fewer memory references in shallow nondeterminate programs, and both make approximately equal numbers of references in deeply nondeterminate programs. Thus the WAM achieves its goal of optimizing the execution of determinate code (with respect to Prolog-10), at the cost of slower nondeterminate execution. What was not known at the time of the design of the WAM, however, was the extent of shallow nondeterminate execution in seemingly determinate programs. As is shown in the next chapter, realistic Prolog programs, although largely determinate, display much shallow backtracking when translated with a simple compiler. The WAM, however, has advantages over Prolog-10, such as higher locality resulting in more efficient use of storage. In realistic implementations, these space saving advantages can outweigh the speed disadvantages caused by inefficiencies in backtracking.

A final sequential environment-stacking architecture, called Lcode, is described in this chapter. Lcode is the actual instruction set emulated and measured for this book. Lcode is closely related to the WAM, and the differences between the two do not significantly affect the measurements presented here. All sequential architectures measured, including the Prolog CIFs and split-stack architectures, are modeled with variations of the Lcode compiler and emulator. The parallel Prolog architecture, PWAM, is modeled with a separate compiler and emulator. These tools are further described in the next chapter.

A high-level description of the PWAM model is also given in this chapter. PWAM is chosen for study because it is closely related to the WAM, allowing a fair comparison of the overheads incurred by the exploitation of parallelism. In addition, it appears promising that the PWAM model can be extended for OR-parallelism, e.g., with the mechanisms introduced in ANLWAM [11].

3 Prolog Architecture Measurements

In this chapter, a methodology is described for measuring the dynamic memory performance of Prolog programs compiled into the instruction set architectures described in the previous chapter. The benchmarks measured with this experimental approach are then described. Next, high-level statistical characterizations of Prolog's memory request behavior are presented. From these high-level statistics, problem areas and performance bottlenecks are noted which give credence to various local memory models. In the next chapter, these memory models are described and simulation measurements are presented and analyzed.

Several important results are presented in this chapter. Shallow backtracking is shown to dominate the Prolog data bandwidth requirement. This is shown by analysis of choice point referencing characteristics, as well as by measurements of the effectiveness of "ideal" indexing in the Prolog CIF. In addition, the WAM stack is shown to exhibit high locality of reference, indicating that various types of stack buffers can effectively reduce Prolog's bandwidth requirement. It is shown, however, that the heap exhibits little locality, and therefore caches will likely be necessary to achieve truly high performance execution. Finally, it is shown that PWAM sacrifices little of the WAM's memory-referencing efficiency to achieve parallelism.

3.1. Methodology

Memory reference behavior is measured with address-trace-driven memory simulators. Traces are produced with an Lcode emulator that executes object files produced by an Lcode assembler. The assembler translates Prolog compiler output. These tools are summarized in Table 3-1 and illustrated in Figure 3-1. The tools run on the Stanford Emulation Laboratory VAX-11/750, under Unix[8] 4.3 BSD.

tool	input	output	implementation
compiler	Prolog source	Lcode assembler	Prolog
assembler	Lcode assembler	binary object	LEX/YACC
emulator	binary object	trace file	C
simulators	trace file	statistics	C

Table 3-1:   Stanford Emulation Laboratory Prolog Tools

3.1.1. Compiler

The compiler is a modified version of the UC Berkeley PLM compiler [89]. The compiler, written in Prolog, is about 2900 source lines. The modifications, listed below, were introduced for another study [83], but do not significantly affect the benchmarks measured here.   Refer to Tick [83] for a complete description of the optimizations.

- **removal of cdr-coding**
  cdr-coding was not deemed a significant attribute of the architecture for the benchmarks considered.

- **static-sized environments**
  environment trimming was removed to simplify the architecture.

- **increased number of registers**
  16 registers were implemented as opposed to eight in the PLM. Of the benchmarks considered in this book, only CHAT is affected by the increase in registers, although not significantly [54].   Since variable-sized choice points are used, as in the WAM, increasing the number of registers does not increase choice point overheads, as in the PLM.

---

[8]Unix is a Trademark of Bell Laboratories.

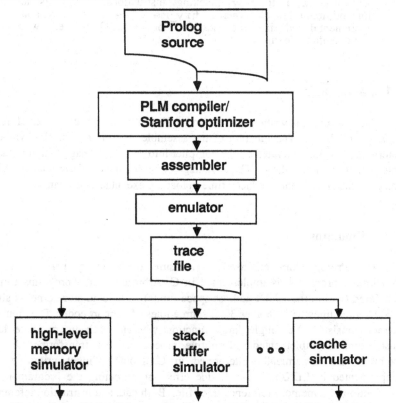

Figure 3-1: Prolog Memory Performance Measurement Methodology

- **arithmetic instructions**
  arithmetic and other primitive operations, e.g., `var/1`, have been
  lifted from built-in predicates to the instruction set.

- **conditional branches**
  a peephole optimization was introduced wherein under certain
  circumstances, simple built-in conditionals, e.g., `>/2`, can be moved
  up into the head of a clause. If a conditional can be moved up in
  front of choice point creation, it is replaced with a conditional
  branch. Subsequently, if the choice point creation meets a cut, both
  are removed.

- **incremental indexing**
  this type of indexing is a slight modification of the method outlined
  by Warren [96], whereby the number of branches is reduced. One

measure of the effectiveness of an indexing method is the ratio of
`try_me_else` to `try` indexing instructions. `try` is an
unconditional branch, whereas `try_me_else` is not. Without
incremental indexing, the ratio is about 3:1 [21], whereas with
incremental indexing, this ratio is about 25:1.

3.1.2. Assembler

The assembler is written in C around a LEX/YACC [47, 40] parser of about
1000 source lines. The function of the assembler is to transform the symbolic
intermediate code generated by the compiler into an object image which is easily
interpreted by the emulator. The advantage of having the emulator read an object
image is the significantly reduced time in loading executable programs.

3.1.3. Emulator

The Prolog emulator, used to measure the memory performance of
benchmark programs, is implemented in C. Arbitrarily large programs can be
emulated (within the UNIX address space limits). The emulator kernel is about
2000 source lines with another 3000 source lines of support code. The emulator
kernel consists of a single large function wherein each intermediate level
instruction is implemented. Primitive procedures not transformed by the
compiler are dynamically interpreted in C. Notably, input primitives are
implemented in LEX/YACC. A side effect of executing the program is the
production of a memory reference trace file. Both data and instruction references
can be traced. An emulator option is procedure profiling, useful in determining
Prolog program hot spots. Memory references made by primitive procedures are
counted as other references; however, these primitives are not restricted to using
the state registers of the WAM model. The assumption is that these primitives
would be microcoded and the required temporary registers would be available.
The emulator also has limited debugging capabilities. The code space can be
displayed through a disassembler and a single break point can be set. Memory
areas and terms can be displayed symbolically. The emulator (with tracing off)
runs at 3900 LIPS for the "naive reverse" benchmark.

The emulator has alternative definitions for certain operations, allowing
emulation of Lcode, the Prolog CIFs (including the split-stack model and ideal
indexing), and shadow register architectures. WAM instructions are emulated in
close correspondence to the detailed semantics given by Warren [96]. Common

simulator	references captured
choice point buffer	data (choice points)
stack buffer	data (choice points and environments)
E-stack buffer	data (environments)
copyback cache	data and/or instructions
"smart" cache	data
write-through cache	data
hybrid cache	data
instruction buffer	instructions
multiprocessor caches	data

Table 3-2: Local Memory Simulators

Lcode operations which lend themselves to alternative semantics include general unification, cut, indexing instructions, and built-ins. The emulator implementations of these operations are described in detail in Tick [84].

3.1.4. Simulators

The memory simulators are C programs that simulate various parameterized local memories driven by trace references. The simulators are summarized in Table 3-2 and described in detail in the next chapters. Note that all memory simulations were conducted with a "cold start," i.e., measurements were taken beginning with the first instruction of each benchmark program, assuming the local memory was initially empty.

3.2. Benchmarks

The four Prolog benchmark programs studied in this book are the CHAT English language parser, the Berkeley PLM Prolog compiler, the Quintus Prolog compiler (QC1), and the Intuitionistic Logic Interpreter (ILI). Two compilers were included because they characterize different programming styles, as described below. CHAT is a database query system written by D. H. D. Warren and L. Periera [95]. Only the front-end parser is used as a benchmark here. The PLM benchmark (not to be confused with the PLM machine) is a slightly modified version of the PLM Prolog compiler, written by P. Van Roy. This compiler does clause and procedure (indexing) compilation. The QC1 benchmark is the Quintus Computer Systems Inc. clause compiler, written by Warren. Neither compiler benchmark generates code — they stop after producing an internal form of WAM code, and both are tested with different input data. ILI, the Intuitional Logic Interpreter, is a natural deduction theorem prover written by S. Haridi.

CHAT, originally written in DEC-10 Prolog, has a simple, pure style, being derived from grammar rules (see [78, p. 256]). PLM, originally written in C-Prolog, has the most complex style, using disjunction and conditionals extensively. PLM originally included code with side effects: an intelligent backtracking register allocator and a garbage collector. The register allocator was retained, by implementing a simplified record primitive, because it has a significant effect on the measurements. The garbage collector was removed. QC1, originally written in Quintus Prolog, has a cleaner style than PLM. QC1 was written to take full advantage of indexing whereas PLM was not. ILI, originally written in IBM-370 Prolog, is the shortest program of the set, being an interpreter. It is pure code, relying on Prolog unification and call to do meta-level reduction.

With only superficial knowledge of the programs, it was expected that CHAT would display the characteristics of a highly nondeterministic program: much backtracking, using choice points and writing environments which are never read because of failure. PLM and QC1 were expected to display characteristics of highly deterministic code: little deep backtracking and more use of the heap. ILI was expected to display characteristics of a meta-level interpreter: much heap and pdl usage. Not all of these predictions are accurate, as is discussed in the following sections.

The benchmarks' characteristics are summarized in Table 3-3. The ratios are approximate, e.g., clauses/procedure is calculated as the total number of clauses divided by the total number of procedures. The mean ratios and *all* mean statistics presented in this thesis are calculated by weighing each benchmark equally. Static measures give an indication of program size, complexity, and consistency. Matsumoto [50] studied 15 large Prolog benchmarks and found similar static characteristics.

Dynamic measures give high-level execution characteristics, e.g., data and instruction references per instruction. A *reference* is a 32 bit word accessed from/to memory. Register-to-register transfers are not considered references. Instruction references are calculated assuming byte encoded formats (see Section 3.3.2). In the queueing models of subsequent chapters, the statistic

program	CHAT	PLM	QC1	ILI	mean
static					
source lines	850	1238	1040	316	
procedures	157	139	133	51	
clauses	500	383	576	141	
Lcode instructions	6439	8694	8269	4478	
clauses/procedure	3.18	2.76	4.33	2.76	3.25
instructions/clause	12.9	22.7	14.4	31.7	20.4
instructions/procedure	41.5	62.5	62.2	87.8	63.5
dynamic					
procedure invocations	47677	36442	41858	17870	
Lcode instructions	587024	616053	674537	283750	
instructions/invocation	12.3	16.9	16.1	15.9	
data references	1347671	1530648	1426098	674013	
instruction references	430715	376236	499043	178908	
data ref/instr ref	3.13	4.07	2.86	3.77	3.46
data ref/instr (v_d)	2.30	2.48	2.11	2.38	2.32
instr ref/instr (v_i)	0.734	0.611	0.740	0.631	0.679

Table 3-3: Summary of Prolog Benchmarks' Characteristics

$v = 3.0$ mean references per WAM instruction[9]
is frequently used. $v = v_r + v_w = v_d + v_i$ corresponding to reads and writes per instruction and data and instruction references per instruction. Huck [39] reports means of 0.524 data words referenced per instruction and 0.837 instruction words referenced per instruction for FORTRAN on the IBM/370. For Pascal/VS on the IBM/370, he reports a mean of 0.84 data words referenced per instruction. For FORTRAN on the VAX 11/780, he reports a mean of 1.31 instruction words referenced per instruction. These results confirm that the WAM instruction set is more potent and more tightly encoded than a conventional instruction set.

---

[9]Throughout the remainder of the book, conclusions drawn about the "WAM" architecture are based on measurements taken of the Lcode architecture, a close variant of the WAM, described in Section 2.2.4.

3.3. WAM Referencing Characteristics

3.3.1. Data Referencing

Memory use statistics are now presented for the benchmarks, assuming a monolithic memory of sufficient size to contain the entire stack, heap, trail, pdl, and code space of the Prolog machine model. Table 3-4 shows the maximum dynamic extent of each data area. The PLM garbage collection facility was turned off, accounting for the runaway heap. The other programs do not have this problem because they do not create large structures (recall QC1 is a *clause* compiler). As hypothesized, ILI makes significant use of the heap — the heap grows about three times larger than the stack. Notice that general unification, which uses the pdl as a call stack (with three word frames) does not deeply recurse for any of these benchmarks.

benchmark	stack	heap	trail	pdl
CHAT	1845	882	258	6
PLM	1577	20013	2628	6
QC1	1571	2675	590	6
ILI	423	1263	84	3

Table 3-4:   Runtime Data Areas in Words

Table 3-5 shows memory data reference statistics broken down by area and by type. The stack references are categorized as choice point (cp) or environment (env). On average the benchmarks do 13% heap referencing and very little trail and pdl referencing. Read to write ratios differ significantly among areas. Heap references are about 2:1 reads to writes, except for CHAT which does the least heap referencing. CHAT does more heap writes than reads, attributed to deep backtracking. Choice point references are consistently about 1:1 reads to writes, indicating that most choice points are restored at least once. Environment references are about 1:2 reads to writes except for QC1, which has a closer ratio. These ratios indicate that most environments are allocated and never read because of failure.

ILI shows the greatest percentage of heap referencing, as expected of an interpreter. As a result of shallow backtracking, PLM shows the greatest percentage of choice point referencing, as expected of a program written without indexing in mind. CHAT shows the greatest percentage of trail referencing, by a wide margin, as expected of a nondeterminate program. Interestingly, CHAT

area	read	%	write	%	total	%
cp	348191	56.4	268918	43.6	617109	45.8
env	132616	35.2	244130	64.8	376746	28.0
heap	109909	45.7	130796	54.3	240705	17.8
trail	51082	50.0	51082	50.0	102164	7.6
pdl	5451	49.8	5496	50.2	10947	0.8
total	647249	48.0	700422	52.0	1347671	100.0

CHAT Data Referencing Profile

area	read	%	write	%	total	%
cp	494678	53.6	428111	46.4	922789	60.3
env	92185	34.7	173151	65.3	265336	17.3
heap	202019	69.5	88755	30.5	290774	19.0
trail	14151	50.0	14156	50.0	28307	1.9
pdl	9669	41.2	13773	58.8	23442	1.5
total	812702	53.1	717946	46.9	1530648	100.0

PLM Data Referencing Profile

area	read	%	write	%	total	%
cp	413119	56.8	314556	43.2	727675	51.0
env	150061	42.4	203864	57.6	353925	24.8
heap	184016	65.4	97166	34.6	281182	19.7
trail	22685	50.0	22685	50.0	45370	3.2
pdl	8859	49.4	9087	50.6	17946	1.3
total	778740	54.6	647358	45.4	14260982	100.0

QC1 Data Referencing Profile

area	read	%	write	%	total	%
cp	215406	58.9	150382	41.1	365788	54.3
env	58638	39.4	90062	60.6	148700	22.1
heap	90146	63.6	51602	36.4	141748	21.0
trail	4568	49.8	4599	50.2	9167	1.3
pdl	4305	50.0	4305	50.0	8610	1.3
total	373063	55.3	300950	44.7	674013	100.0

ILI Data Referencing Profile

Table 3-5: Data Referencing Characteristics of Benchmarks

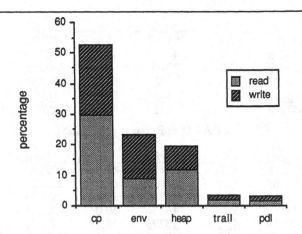

Figure 3-2:   Data References By Area

shows the *least* percentage of choice point referencing, indicating that even for well-written determinate programs, such as QC1, shallow backtracking dominates Prolog referencing characteristics.

Note that the environment `allocate` instruction, as implemented in the Lcode emulator, writes four words of bookkeeping information. Warren claims this can be reduced to two words [96] at the cost of impacting other instructions; however, four words of bookkeeping information is more appropriate for modeling real systems (e.g., PLM and PSI-II). The data in Table 3-5 are summarized in Figure 3-2, which shows the data areas by percentage for the mean of all benchmarks.

Approximately 47% of Lcode data references are writes. Huck [39] reports that both IBM/370 and VAX FORTRAN programs display approximately 18% data writes. Mulder [55] reports approximately 25% data writes for Pascal programs, independent of architecture. The increased Lcode write traffic is attributed to setting up for backtracking, failure and structure copying. The high percentage of choice point writes is due to the method used to implement backtracking. As mentioned above, the high percentage of environment writes is an indirect result of failure. The high percentage of heap writes is caused by the policy of structure copying.

The statistics collected by the high-level memory simulator are listed below. For each of these statistics, frequency distributions are shown for each benchmark as well as the average of the benchmarks. Note that the total area

statistic	area	mean	95%†
object size	cp	11.0 words	13
	env	9.3	15
read depth	cp	10.8	30
	env	22.1	64
	heap	345	>1200
write depth	cp	5.0	10
	env	9.7	29
	heap	86.8	>120
total depth	cp	8.2	21
	env	14.2	40
	heap	261.5	>1200
reset depth	cp	39.6	55
	env	17.7	75
	heap	17.9	50

† refers to 95% quantile

Table 3-6: Summary of High-level Prolog Memory Statistics

under each distribution is one. The mean and 95% quantile of the mean distributions are summarized in Table 3-6. The area under each distribution to the left of the 95% quantile sums to 0.95.

- **object size**
  - **choice point size** — A choice point consists of an entry indicating its size, entries corresponding to the values of six state registers, and the parameters being passed, taken from the temporary registers. Thus the minimum choice point size is seven words, corresponding to a procedure with no arguments. Choice point size is sampled for each choice point reference.
  - **environment size** — An environment consists of an entry indicating its size and entries corresponding to the values of three state registers and the clause's permanent variables. Thus the minimum environment size is four words, corresponding to a procedure with no permanent variables. Environment size is sampled for each reference to the current environment. The sizes of deep environments referenced during dereferencing are not counted.
- **reference depth** — Note that this statistic is measured for read, write, and total references.
  - **choice point depth** — This statistic is sampled for each choice point reference. It is the distance from the reference to the top of stack. Reference depths of less than seven words

are guaranteed to reference a choice point on the top of stack. The read depth indicates the *type* of backtracking because most choice point read references are generated during procedure failure. Shallow backtracking is evident when the choice point read depth is small. Large read depths imply deep backtracking.

- **environment depth** — This statistic is sampled for each environment reference. It is the distance from the reference to the top of stack. Reference depths of less than four words are guaranteed to reference an environment on the top of stack. Environment depth indicates the proportion of references to *deep environments*, i.e., environments hidden by choice points.

- **heap depth** — Sampled for each heap reference, this is the distance from the reference to the top of heap. Heap depth indicates the locality of heap references.

- **reset depth**

  - **choice point reset depth** — This statistic is sampled for each instruction which resets the current choice point. It is the distance from the top of stack *after* resetting the choice point, to the previous top of stack. Recall that the top of stack is defined as the topmost environment or choice point. Deallocating choice points may or may not affect the top of stack. This statistic is a measure of stack locality and type of backtracking. Large reset depths indicate deep backtracking. Zero reset depth often corresponds to cuts.

  - **environment reset depth** — This statistic is sampled for each instruction which resets the current environment, namely **deallocate** and **fail**. It is the distance from the top of stack *after* resetting the environment, to the previous top of stack. A large reset depth signifies that a series of environments has been popped from the stack, i.e., nested determinate procedure calls have terminated (either successfully or otherwise). Zero reset depth signifies termination of a nondeterminate procedure call, i.e., one that left at least one choice point on the stack.

  - **heap reset depth** — This statistic is sampled for each failure. It is the distance from the top of heap *after* failure to the previous top of heap. Recall that during failure, the heap pointer, **H**, is reset to the heap backtrack pointer, **HB**. This statistic indicates the efficiency of this automatic type of garbage collection. Zero reset depth indicates that no heap space has been reclaimed.

- **deference chain length** — This statistic is sampled for each dereference operation executed by an instruction or built-in procedure. Recall that the Lcode architecture may bind a variable to an object by creating a pointer from the variable to the object. Binding a variable to another variable may result in a double pointer chain and so forth. The dereference chain length is the number of memory references needed to fully dereference a variable. Zero length indicates that the variable is bound to an immediate value.

Figures 3-3 and 3-4 show distributions of stack object size. The maximum size choice point is 21 words, generated for the nondeterminate procedure with the greatest number of arguments. The mean size is 11.0 words, and so a nondeterminate procedure contains an average of 4.0 arguments. The 95% quantile is 13 words. 98.0% of all dynamically created choice points are less than 16 words long (hold fewer than nine arguments). The PLM architecture constrains choice points to be fixed at 15 words — this upper bound appears to be a reasonable choice. CHAT procedures have more arguments on the average than the other benchmarks because of the method of translation from grammar rules to simple clauses.

The maximum size environment is 24 words, generated for the procedure with the greatest number of permanent variables. The mean size is 9.3 words, and so an environment contains an average of 5.3 permanent variables. The 95% quantile is 15 words. The statistics indicate that the four bookkeeping words per environment occupy 43% of the environment on average. A 43% overhead is extremely high and skews the read:write ratio for environment references. The ratio is skewed because the overhead entries are always written in the `allocate` instruction, whereas the number of subsequent environment references may be reduced by failure. CHAT procedures have more permanent variables on the average than the other benchmarks because of the complexity of the grammar rules.

Figure 3-5 shows the mean choice point reference depth distributions broken down into read and write distributions. Most references are made near the top of stack. Depths 0-6, referring to a choice point at the top of stack, are unevenly distributed because this information is not used uniformly. For instance most writes are made at a depth of six because `retry` instructions overwrite the P pointer saved in entry seven of the current choice point. The maximum read depth is greater than 120 words and the long read depth tail significantly influences the mean distribution. Whereas the mean write depth is 5.0 words, the mean read depth is 10.8 words. The mean choice point reference depth is 8.2 words with 95% quantile at 21 words.

Figure 3-6 shows the mean environment reference depth distributions. The mean depth is 14.2 words. More significant is a 95% quantile of 40 words indicating a long tail due to referencing deep environments. Of the benchmarks measured, CHAT displays the longest tail. The maximum depths of all the benchmarks exceed 120 words. The split-stack model was proposed as a partial solution to this problem.

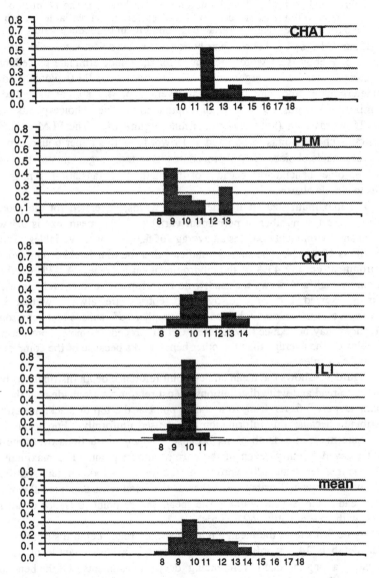

Figure 3-3: Choice Point Size Frequency Distributions (words)

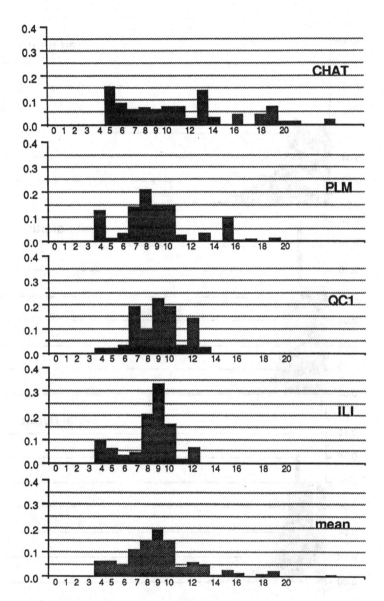

Figure 3-4: Environment Size Frequency Distributions (words)

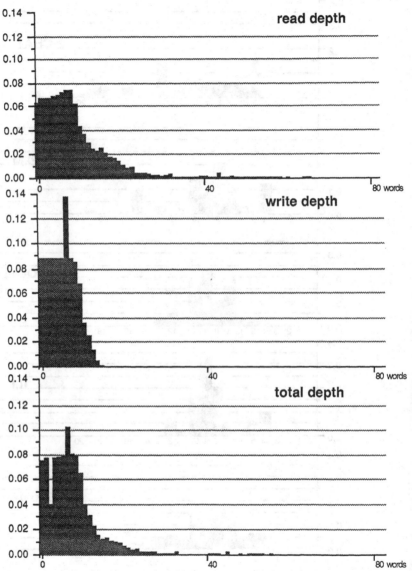

Figure 3-5: Choice Point Depth Frequency Distributions (words)

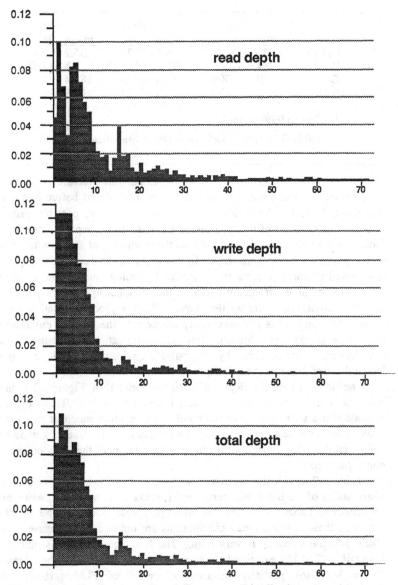

Figure 3-6: Environment Depth Frequency Distributions (words)

	read		write		total	
	mean	95%†	mean	95%	mean	95%
CHAT	74.2	350	5.6	21	36.2	210
PLM	984.6	>1200	291.9	>120	772.8	>1200
QC1	259.5	900	43.3	>120	184.4	800
ILI	62.0	430	6.3	14	41.4	160

† refers to 95% quantile

Table 3-7: Heap Reference Depth Statistics (in words)

An important statistic of a conventional architecture is *call depth distribution*, i.e., the number of nested procedures entered before one is exited. Call depth indicates the locality of the activation stack, possibly justifying a hardware stack buffer of the type discussed in the next chapter. For Prolog, call depth is not an accurate statistic because the environment stack (with or without choice points) is not a *true* stack. In a true stack, the current scope is always represented by the top frame in the stack. In Prolog, the current scope may be represented by an environment buried in the stack because choice points created after that environment freeze the stack. When a procedure call is made, the caller's environment is not necessarily adjacent to the callee's environment (at the top of stack). In addition, last call optimization can cause the caller's environment to be replaced by the callee's environment. These two effects lessen the usefulness of the call depth statistic.

The stack reference depth distributions given in Figures 3-5 and 3-6, however, give a more general statistic useful for Prolog. These distributions indicate that a small hardware stack buffer can capture much of the locality of choice point and (less of) environment references. These statistics indicate that a single choice point buffer will capture more references than any other buffer of comparable cost.

Table 3-7 shows the mean and 95% quantile of the heap reference depth distributions of the individual benchmarks, broken down by read, write, and total references. Table 3-6 gives the average statistics across the benchmarks; however, these and the mean distributions are not accurate because, as seen in Table 3-7, the variance is very high. The heap referencing distributions have long tails. PLM has extreme behavior with respect to the other benchmarks (see Figure 3-4 also), partially because the specialized PLM garbage collection facility was removed. The write depths are shallow because most heap writes occur during structure creation, at the top of heap. Reads, however, often occur deep in the heap, during unification of passed structures. The distribution statistics suggest that the high spatial locality exhibited by writes can be exploited by local memories that capture the top of heap. The write distribution statistics indicate that a "smart" memory, which does not continually prefetch the top portion of the heap (because it will be overwritten), can significantly reduce heap traffic.

Figure 3-7 shows the choice point reset depth distributions. The mean is 39.6 words with 95% quantile at 55 words. The maximum reset depth is greater than 120 words. CHAT differs from the other benchmarks because it has no cuts and therefore no zero depths. Figure 3-8 shows the environment reset depth distributions. The mean is 17.7 words with 95% quantile at 75 words. The maximum reset depth is greater than 120 words. All these benchmarks have approximately equal zero reset depths. This indicates the prevalence of shallow choice points on the stack, even for supposed determinate programs, such as QC1 (which, in fact, has the highest mean reset depth of 21.5 words).

Figure 3-9 shows the heap reset depth distributions. The mean is 17.9 words with 95% quantile at 50 words. Heap reset depth indicates the amount of heap space automatically reclaimed during backtracking. On average, resetting the heap cleans up only a small portion of the heap. Figure 3-9 indicates however that this behavior is highly program dependent — ILI and CHAT display instances of larger reclamations. In comparison, consider that *explicit* Prolog garbage collection reclaims about 50% of the heap on average [100]. This statistic, however, is also highly program dependent.

Figure 3-10 shows the dereference chain length distribution for the combined benchmarks. The mean is 0.32 references. The PLM benchmark has a procedure that unravels terms in the input source program. This procedure can produce arbitrarily long dereference chains, e.g., unraveling a term nested ten levels deep produces a chain of length ten. Since deeply nested Prolog source terms are rare, this benchmark rarely produces long dereference chains. These results indicate that optimizations to further shorten pointer chains are not needed.

3.3.2. Instruction Referencing

Instruction bandwidth requirements are measured in several different ways in this section, clarifying design tradeoffs between encoding efficiency and decoding complexity. An instruction is encoded into an *opcode, format,* and *operand(s).* The opcode and format are not clearly separated in the Lcode instruction set because there is little *orthogonality,* i.e., reuse of the same format among different opcodes. Instructions can be encoded with a fixed (e.g., IBM/370) or variable (e.g., VAX/11) number of operands. In addition, the

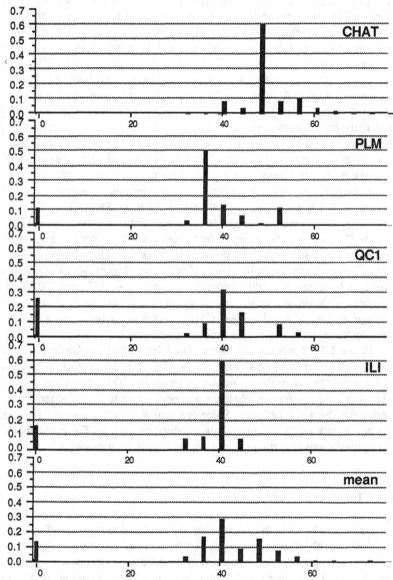

Figure 3-7: Choice Point Reset Depth Frequency Distributions (words)

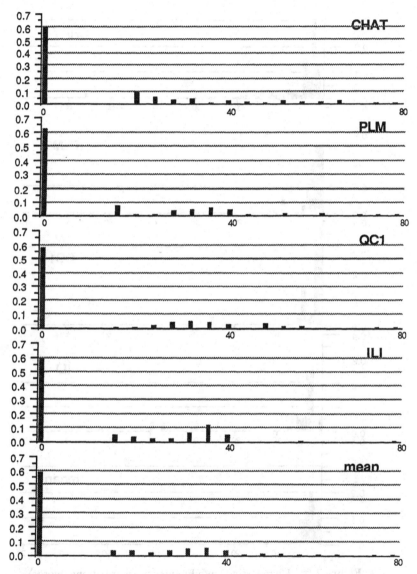

Figure 3-8: Environment Reset Depth Frequency Distributions (words)

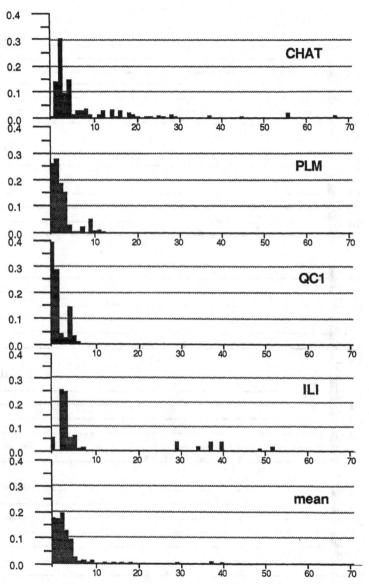

Figure 3-9: Heap Reset Depth Frequency Distributions (words)

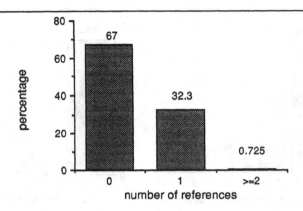

Figure 3-10: Dereference Chain Length Distribution

instruction may be aligned on word, halfword, byte, or bit boundaries. These storage units are called instruction *syllables*. Bit alignment allows tight encoding using $\log_2$ encoding schemes as in ADEPT [91]. The size and placement of immediate constants and branch offsets and addresses also offer variability of design. These parameters are difficult to design without analysis of many large programs, where the mean and peak numbers of interned constants (in the symbol table) and accurate branch distance distributions can be calculated. Because only a small set of benchmarks is analyzed in this book, no definitive statement is made concerning the "best" instruction formats. Instead, several alternatives are presented.

Table B-1 in Appendix B summarizes the sizes of each Lcode instruction. In this table, a word and byte count is given for each instruction. Instructions with two byte (or word) counts indicate local branch target operand(s) which can be encoded as either one or two byte offsets. Figure 3-11 shows the distribution of instruction size (assuming one byte offsets) for all instructions referenced during execution of the benchmarks. The mean distribution is calculated weighing each benchmark equally. The mean of the distribution is 2.6 bytes. Huck [39] reports mean instruction lengths for typical FORTRAN programs of 3.35 bytes on an IBM/370, and 5.23 bytes on a VAX 11/780.

Instruction bandwidth is measured for the benchmarks in the following seven ways.

1. word boundaries, halfword offset (from P) for local branch target

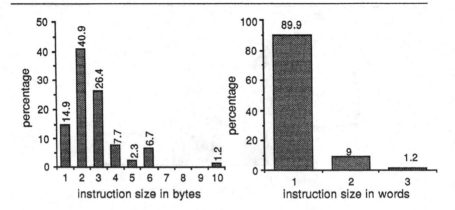

Figure 3-11: Instruction Format Distribution

2. word boundaries, byte offset

3. byte boundaries, halfword offset

4. byte boundaries, 8/16 offset

5. byte boundaries, byte offset

6. bit boundaries, 8/16 offset

7. bit boundaries, 8/16 offset, $\log_2$ encoding of permanent register specifiers (these specifiers can be decoded because the fixed size of each environment is known).

The local branch offset in these encodings is either a byte, halfword, or "8/16" (a combination of both). The 8/16 encoding uses whichever offset is appropriate for an individual instruction. Thus byte offset encoding is somewhat optimistic and halfword offset encoding is somewhat pessimistic. Table 3-8 lists the *relative* instruction reference counts of the seven encoding schemes. These counts are relative to the first encoding with word boundaries and halfword offsets. As indicated, byte encoding (halfword offset) generates about 63% of the instruction traffic of word encoding (halfword offset). Calculated over all references (including data), traffic is reduced by about 8%. This savings, representing the added efficiency of using smaller syllables, is significant compared to that of other encoding attributes.

The savings in instruction traffic generated by the 8/16 offset byte encoding over the pessimistic (halfword offset) byte encoding is about 5%. This is a savings of about 1% for the mean total references. The cost of the more efficient

	instr bound	branch offset	CHAT	PLM	QC1	ILI	mean
1.	word	16	1.0	1.0	1.0	1.0	1.0
2.	word	8	0.977	0.982	0.958	0.981	0.975
3.	byte	16	0.654	0.597	0.652	0.603	0.627
4.	byte	8/16	0.627	0.564	0.608	0.572	0.593
5.	byte	8	0.626	0.561	0.604	0.567	0.590
6.	bit	8/16	0.584	0.501	0.558	0.520	0.541
7.	bit†	8/16	0.550	0.469	0.525	0.478	0.506

† $\log_2$ encoding

Table 3-8: Instruction References for Benchmarks (per Encoding 1)

encoding is a more complex assembler and two versions (one with byte offsets, one with halfword offsets) of each local branch instruction.

The savings in instruction traffic generated by the standard bit encoding over the byte encoding is about 9%. $\log_2$ encoding of permanent register specifiers saves about 6% over standard bit encoding. Again, calculated over all references, the savings are insignificant. Mitchell [53] gives similar results for Pascal programs. He reports that a Pascal DCA with bit encoded identifiers saves 15% of the instruction traffic over byte encoding. The savings for Prolog are lower because the instruction set is not as orthogonal as DCAs based on arithmetic operations.

3.4. CIF Referencing Characteristics

In this section, measurements of CIF attributes are presented and compared to WAM measurements. Recall that in Chapter 2, three Prolog CIFs are introduced:

- **naive CIF** — this model, based on a frame stack, assumes a simple host that requires a memory access for every data reference.

- **traditional CIF** — this model, also based on a frame stack, assumes a complex host that requires *no* memory accesses to reference frames in the stack.

   'ster-based CIF — this model, based on separate choice point environment stacks, requires *no* memory accesses to reference gister set.

instr	CHAT	PLM	QC1	ILI
traditional CIF	1.00	1.00	1.00	1.00
naive CIF	1.00	1.00	1.00	1.00
register-based CIF	1.19	1.18	1.14	1.17

data	CHAT	PLM	QC1	ILI
traditional CIF	1.00	1.00	1.00	1.00
naive CIF	4.64	4.83	4.74	4.65
register-based CIF	3.73	4.34	4.03	4.09

Table 3-9: Comparison Between Prolog CIF Memory Bandwidths

	CHAT	PLM	QC1	ILI
CIF†	1.00	1.00	1.00	1.00
WAM	1.19	1.29	1.21	1.25

† assuming standard indexing

Table 3-10: WAM Instruction Bytes Referenced (per CIF)

		CHAT	PLM	QC1	ILI
CIF	total	1.00	1.00	1.00	1.00
WAM	data	1.30	1.24	1.55	1.31
	instr†	1.21	1.28	1.39	1.31
	total	1.28	1.25	1.51	1.31
naive‡	data	1.77	1.35	2.37	1.57
	instr†	1.49	1.36	1.69	1.53
	total	1.71	1.35	2.21	1.56

† assuming bit encoding
‡ no indexing

Table 3-11: Standard (WAM) Indexing Memory Bytes Referenced (per CIF)

	CHAT	PLM	QC1	ILI
CIF	1.00	1.00	1.00	1.00
WAM†	1.01	1.16	1.24	1.08
naive‡	1.53	2.43	2.49	3.07

† trail test only
‡ trail all

Table 3-12: WAM (De)trailing Memory Bytes Referenced (per CIF)

Table 3-9 shows the relative instruction and data references generated by these CIF models for the benchmarks studied. The traditional CIF, because it generates the lowest bandwidth of the models considered, is used as the baseline of this comparison, i.e., all reference counts are given relative to the traditional CIF. Notes on Table 3-9 follow.

- The traditional CIF assumes tightly encoded instructions on bit boundaries. All frame variable specifiers are $\log_2$ encoded. Recall that the CIFs use variable length get/put_list/structure instructions with n operands, where n is the arity of the structure. This obviates unify instructions, but requires an additional three bit tag per operand, indicating how the operand is to be processed (e.g., as variable, value, constant, etc.). This also obviates the need for read/write mode in the image architecture.

- The naive CIF is encoded identically to the traditional CIF.

- The register-based CIF assumes similarly encoded instructions; however, only permanent variable specifiers are $\log_2$ encoded. Register specifiers require four bits.

- Standard (single argument) indexing, a trail test, and a single stack are assumed.   These attributes are subsequently analyzed individually.

Whereas, for the benchmarks measured, the register-based CIF instruction bandwidth can be as much as 19% greater than the traditional CIF, data bandwidth can be as much as 330% greater. This difference indicates the relative importance of the instruction encoding and unlimited stack buffer assumptions in the traditional CIF. The register-based CIF can decrease the worst-case data referencing of the naive model by only about 14%, compared to the 79% savings of the traditional CIF.

Throughout the remainder of this section, the register-based CIF (simply called "the CIF") is compared in greater detail with the WAM. Tables 3-10, 3-11, and 3-12 show the WAM reference counts relative to those of the CIF, for various attributes. Each attribute is measured independently of the others.

Table 3-10 compares the instruction traffic of a standard byte encoded WAM (with byte local branch offsets) with the tightly encoded CIF. The table gives the number of WAM instruction bytes referenced per CIF instruction byte. As indicated, the WAM encoding causes from 19% to 29% more instruction traffic than the CIF encoding. For this comparison, both use standard (single argument) indexing.

Table 3-11 compares the data and instruction traffic of WAM (single argument) indexing with   CIF ideal indexing. Also given is the traffic for a naive architecture (not to be confused with the *naive CIF*) with no indexing. The table gives the number of memory bytes referenced per CIF memory byte. For

	CHAT	PLM	QC1	ILI
depth(B-stack)	845	997	599	210
depth(E-stack)	1007	600	632	166
depth(single)	1845	1577	1571	423
%	100	101	78	89
data(single)	1.000	1.000	1.000	1.000
data(split)	1.015	1.025	1.018	1.023

Table 3-13: Data Referencing of Single and Split-Stacks (Per Single)

	single-stack		split-stack	
statistic	mean	95%†	mean	95%
cp depth	8.2	21	5.6	11
env depth	14.2	40	7.0	18
cp reset depth	39.6	55	42.1	55
env reset depth	17.7	75	14.6	51

† refers to 95% quantile

Table 3-14: Comparison Between Single and Split-Stack Models

this comparison, all the architectures use similarly tightly encoded instructions. As indicated, single argument indexing generates from 25% to 50% more memory traffic than ideal indexing. Lack of indexing generates up to 120% more traffic than ideal indexing.

Table 3-12 compares the memory traffic devoted to (de)trailing (i.e., trailing *and* detrailing) for the WAM (with a trail test) and the CIF (with both a trail test and an inverse trail test). Also given is the traffic for a naive architecture with no trail tests. Without a trail test, up to three times the memory traffic is generated during (de)trailing. The inverse trail test saves from 1% to 24% of the (de)trailing traffic generated with a trail test. Since (de)trailing accounts for a small percentage (on average less than 5%) of all memory references, this attribute reduces memory references by very little.

Table 3-13 compares the maximum stack depths and data reference counts of the single and split-stack models, relative to the single stack model. The register-based CIF model with standard indexing is assumed here. Since the maximum depths of both the E-stack and B-stack may not occur simultaneously, comparison with the single stack depth must be made carefully. In most cases however, splitting the stack *decreases* the absolute stack depth.

The split-stack always makes more data references than the single stack, by

1.5% to 2.5%. This is because management of two stacks requires an additional state register, C, as discussed in Section 2.2.4. References to C itself are not counted (just as with B in the single stack model), but management of two stacks requires saving/restoring C from memory.

Table 3-14 compares the high-level memory characteristics which differ between the single and split-stack models. As expected, the split-stack model lessens object depth. Notice the 95% quantile of environment depth has been halved to 18 words.

3.5. PWAM Referencing Characteristics

In this section, the Restricted-AND Parallel Prolog architecture (PWAM) tools and the RAP-Prolog benchmark studied in this book are described. High-level memory referencing characteristics of the benchmark are then presented.

The PWAM tools [35] are illustrated in Figure 3-12. PWAM traces differ from the WAM traces previously described in that each reference is marked with a *processor identifier*. The PWAM emulator produces trace records in a round-robin fashion as it emulates an instruction on each of multiple processors. References are not time-stamped, so this method is not entirely accurate; however, since the PWAM emulator time slice is one instruction, inaccuracies are not significant. The RAP-Prolog benchmark studied is deterministic in the sense that the control flow of the program cannot depend on the execution timing of the program.

The PWAM emulator uses the following control policies in addition to those outlined in Section 2.3:

- When a parallel call is entered, i.e., the CGE condition evaluates to true, the goals are executed sequentially if all PEs are busy.
- The parent process of a parallel call waits for either all of its child processes to succeed, or one of its child processes to fail.

Sderiv, the simple parallel benchmark measured in this book, is shown in Figure 3-13. The program is a *synthetic* variation of the symbolic differentiation program given by Warren [93]. The original program has been modified by adding two new differentiation rules which offer greater parallelism than the original rules. The initial mode declaration states that the first two (input) arguments of the d/3 predicate are completely ground, and that the third (usually output) argument contains no shared unbound variables. This declaration ensures that no checks are required in the CGEs. Because all body goals are placed in the CGEs, last call optimization cannot be exploited; however, the lack of this

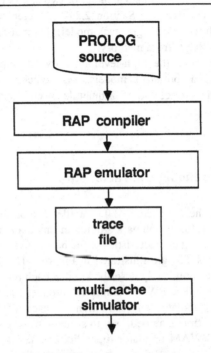

Figure 3-12: RAP-Prolog Performance Measurement Methodology

optimization does not significantly affect the memory referencing behavior of the program.

The Sderiv input datum is an irregular expression composed of summations of irregular expressions. The summations are highly regular trees of additions, and are nicely split by the first differentiation rule. The decomposition of the irregular expressions represent a much finer grain size and higher communication.

High-level characteristics of the Sderiv benchmark are presented in Table 3-15. The dynamic statistics were collected during a simulation of four processing elements (PEs). Instruction references were not measured; however, they have approximately the same high-level characteristics as in the WAM (Table 3-3).

Table 3-16 compares the number of data words referenced by Sderiv

```
:- mode d(g, g, i).

sderiv :- expr(X), d(X, x, Y).

d(A+B+C+D,X,DA+DB+DC+DD) :- !,
    (true | d(A,X,DA) & d(B,X,DB) & d(C,X,DC) & d(D,X,DD)).

d(A*B+C*D,X,DA*B+A*DB+DC*D+C*DD) :- !,
    (true | d(A,X,DA) & d(B,X,DB) & d(C,X,DC) & d(D,X,DD)).

d(U+V,X,DU+DV)              :-!,(true | d(U,X,DU) & d(V,X,DV)).
d(U-V,X,DU-DV)              :-!,(true | d(U,X,DU) & d(V,X,DV)).
d(U*V,X, DU*V+U*DV)         :-!,(true | d(U,X,DU) & d(V,X,DV)).
d(U/V,X, (DU*V-U*DV)/V^2)   :-!,(true | d(U,X,DU) & d(V,X,DV)).
d(U^N,X, DU*N*U^N1)         :-!,integer(N), N1 is N-1,
                                 d(U,X,DU).
d(-U,X,-DU)                 :-!,d(U,X,DU).
d(exp(U),X,exp(U)*DU)       :-!,d(U,X,DU).
d(log(U),X,DU/U)            :-!,d(U,X,DU).
d(X,X,1):-!.
d(C,X,0).

value(((3*x + (4*exp(x^3)*log(x^2)) -2) /
       ( -(3*x) + 5/(exp(x^4)+2))))).

expr( E+E-E*E/E*E/E   ) :-
       value(F),
       E = F+F+F+F+F+F+F+F.
```

Figure 3-13: RAP-Prolog Program Example: Sderiv

executing sequentially in the WAM and on PWAM multiprocessors with one to eight PEs. For PWAM, the number of process management references increases steadily for Sderiv. On eight PEs, the parallelism exploited is so fine grained that management overheads increase dramatically — data references increase by 8%. This is mostly due to busy waiting. The PWAM emulator is organized to force quickly succeeding parallel processes within a CGE *to wait for* slower processes to complete. This busy waiting entails continuously reading a process management flag to determine if all sibling processes have completed. The memory bandwidth required by these extra reads can be almost completely removed with local memories. In fact, the busy wait loops generate atypical reference patterns because the references display 100% temporal locality, which skews the overall measure of program locality. Discounting busy wait references, the low number of extra references in comparison to the WAM is

Program	Sderiv
static	
PWAM instructions	324
dynamic	
procedure invocations	1494
PWAM instructions	34675
instructions/invocation	23.2
data references	87890
data ref/instr	2.53

Table 3-15: Summary of PWAM Sderiv Benchmark on Four PEs

Sderiv	PEs	data ref
WAM	1	74358
PWAM	1	85709
	2	86180
	4	87890
	8	94922

Table 3-16: PWAM Sderiv Data Bandwidth Efficiency

area	read	%	write	%	total	%
cp	19062	49.3	19566	50.7	38628	43.9
env	10606	40.1	15866	59.9	26472	30.1
heap	8912	46.7	10182	50.3	19094	21.7
trail	0	0.0	1514	100.0	1514	1.7
pdl	0	0.0	0	0.0	0	0.0
pf-local	24	40.0	36	60.0	60	0.1
pf-slot	24	51.1	23	48.9	47	0.1
pf-lock	1391	92.2	118	7.8	1509	1.7
marker	46	20.0	184	80.0	230	0.3
goal	168	50.0	168	50.0	336	0.4
message	0	0.0	0	0.0	0	0.0
total	40233	45.8	47657	54.2	87890	100.0

Table 3-17: PWAM Sderiv Data Referencing Characteristics on Four PEs

consistent with the results given by Hermenegildo [35] and helps confirm the efficiency of the PWAM model.

Table 3-17 shows the Sderiv memory data reference statistics broken down by area and by type. This data was collected for a simulation of four PEs. Although each process references its own storage areas, the separate areas are lumped together in Table 3-17. The PWAM-specific storage areas include the Parcall Frames and Markers (marker) on the stack, Goal Frames in the Goal Stack (goal), and Message Buffer (message) (refer to Table 2-7). References to Parcall Frames are broken down into the local area (pf-local), and the global area. The global area is further split into the Process Slots (pf-slot) and the two semaphores (pf-lock). The profile is similar to the WAM benchmarks (Table 3-5). Less than 3% of the memory references are PWAM overheads, and most of these are lock reads during busy waiting.

3.6. Summary

In this chapter, an empirical methodology is described for measuring the dynamic memory-referencing characteristics of Prolog programs. This methodology consists of a Prolog-to-Lcode compiler, Lcode assembler, Lcode instruction-set emulator, and various memory simulators. A set of four Prolog benchmarks (CHAT, PLM, QC1, and ILI) and one RAP-Prolog benchmark (Sderiv) are described. High-level memory-referencing characteristics of the benchmarks, measured with the tools described, are given. Characteristics of the WAM, Prolog CIFs, and PWAM architectures are presented.

The WAM statistics indicate that even for well-written determinant Prolog programs, shallow backtracking dominates the Prolog data bandwidth requirement. The referencing localities of objects on the stack and heap roughly indicate the relative merits of different types of local data memories for reducing the memory bandwidth requirement. 95% of all references to choice points land within the top 21 words of the WAM stack. 95% of all references to environments land within the top 40 words of the stack. It is shown that in a split-stack architecture, 95% of all environment references land within the top 18 words of the stack. For the heap, even the top 1200 words of the heap do not always capture 95% of all heap references. From these high-level statistics, choice point buffers, stack buffers, split-stack buffers, and general data caches appear to be viable alternatives for reducing memory traffic. Low-level memory-referencing measurements of the benchmarks executing on these local data memories are presented in the following chapters.

Several alternative WAM instruction encodings are considered in this chapter. Measurements are presented indicating that byte encoding generates about 63% of the instruction traffic of word encoding, all other encoding attributes being equal. Other encoding attributes, such as branch offset size and bit encoding, do not reduce the instruction bandwidth requirement as significantly.

High-level memory-referencing statistics of three (naive, traditional, and register-based) Prolog CIFs are presented. The register-based CIF generates as much as 330% more data traffic than the traditional CIF, yet only as much as 19% more instruction traffic, indicating that the unlimited stack buffer assumptions in the traditional CIF far outweigh its instruction encoding advantages. Compared to the naive model, the register-based CIF reduces data traffic by about 14%, whereas the traditional CIF achieves a 79% reduction in traffic. Measurements of more detailed CIF attributes are presented for the register-based CIF, which corresponds most closely to the WAM. Among these attributes, ideal indexing offers the greatest traffic reduction — single argument (WAM) indexing generates 25%-50% more memory traffic than ideal (CIF) indexing. This result indicates that efforts to improve the WAM and its related compiler technology should concentrate primarily on indexing. As is discussed in the next chapter, poor indexing can alternatively be improved with hardware, in the form of local memories.

The RAP-Prolog memory-referencing characteristics of the Sderiv benchmark are also presented in this chapter. On a single processor, PWAM generates about 15% more memory references than the WAM. This overhead increases to 28% for eight processors (where most of the overhead is due to busy waiting). These high-level statistics indicate that PWAM does not sacrifice much of the WAM's efficiency to achieve parallelism. Further measurements of Sderiv presented in Chapter 5 explore the PWAM overheads in more detail.

4 Uniprocessor Memory Organizations

In this chapter, two-level memory hierarchies are defined and measurements are presented and analyzed for sequential Prolog architectures. The first level consists of a local memory. The second level consists of an interleaved main memory. Both traditional local memory models, as well as models suited specifically to the Prolog architectures previously introduced, are examined. Queueing models are used to determine the main memory interleaving required to support the local memory configurations. In the next chapter, these memory hierarchy designs are extended to multiprocessor systems.

Local data memories include a choice point buffer, stack buffer, environment stack buffer, copyback cache, and "smart" cache. Local instruction memories include an instruction cache and look-ahead instruction buffer. In addition, combined instruction/data copyback cache measurements are presented. Local memory configurations are presented, consisting of a combination of these memories, ranging from low cost/low performance to high cost/high performance systems. Local memory performance measurements are given in terms of *hit ratio, traffic ratio, copyback ratio*, and *dirty line ratio*. These measures allow comparison between the local memory designs and supply the main memory queueing models with critical design parameters. It is shown that small local buffers perform quite well — a 12 word single choice point buffer reduces the memory data bandwidth requirement by 38%. Larger, sophisticated local memories perform significantly better — a 1024 word "smart" data cache reduces the memory data bandwidth requirement by 93%.

The second-level main memory and memory bus are modeled, with asymptotic M/G/1 queueing models, for typical system configurations: a combined I/D cache, and a look-ahead instruction buffer + stack buffer configuration. The measurements presented indicate that although the stack buffer configuration can make more efficient use of an interleaved main memory than can the cache, the cache performs better because it captures heap references and code loops, which the stack and instruction buffers cannot capture.

Both uniprocessor and shared memory multiprocessor architectures are studied in this book. For both of these host organizations, motivations are now given for reducing, with local memory, the memory bandwidth requirement and the effective memory latency. From the previous chapter, the benchmarks studied have an average number of 3.0 words referenced per instruction executed. The average number of instructions executed per "logical inference" is 15.0. Therefore to attain one MLIPS (millions of logical inferences per second) average performance, or 15 MIPS (millions of WAM instructions per second), 180 Mbytes/sec sustainable memory bandwidth is required.

Even if a shared memory multiprocessor is used to deliver this performance, the bandwidth requirement must still be satisfied by a single (possibly interleaved) main memory if no local memory exists. In addition, multiprocessors have communication overheads which imply an even greater bandwidth requirement. A main memory suitable for symbolic processing applications must be large and therefore cost and packaging constraints typically prevent it from having a fast access time. A suitably interleaved memory, for instance, may achieve the bandwidth requirement under ideal conditions. In general, however, contention between requests to the same main memory module will reduce the deliverable bandwidth. Considering single bus interconnections, current technology buses can deliver only a fraction of the required bandwidth (e.g., the current Sequent can deliver 32 Mbytes/sec peak bandwidth). Emerging technology buses, however, may be able to deliver up to 200 Mbytes/sec peak bandwidth [5] (sustained bandwidth will be lower). These considerations indicate that the target of one MLIPS will tax the bandwidth capabilities of single memory systems. The introduction of local memory can reduce the bandwidth requirement, allowing the processor(s) to operate closer to their peak performances.

More important than the reduction in bandwidth requirement is the necessity to reduce the memory latency, i.e., the delay in servicing a given memory request. With only a single memory, each request requires the full access time of the memory. As previously argued, large memory systems have slow access times, and therefore long latencies. From the results of the previous chapter, about 40% of all memory references generated by the WAM are data reads. Assuming that the processor must stall until a data read is serviced, and assuming that the memory request rate of the processor is much higher than the service rate of the memory, only about 60% of the target performance can be achieved. Under the more optimistic assumption that a processor can sustain up to two data reads on average before stalling, approximately 80% of the target performance can be achieved, etc. The introduction of local memory can reduce the effective memory latency, thereby allowing the processor(s) to operate closer to their peak performances.

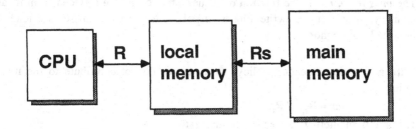

Figure 4-1: Uniprocessor Memory Model

4.1. Memory Model

The memory model, illustrated in Figure 4-1, consists of a single processing unit making requests to a two-level memory hierarchy. The closest level to the CPU is a *local* memory of limited capacity. The second level in the model is a slower main memory of unlimited capacity. The local memories examined are queues, buffers, and caches. Certain local memories capture only select types of references, accessing others directly from main memory. These memories are managed with a *copyback policy*: write references contained in the local memory are serviced there without immediately updating main memory. Main memory is later updated when the modified local memory location (called a *dirty* location) is chosen for replacement.

In Section 5.3, local memories managed with a *write-through policy* are examined. Write references are issued to both the local and main memories, thus keeping the two consistent. In addition, a hybrid policy of copyback and write-through for different types of requests is examined. As is discussed in Section 5.2 these local memories solve coherency problems inherent to multiprocessors.

For a given program, the processor issues R requests or references, broken down into reads, R_r, and writes, R_w. Requests are in units of words. The requests can also be broken down into hits, R_h, and misses, R_m, indicating whether the request is serviced from local or main memory:

$$R = R_r + R_w = R_h + R_m.$$

In addition, read request misses, $R_{r,m}$, write request hits, $R_{w,h}$, etc., are defined. The *miss ratio*, *mr*, is the fraction of requests that cannot be serviced from local memory. Assuming a write-allocation policy, where write misses are loaded into the local memory,

$$mr = R_m / R.$$

With a no-write-allocation policy, write misses do not contribute to the miss ratio,

$$mr = R_{r,m} / R_r.$$

Hit ratio is an alternative measure to miss ratio,

$$hr = 1 - mr.$$

For a copyback local memory, the main memory traffic, R_s, is the requests made to main memory,

$$R_s = (R_m + C)B,$$

where C is the number of copyback requests and B is the size of blocks (in words) transferred between main and local memory. For a write-through local memory, the main memory traffic is

$$R_s = R_{r,m}B + R_w.$$

This is easily generalized for a hybrid local memory that copies back certain request types and writes-through others.

The *traffic ratio*, *tr*, is the ratio of main memory traffic to local memory traffic. An alternative definition is the ratio of the number of references serviced by the main memory *with* local memory, to the number of references serviced by the main memory *without* local memory.

$$tr = R_s / R.$$

The *copyback ratio*, *cr*, is the ratio of the copyback traffic (to main memory), to the write traffic (to local memory),

$$cr = C*B / R_w.$$

The *dirty line ratio*, *dr*, is the fraction of local memory replacements which require copyback, i.e., the ratio of copybacks to misses,

$$dr = C / R_m.$$

By definition, hit and dirty line ratios are less than one, whereas traffic and copyback ratios can be greater than one. The latter can happen if the replacement granularity (a block) is greater than one word (the reference size). Large blocks increase hit ratio by virtue of prefetching sequential locations, i.e., exploiting spatial locality. A well-balanced model must have both high hit ratio and low traffic ratio (significantly less than one if possible). The copyback ratio indicates the efficiency of the copyback policy. A low (less than one) copyback policy is desirable, although it is not critical if the traffic ratio is low. A high copyback ratio indicates that a write-through policy is possibly better. A low dirty line ratio is desirable, indicating that not much copyback traffic is necessary.

In the remainder of this chapter, measurements of these statistics are presented for various local memory models. The performance of configured models, e.g., a choice point buffer combined with a instruction buffer, are calculated by combining the statistics of the singular models in the following manner. Consider partitioning all memory references into an exhaustive and mutually exclusive set of *reference types*. A reference type, in contrast to a data type, corresponds to a storage area, e.g., the heap, trail, etc. When combining local memory models which capture certain memory types, the following relations hold:

$$hr = \sum hr_j Pr(j)$$

$$tr = \sum tr_j Pr(j)$$

where $Pr(j)$ is the fraction of references of type j. A reference type i that is not captured by any local memory in the configuration, has $hr_i=0$ and $tr_i=1$.

These statistics are then used to derive the main memory *interleaving factor* necessary to increase memory bandwidth. An interleaved memory consists of m modules, where each memory module can be accessed independently and multiple requests to the same module are queued. For a sequential processor, as the number of modules is increased, a local memory with a larger block size, B, can be accommodated. This can increase local memory performance. For a multiprocessor, as the number of modules is increased, contention at the modules between different processor requests is reduced, thus increasing performance.

4.2. Data Referencing

4.2.1. Choice Point Buffer

A choice point buffer offers maximum data bandwidth reduction at minimal cost. An example of a choice point buffer design is that of the PLM [21]. A buffer holding the current choice point is simple and directly reduces the primary data bandwidth requirement caused by shallow backtracking. In the WAM, choice point references are always made to the current choice point defined by B. This facilitates designing a simple yet efficient buffer as illustrated in Figure 4-2.

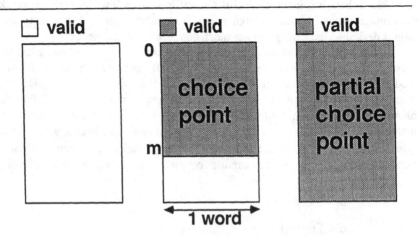

Figure 4-2: Choice Point Buffer Model

Figure 4-2 shows the three possible states of the buffer: invalid, valid, and partially valid. The buffer has a valid bit indicating whether it contains a choice point or partial choice point. m, ranging from zero to *BufferSize*, indicates the number of valid entries if the valid bit is set. Instructions which create choice points copyback the valid portion of the buffer to memory and load the new choice point. Instructions which reset the current choice point simply invalidate the buffer.

The choice point buffer management scheme is summarized below (refer to Figure C-1 in Appendix C for the detailed algorithm). If the buffer is invalid, choice point references are serviced from memory. If the buffer is valid, a choice point reference is not guaranteed to be contained by the buffer. A reference to a choice point larger than the buffer size may require service from memory. It is assumed that when referencing large choice points, the host (by either microcode or reduced native code) will access the valid portion (up to *BufferSize*) from the buffer and the invalid portion directly from main memory. This obviates the need for runtime checks.

The following variations of this management policy were examined:

- *Use dirty bits to reduce memory traffic* — A dirty bit is a flag associated with each buffer entry indicating if that entry holds a value not updated in main memory. This policy does not significantly affect traffic or copyback ratios because choice points are only allocated in the buffer when they are created.

- *Always load the current choice point into the buffer* — This policy ensures that all instructions which modify B also load the new current choice point into the buffer. Higher hit ratios are attained at the cost of increased traffic ratios. Even with dirty bits, the buffer's traffic ratios are over three times that of the former policy.

Figure 4-3 shows the choice point buffer performance measurements. These statistics account for choice point references only, i.e., the only memory requests counted are choice point requests. In this and all subsequent memory simulations, "cold start" measurements are presented. Hit and traffic ratios level off at a buffer size of 12 words. An eight word buffer, which contains at most one saved argument, achieves a hit ratio of 0.70. A 12 word buffer increases the hit ratio to 0.84 and reduces the traffic ratio to 0.28. QC1 exhibits significantly higher hit ratios and lower traffic and copyback ratios than the other programs. CHAT exhibits significantly lower hit ratios and higher traffic and copyback ratios than the other programs. This behavior can be attributed to CHAT's highly nondeterminate style and QC1's highly determinate style.

The choice point buffer has two additional advantages:

- Simplicity of design and small size map well onto VLSI.

- The buffer can be distributed over the state and argument registers, as *shadow registers*. This reduces the time required to read and write a choice point. This idea was first reported in Tick [82] and implemented in the Pegasus Prolog processor [71].

4.2.2. Stack Buffer

An alternative to the choice point buffer is a more ambitious buffer which captures portion(s) of the stack. A reasonable design is a directly addressable wrap-around buffer containing the top portion of the stack. The advantage of a stack buffer over a choice point buffer is that the stack buffer captures both environment and choice point references. In addition, the stack buffer can capture deep choice points.

Examples of stack buffer designs include the Symbolics 3600 stack buffer [80], DCA contour buffers [2], and the C Machine stack cache [19]. The Symbolics 3600 stack buffer is composed of four 256 word pages. Management is based on pages — upon overflow, a page is spilled and upon underflow, a page is restored. Alpert's contour buffer holds variable sized *contours*, similar to activation records. Management is based on contours — upon overflow, the oldest contour is spilled and upon underflow, the topmost contour is restored. Ditzel's stack cache is similar to the DCA contour buffer.

The Prolog stack buffer model is illustrated in Figure 4-4. The stack buffer

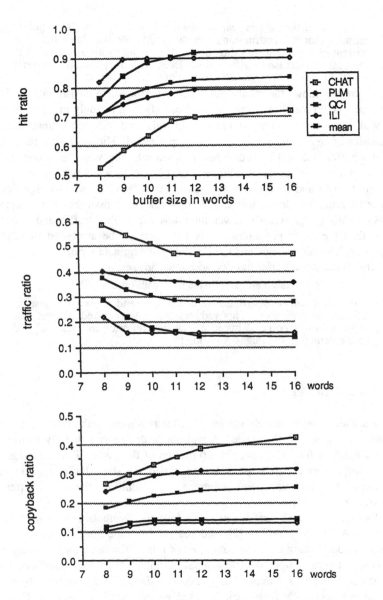

Figure 4-3:   Choice Point Buffer Performance Measurements

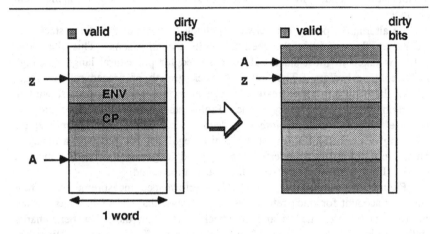

Figure 4-4: Stack Buffer Model: Object Allocation

management scheme is summarized below (refer to Figure C-2 in Appendix C for the detailed algorithm). Assume that the stack grows upward in addresses. In Figure 4-4, physical buffer addresses increase downward. A points to the highest valid stack address in the buffer. Z points to the lowest valid stack address in the buffer. E and B point to the current environment and choice point, respectively. TOS is the top of stack pointer.

The buffer is managed by instructions which allocate and deallocate stack objects (environments and choice points). Instructions which create an object load the new object into the stack buffer if the object is not larger than the buffer. If the object fits in the buffer, the appropriate portion of the buffer is copied back to make room for the new object. Dirty bits are used to minimize the number of buffer entries requiring copyback. If the new object does not fit in the buffer, the entire buffer is copied back and invalidated.

Instructions which deallocate objects reset TOS to the new top of stack. If Z>TOS, the buffer is invalidated. If Z<TOS, the buffer remains valid. No copyback is necessary in these situations because objects more recent than the new top of stack are not needed.

If the buffer is invalid, stack references are serviced from memory. If the buffer is valid, stack references are not guaranteed to be contained by the buffer. For instance, references to a deep environment may not be in a valid buffer. Thus the model requires runtime address comparison to detect a buffer hit. The model can be extended, in obvious ways, to avoid runtime comparisons in certain instances.

An alternative policy is to always prefetch the top portion of the stack into the buffer, thus avoiding the need for runtime comparisons. This alternative policy is taken in most stack buffers designed for procedural languages, e.g., DCA contour buffers. The "regular" stack growth of procedural languages allows these buffers to be restored when a buffer underflow occurs, without generating excessive memory traffic. Prolog stack behavior is more irregular because of choice points protecting deep environments, and failure and cut releasing large portions of the stack. This irregularity coupled with a policy of buffer restoration upon underflow is expected to generate excessive memory traffic. Therefore the alternative policy was not measured.

Figure 4-5 shows the stack buffer performance measurements. These statistics account for stack references only. Notice that CHAT exhibits a lower hit ratio and higher traffic and copyback ratios than the other benchmarks, indicating less locality. In fact, CHAT significantly affects the mean ratios. The statistics indicate that a stack buffer of 64 words, with a hit ratio of 0.95 and traffic ratio of 0.08, is sufficient to capture most locality in the benchmarks. Figure 4-6 shows the effect of the dirty bits on reducing memory traffic. The traffic is reduced in the range of 27% to 42%, for buffer sizes 128 and 16 words respectively.

Note that both the stack buffer and the choice point buffer models are organized around one word entries. This assumption may not be realistic for a system with a wider bus (i.e., a wider *physical* memory word). Realistic local memories are organized around *blocks* or *lines* of multiple physical words. The advantage of blocks is that block access time can be reduced by pipelining memory module accesses in an interleaved memory. The disadvantage of blocks is that excess traffic is generated whenever the entire block need not be transferred (e.g., if a dirty block to be copied back is not *entirely* dirty). Thus the buffer statistics presented here may be optimistic in terms of raw traffic. However, estimates of burst mode traffic may be pessimistic.

Figure 4-7 shows the choice point reference hit ratios for the stack buffers and choice point buffers. The stack buffer captures a significant portion of deep choice point referencing that a single choice point buffer cannot capture. Recall, however, that the choice point buffer, because of its simplicity, does not require runtime address comparisons to determine a hit, as does the stack buffer. In addition, a choice point buffer can be distributed in implementation (as shadow registers), whereas the stack buffer cannot.

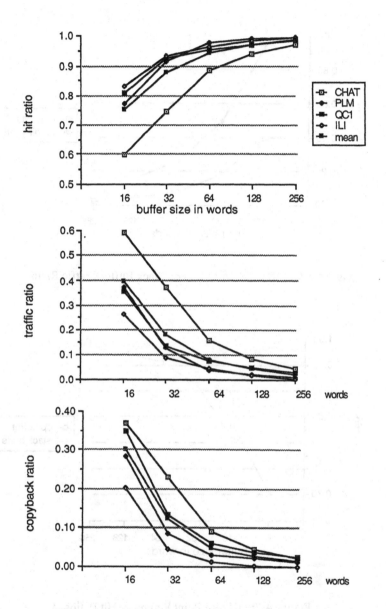

Figure 4-5: Stack Buffer Performance Measurements

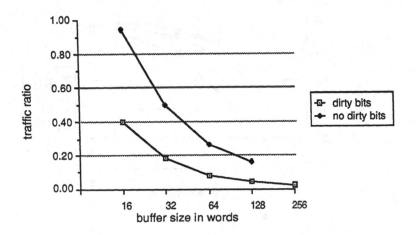

Figure 4-6: Effect of Dirty Bits on Stack Buffer Traffic Ratio

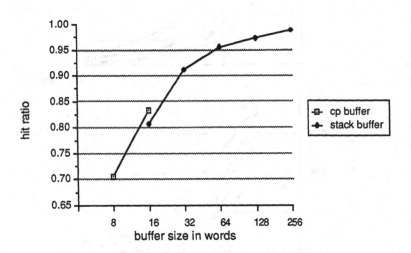

Figure 4-7: Choice Point Reference Hit Ratios

4.2.3. Environment Stack Buffer

The split-stack architecture, introduced in Section 2.2.4, increases the locality of environment references. A reduction in the memory bandwidth requirement was anticipated as a result of increased environment locality. Environment bandwidth reduction was measured by modeling an environment stack (E-stack) buffer. The E-stack buffer model is similar to the stack buffer illustrated in Figure 4-4, except that only environments reside within the buffer.

The E-stack buffer management scheme is summarized below (refer to Figure C-4 in Appendix C for the detailed algorithm. Definitions of *set(n)* and *copyback(d)* are given in Figure C-2). Assume that E points to the current environment, TOS points to the top of the E-stack, and Z points to the lowest E-stack address valid in the buffer.

As with the stack buffer model, the E-stack buffer is managed by instructions which allocate and deallocate environments and choice points. A newly created environment is allocated in the buffer, possibly causing a copyback. Deallocated objects, both environments and choice points, possibly cause the the top of stack to be reset. If Z>TOS, the buffer is invalidated. If Z<TOS, the buffer remains valid. No copyback is necessary in these situations because objects more recent than the new top of stack are not needed. Alternative policies are to always prefetch the top portion of the E-stack into the buffer or to always load the current environment into the buffer. These approaches are expected to cause excessive memory traffic and were not measured.

Figure 4-8 shows the E-stack buffer performance measurements. These statistics account for environment references only. Figure 4-9 shows a comparison of the single and split-stack model environment reference hit ratios. A 32 word E-stack buffer and 64 word stack buffer give similar performance. Choice point locality in the split-stack model is also increased. This effect is immaterial, however, if a choice point buffer, which buffers only one choice point, is used.

4.2.4. Copyback Cache

An alternative to the previously described local memories is a data cache, which can capture all types of references, i.e., heap and trail references as well as stack references. A cache, in contrast to the buffers previously described, is not included in a conventional processor architecture. In other words, a cache exploits locality without explicit knowledge of architecture. Whereas the buffers are managed *explicitly* by instructions, matching expected referencing patterns to

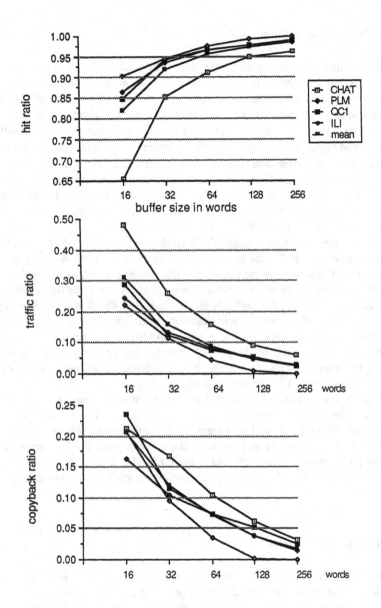

Figure 4-8: Environment Stack Buffer Performance Measurements

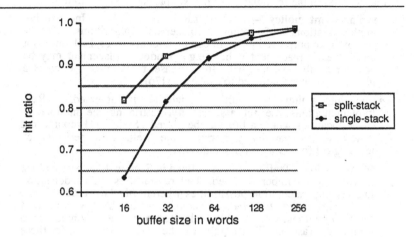

Figure 4-9: Comparison of Environment Reference Hit Ratios

program semantics, the cache is managed *implicitly* by replacing fixed sized objects on a demand basis. In this section, a data cache model is described and measurements are presented.

The cache model considered in this section is line (block) oriented, i.e., all transfers to/from main memory are line transfers. A *write-allocation* policy is used wherein both read and write misses cause fetching of the target. A *copyback* or *write-back* policy is used wherein writes to the cache do not immediately update main memory. Main memory is updated only upon cache replacement. The cache is categorized by a number of *blocks* or *lines* of a given size (in words). The cache is modeled as a *fully associative* memory, i.e., any line within the cache can contain any line from main (or virtual) memory. A perfect *least recently used* (LRU) replacement algorithm is used — the block least recently referenced is replaced next. Dirty bits are used to minimize the number of blocks requiring copyback.

An alternative cache model uses a *write-through* policy, where all writes are issued to both the cache and main memory. The copyback policy is superior to the write-through policy because the copyback policy reduces memory traffic more effectively. This is especially important in Prolog, where the read to write ratio is almost 1:1 (see Section 3.3.1). The write-through policy, however, maintains a consistent main memory, whereas the copyback policy does not. Variations of the write-through policy are studied in the next chapter because these strategies facilitate solving the multiprocessor consistency problem.

Inaccuracies in the formulation of this simple cache model follow.

- **replacement policy** — Pure LRU is assumed. Inexpensive implementations of other replacement algorithms closely approximate pure LRU [79]. In certain circumstances, LRU may not be the best replacement policy, e.g., random replacement may be best for small I-caches [76]. In any case, replacement policy is a minor parameter compared to cache size [76].

- **mapping policy** — Full associativity is assumed. Real implementations use set associativity, restricting the number of cache locations where a line can be placed. Smith [74] reports that 2-way set-associativity performs quite well, with performance leveling off for 4-way set-associativity.

- **traffic ratio** — Traffic ratio, as defined in Section 4.1, treats a block transfer as a number of B equal word transfers. This definition ignores implementation possibilities wherein *blocks are transferred at rates faster than the sum of the constituent words*. This method of *burst mode* transfer is possible with interleaved memory modules in a pipelined fashion. Traffic ratio can be *scaled* to account for these effects [38]. Instead, in later sections, queueing models are developed incorporating burst mode effects. Unscaled traffic ratio can be viewed as a conservative statistic to be used for comparison of local memories.

- **block/sub-block sizes** — The simple allocation policy used here requires transfer of an entire block on a cache miss. An alternative policy transfers only a portion of a block, called a *sub-block*, while allocating an entire block. This alternative policy reduces traffic and cache map size, at the cost of increasing miss ratio. Miss ratio is increased because spatial locality is no longer exploited. An optimal trade-off between block and sub-block sizes can often be found [38]. Larger sub-blocks give optimum performance for *scaled* traffic, i.e., traffic accounting for burst mode transfers of blocks [38]. In the main memory models of the next chapter, interleaving is assumed, implying that the simplifying assumption used here (block size = sub-block size) is reasonable.

- **write-allocation policy** — This policy refers to the fetching of the target of a write miss into the cache. A no-write-allocation policy consistently generates less memory traffic for small caches (64 words or less). Another method of reducing traffic in small caches is the use of sub-block allocation, as previously described.

- **cache size** — Cache size, as defined here, is *net size*, i.e., "offered data" size, discounting space required for addressing tags. To be more accurate, especially for small caches and caches with small lines, *gross size* should be calculated.

Figure 4-10 shows the data cache performance measurements. The copyback cache simulator used to make these measurements is a translation of the DELCACHE program written by D. Alpert [2]. Large caches and caches with small block size satisfy the criteria of low traffic and copyback ratios.

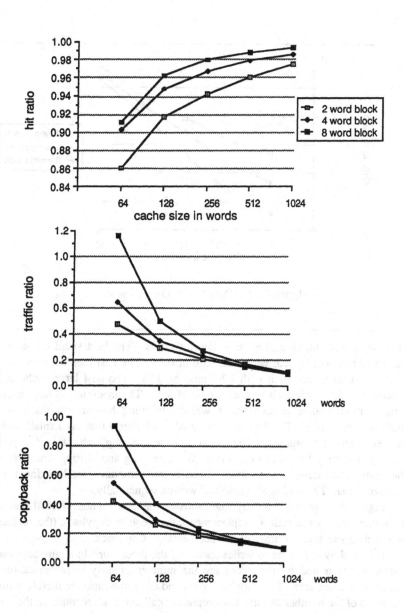

Figure 4-10:   Data Cache Performance Measurements

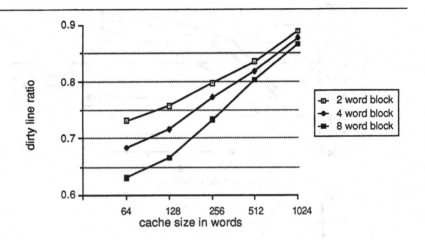

Figure 4-11:   Data Cache Dirty Line Ratio

However, small block caches have low hit ratios. The best small cache is 32 blocks of two words each with a hit ratio of 0.84. The best medium cache is 32 blocks of four words each with a hit ratio of 0.94. The best large cache is 32 blocks of eight words each with a hit ratio of 0.97. The medium and large caches retain similar traffic characteristics while improving hit ratio at the cost of doubling cache size. The data cache simulations indicate that even small caches deliver high performance. Heap and trail referencing exhibit more spatial locality than may have been expected. When reading and writing structures on the heap, referencing is sequential. Even nested structures are laid down in a localized area. The trail is also read and written sequentially.

Figure 4-11 shows the dirty line ratios of the data caches. Recall that the dirty line ratio is the ratio of replacements that require copyback (the replaced line is dirty) to total number of replacements. Copyback ratio is the ratio of writes issued by the cache to writes issued by the processor. In a pure copyback cache, writes issued by the cache are the number of dirty lines copied-back, scaled by the line size. The copyback ratio and dirty line ratio are therefore both functions of the number of dirty lines replaced, called the *dirty total*. In the dirty line ratio, the dirty total is inversely scaled by the number of misses. In the copyback ratio, the dirty total is directly scaled by the line size. Removing the scaling from the copyback ratio statistics (Figure 4-10) indicates that small line sizes have the greatest dirty total. Thus the result shown in Figure 4-11, where the dirty line ratio is inversely proportional to line size, is not surprising.

Another unexpected result is that copyback ratios are inversely proportional to cache size whereas dirty line ratios are directly proportional to cache size. Dirty line ratio is directly proportional to dirty total and inversely proportional to miss total. In the data cache, the number of misses (and the miss ratio) drops off very fast as cache size increases, whereas the dirty total does not. As a result, the dirty line ratio increases. This may be explained as many write hits in the cache create many dirty lines, so that for the rare miss, replacement has a higher probability of selecting a dirty line.

4.2.5. Smart Cache

In contrast to the traditional caches analyzed in the previous section, *smart* caches are not ignorant of the instruction set architecture. A smart cache, as defined here, avoids fetching or copying back lines that are not contained in the current valid storage areas of the machine model, e.g., invalid portions of the stack and heap. The PSI-II and Firefly machines both utilize one word line caches with write-allocation. These caches implement the smart feature of avoidance of fetching a write miss on the top of stack. Note that avoiding a stack or heap fetch can be implemented by a host instruction (e.g., PSI-II's **write-stack** operation [56]), whereas avoiding copyback requires a runtime check by the cache.

Ross and Ramamohanarao [69] present and measure a similar management strategy but at the next higher level: the transfer of pages between main memory and disk. Their results show that for compiled Prolog programs, page traffic is reduced by a factor of two over a conventional paging strategy. This suggests that a similar cache line transfer management policy may be beneficial. The smart cache strategy essentially introduces the management policies of the stack buffer into the cache.

The potential bandwidth reduction offered by a smart cache is indicated by the high-level statistics presented in Section 3.3.1. Almost all writes to the stack occur at the top — the mean choice point write depth is 5.0 words and the mean environment write depth is 9.7 words. In addition, certain benchmarks display frequent writes to the top of heap — CHAT and ILI have a mean heap write depth of 6.0 words. Therefore avoidance of fetching the line at the top of the stack or heap, on a write miss, has the potential to significantly reduce memory traffic.

Avoidance of copying back dirty yet invalid portions of the stack appears beneficial because on average, 40 words at the top of the stack are freed by each choice point deallocation. Environment and heap deallocations are only half as effective, freeing up 18 words on average.

A smart copyback cache was simulated, based on the previous copyback cache. The smart cache avoids fetching and copying back lines not contained within the current valid storage boundaries, as defined by **H**, **B** and **E**. Figure 4-12 compares the smart cache and standard copyback cache data traffic ratios. Both models give identical hit ratios. The percentage reduction in traffic ratio afforded by the smart cache over the standard cache is given in the last graph in Figure 4-12. As indicated, savings of 20% to 30% are expected.

Figure 4-13 shows the breakdown of references saved by the smart cache, for each benchmark. For each benchmark, four percentages are given, adding up to 100% of the traffic savings: heap fetches (heap-f), heap copybacks (heap-cb), stack fetches (stack-f), and stack copybacks (stack-cb). Removal of heap fetches contributes the most to the traffic savings, with removal of stack copybacks second. Note that removal of stack fetches consistently offers the least savings.

4.2.6. Comparison of Data Memories

In Section 4.2.1, choice point buffer performance statistics are presented considering only choice point references. Similarly, the stack buffer and environment buffer performance statistics presented concerned only reference types that could be stored in the associated memory. These statistics show how well the buffer exploits the locality of its associated data storage area. Total memory system performance includes both local memory performance and the performance of other reference types. In some cases, these other references bypass the local memory, and total memory system performance is significantly lower than the local memory performance. Figures 4-14 and 4-15 show the statistics accounting for all data reference types (instruction reference types will be included in Section 4.4). Included in these figures are 8 and 16 word choice point buffers, 16 - 256 word stack buffers, 64 - 1024 word caches (with four word line), and 16 - 256 environment stack buffers combined with a 16 word choice point buffer.

The environment stack buffer + choice point buffer configuration statistics are calculated from the individual simulator measurements, with the method given in Section 4.1. Although the number of references to the stack and heap in the WAM and split-stack architectures are different, the counts are approximately the same (to within 2.5% worst case — see Section 3.4). The WAM counts are used here.

With the equations of Section 4.1, a choice point buffer configured with an environment buffer is modeled as:

$$hr_{cp+env} = hr_{cp}P_{cp} + hr_{env}P_{env}$$

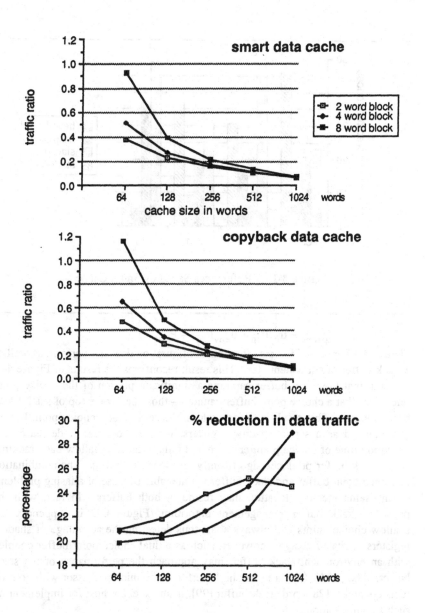

Figure 4-12: Comparison of Copyback and Smart Caches

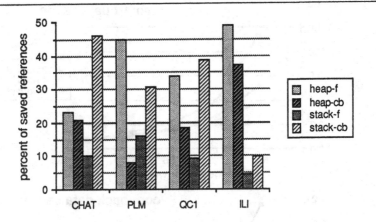

Figure 4-13:   References Saved by Smart Cache

$$tr_{cp+env} = tr_{cp}P_{cp} + tr_{env}P_{env} + P_{rest}.$$

Figures 4-14 and 4-15 indicate that this configuration does not perform as well as a stack buffer of equivalent size. This result reconfirms the results of Figure 4-7, showing that the stack buffer captures a significant portion of the choice point references that a choice point buffer cannot — those below the top of stack (deep backtracking). This result is unfortunate in the sense that a choice point buffer, implemented as a set of shadow registers, is useful because it decreases the execution time of choice point creation and failure, during shallow backtracking. Yet a stack buffer produces significantly less memory traffic. The combination of choice point buffer and stack buffer is untenable because of aliasing problems — the same memory location may reside in both buffers. In fact, with the proposed stack buffer management algorithm (Figure C-2 in Appendix C), shallow choice points will always alias, thus defeating the advantage of shadow registers. Related designs, however, such as a dual choice point buffer coupled with an environment stack buffer, may approach the performance of the stack buffer. The AM29000, a recent high-performance microprocessor with both 64 registers and a 128 word stack buffer [99], is an excellent host for implementing such a configuration.

The data cache displays significantly higher hit ratios than the buffers (note that both the copyback cache and "smart" cache have identical hit ratios). For small caches, the hit ratio is paid for with a correspondingly high traffic ratio.

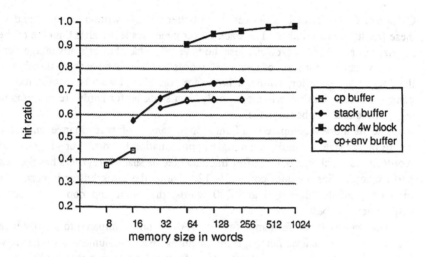

Figure 4-14: Local Data Memories: Hit Ratio

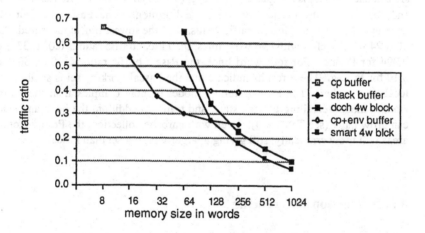

Figure 4-15: Local Data Memories: Traffic Ratio

Caches of 64 words or less, however, do better without write-allocation, and so these results are disputable. The stack buffer generates less traffic than the cache for sizes of about 200 words and less; however, the stack buffer's advantage over the smart cache is for sizes of about 130 words and less. Above these thresholds, the caches are superior, although hardware cost should also be considered — generally, cache hardware is more costly than stack buffer hardware in terms of access time and number of gates.

The memories compared fall into three ranges of performance and cost, where buffer size in words is a simple approximation to cost. For low cost, 16 words or less, a choice point buffer implemented as shadow registers has the best performance. For medium cost, 32 - 128 words, the stack buffer is best. For high cost, greater than 130 and 200 words, the smart and copyback caches respectively are best.

The data cache performance for the WAM is now compared to similar local memories for procedural language architectures. Because numerous studies have been made of the memory characteristics of procedural languages, and this book is one of the first studies of Prolog memory characteristics, it is helpful to the intuition to understand their relationship. Mulder [55] measured the data memory performance of typical Pascal programs. Only traffic ratio, the most significant statistic, is compared here. Figure 4-16 shows the traffic ratios of two and four word line caches for Pascal and Prolog. The Pascal benchmarks generated significantly lower traffic ratios. For the lowest traffic measured, that of 1024 word caches with two word lines, the Pascal traffic ratio is 0.031, 33% of 0.094 for Prolog. For four word lines, the Pascal traffic ratio is 0.049, 50% of 0.10 for Prolog. These results indicate that the Pascal working set is smaller and locality is higher. The Prolog storage model is more complex than the Pascal storage model, entailing a heap, stack and trail. In addition, the heap and stack can grow large (see Table 3-4). Even with garbage collection, the Prolog storage areas will grow erratically, still giving a larger working set than Pascal.

4.3. Instruction Referencing

Local memory buffers capturing instruction references are introduced in this section. A look-ahead instruction buffer, instruction cache, and combined instruction/data (I/D) cache are described and measurements are presented. The functions of an instruction buffer and cache are complementary. An instruction buffer prefetches the instruction stream, attempting to supply the CPU with a

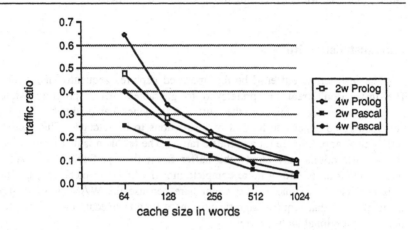

Figure 4-16:   Pascal and Prolog Copyback Data Cache Measurements

constant supply of instructions. An instruction cache reduces the effective access time of instruction references and prefetches instructions by block. Often a simple instruction buffer that cannot capture loops is configured with an instruction cache, or I/D cache, which does.

All local instruction memory performance measurements presented in this book are based on the most realistic, fixed-size byte-encoded formats defined in Section 3.3.2. The Lcode emulator, however, executes loosely encoded instructions, most of which are either one or two words in length. Although this facilitates fast emulation, it makes accurate instruction trace production difficult for other encoding schemes. There are two reasons for this. First, program size varies with encoding scheme, therefore branch target distance varies. Second, individual instruction sizes vary with encoding scheme. A mapping is made from Lcode addresses to byte-encoded instruction addresses, which solves the above problems, while generating the instruction trace file.[10]

4.3.1. Instruction Buffer

The instruction buffer (I-buffer) modeled captures sequential instructions. The instruction stream is prefetched to guarantee that a program without branches will never miss in the buffer. Branches cause the buffer to be invalidated and a new buffer full of instructions to be fetched. This model is sufficient to approximate hit and traffic ratios. The problem is that a sequence of simple instructions may empty the buffer faster than prefetching can keep it filled. See Rau [65] for a more complete model which can measure this effect. This problem is assumed to be minor here because the WAM is a high-level instruction set that requires significantly more time to execute most instructions than a conventional architecture.

The degree of prefetching, d, is defined as the number of bytes prefetched when a reference misses in the buffer (d bytes *beyond* the missed reference itself). Each decoded instruction prefetches a number of bytes equal to the size of that instruction. Therefore the model retains d bytes of unseen instructions in the buffer at all times. In other words, the model simulates buffers of size d. As d is varied, the hit ratio remains constant, limited only by the number of branches in the instruction stream. Lcode branches occur after instructions such as `call` and `try`. Instructions between branches are called   *runs*.   Run length distributions (in words) for the benchmarks are shown in Figure 4-17. These distributions assume a byte-encoded instruction set. The mean run length is 17 bytes and the 95% quantile is 42 bytes. (A word encoded instruction set has a mean run length of 6 words and a 95% quantile of 16 words). Given the simple run length distribution, it doesn't pay to make d significantly greater than the mean run length.

---

[10]The mapping is *approximated* in the following manner. A psuedo program-counter, **Pb**, is used to track the Lcode program-counter, **P**. For sequential execution, both **P** and **Pb** are incremented by the instruction size (in bytes). For branches, however, **P** = **A** and **Pb** = **k*(A - codebot)**, where **k<1** is the ratio of byte-encoded program size to Lcode program size and **codebot** is the base address of the program. This mapping has the advantage that *each domain maps into a single range*. In addition, sequential instruction addresses are accurate. The mapping has the disadvantage that branch targets are inaccurate because of the inaccuracy of scaling. This inaccuracy slightly perturbs cache performance statistics because determining whether a target instruction is in the cache is dependent on where the branch is located. This perturbation is assumed to be minor because recursive loops usually branch from a fixed location, thus accurately branch to the same target.

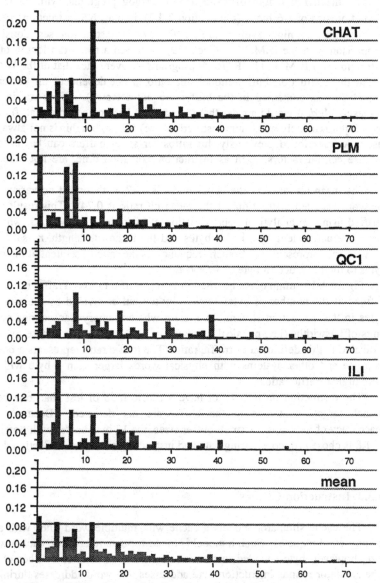

Figure 4-17:   Instruction Run Length Distribution (bytes)

The mean run length of 17 bytes for Prolog programs, with an average instruction size of 2.6 bytes (see Section 3.3.2), implies 6.5 instructions per run. To illustrate the high-level nature of the WAM instruction set, consider a comparison with the IBM/370. Huck [39] measured a mean run length of 16.9 instructions for IBM/370 FORTRAN programs — over twice that of the WAM.

In the instruction buffer model, hit ratio is not dependent on buffer size (branch targets contained in the buffer are *not* detected). Since traffic ratios increase with d, it would appear that the smallest buffer size (minimal d) of four bytes (approximately maximum instruction size) is best, but this is not always the case. As mentioned previously, hit ratios for small buffers can be inaccurate because certain factors, such as instruction execution time, are not taken into account.

The mean hit ratio for the benchmarks is 0.82, with almost no variance (for the word encoded instruction set the mean hit ratio is 0.74). This result can be verified using an analytical approximation of hit ratio, $(r-i)/r = 0.85$, where the mean instruction length, i, is 2.6 bytes and the mean run length, r, is 17 bytes. This statistic represents the branch frequency as the ratio of sequential instruction bytes to total instruction bytes referenced.

Figure 4-18 summarizes instruction buffer traffic ratios. Traffic ratio here is defined as the number of bytes fetched by the buffer divided by the number of bytes in the instruction stream. A system where memory transactions occur in units of buswidths (i.e., physical words) may be forced to move more bytes than indicated in this definition of traffic ratio. The traffic ratio represents a best case estimate and other systems with physical words larger than a byte will likely have higher traffic ratios.

The instruction buffer cannot have a traffic ratio of less than one because branch targets contained in the buffer are not detected. Because of the inaccuracy of hit ratios for small buffer sizes, the 12 byte buffer with traffic ratio of 1.8 is chosen for configuring data and instruction memories in Section 4.4.

4.3.2. Instruction Caches

The cache simulator models a cache with multiple word lines with a CPU issuing word requests. Such a model is tuned for data references, each a word in size; however, byte-encoded instructions consist of a variable number of bytes. The emulator rounds instruction byte addresses into word addresses during trace production. For example, a two byte instruction straddling a word boundary causes two word references in the trace. This method of trace production allows the use of the standard copyback cache simulator (Section 4.2.4) to collect

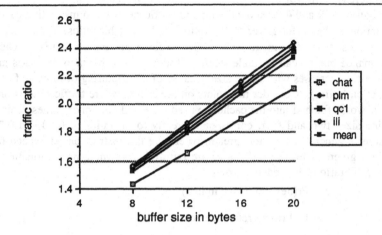

Figure 4-18:   Instruction Buffer Traffic Ratios

instruction referencing statistics. With this method, however, hit and traffic ratio statistics must be carefully interpreted, as described below.

In the system without a cache, the assumption is made that instructions are fetched independently with no buffering. For example, a word is fetched for a byte instruction, and extra bytes are ignored. Since there are no instruction writes, there is neither copyback nor write-through in an instruction cache. Therefore traffic ratio is

$$tr = R_m * B / R,$$

where, using the notation of Section 4.1, R is the number of CPU requests, R_m is the number of requests which miss in the cache, and B is the cache line size in bytes.

In the data cache simulator, miss ratio is calculated as the number of (word) references missing in the cache over the total number of (word) references. An alternative definition is the number of *bytes* referenced missing in the cache over the total number of *bytes* referenced. For a data cache these two definitions are equivalent because all references fall on word boundaries. The alternative definition, although desirable for the instruction cache, cannot be calculated with the standard cache simulator because of the trace production method previously described. For a byte-encoded instruction stream, the two definitions produce different results; however, the difference is expected to be small.[11]

Figures 4-19 and 4-20 show the hit and traffic ratios of an instruction cache. Instruction caches offer lower traffic ratios (and lower hit ratios) at the cost of larger sizes than the instruction buffer (shown in Figure 4-18). These performance curves can be understood as follows. The hit ratio increases and traffic ratio decreases with cache size because of the capturing of loops (c.f., the instruction buffer). Consider the points on the curves where traffic ratio is one, i.e., all words fetched into the cache are used once and only once. These points, for line sizes two and four, correspond directly to hit ratios of 0.50 and 0.75. Consider a general instruction stream, where the last instruction referenced fell within a given cache line. For a traffic ratio of one (where no information is reused), hit ratio is defined as follows.

$$\text{hr} = \text{Pr(next reference in line)}$$

$$= 1 - \text{Pr(next reference not in line)}$$

$$= 1 - \{\text{Pr(branch)} + \text{Pr(not branch)}*\text{Pr(overruns line)}\},$$

where

$$\text{Pr(overruns line)} = \text{mean instr length / line length.}$$

The probability of a branch, Pr(branch), was measured as 0.17, the miss ratio of the instruction buffer in the previous section:

$$\text{Pr(branch)} = 0.17$$

---

[11]Consider a branch to a two byte instruction target not in the cache. Suppose the target instruction straddles a word boundary within a line. The method used here gives a miss ratio of 0.5, whereas the alternative miss ratio is 1.0. This large error, of 100%, occurs *only* for branch targets which straddle word boundaries, and decreases in magnitude with increasing run length. Over the total program execution, this error is expected to be small, as is shown here.

An upper bound on the expected error is calculated as follows. The maximum error of 100% is caused by a branch to a target straddling a word boundary within a line. Thus an upper bound of the expected error is equal to the probability of an error occurring. The probability of a branch, Pr(branch) = 0.17, was measured in the previous section as one in 6.5 instructions. The probability that a branch target straddles a word boundary within a line, assuming uniform distribution of branch targets, is Pr(straddle) = $(m-1)(n-1)/4m$, where m is the number of words per line and n is the number of bytes per branch target. Since $(m-1)/m < 1$, Pr(straddle) < $(n-1)/4$. Using the instruction size distribution (Figure 3-11) as an approximation of branch target size distribution, Pr(straddle) < $\sum \text{Pr}(n)*(n-1)/4 = 0.40$. Therefore, E(error) < $1*\text{Pr(error)} = \text{Pr(branch)} * \text{Pr(straddle)} = 0.07$. Again, this upper bound of expected error is pessimistic because it assumes that each time an error occurs, the statistics are in error by the maximum of 100%. However, the error drops off rather quickly with increasing run length, so that this cache simulation model is certainly accurate to within 7%.

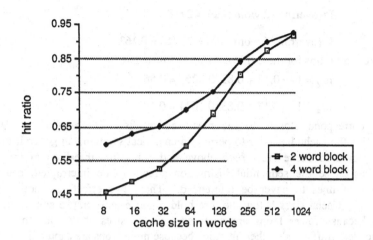

Figure 4-19: Instruction Cache Hit Ratio

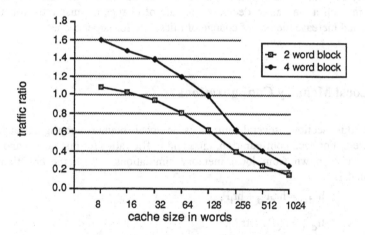

Figure 4-20: Instruction Cache Traffic Ratio

Pr(overruns 2 word line) = 2.6/8 = 0.325

Pr(overruns 4 word line) = 2.6/16 = 0.163.

Therefore hit ratios for these line sizes are estimated as

$$hr_2 = 1 - \{0.17 + 0.83*0.325\} = 0.56$$

$$hr_4 = 1 - \{0.17 + 0.83*0.163\} = 0.69.$$

These correspond closely to the measured results. The previous analysis simplified the cache behavior to permit an analytical solution. In general, loops are captured in cache sizes *both* above and below the threshold of tr = 1. Branches cause the sequential instruction stream to be interrupted, causing portions of lines to never be referenced. These two effects balance at the threshold. Cache sizes below the threshold produce more traffic and lower hit ratios because fewer loops are captured. Cache sizes above this threshold produce less traffic and higher hit ratios because more loops are captured.

Figure 4-21 shows the performance statistics of a combined instruction/data (I/D) cache. Figure 4-22 shows the dirty line ratios of the I/D caches. Note that the dirty line ratios are non-monotonic. In the I/D cache, instructions fill the cache in such a way as to decrease the rate of change of miss ratio for small caches and increase the rate of change of miss ratio for larger caches.

4.4. Local Memory Configurations

In this section, several uniprocessor local memory configurations are presented. For each configuration, miss and traffic ratios for instruction and data are already known from local memory simulations. With the equations of Section 4.1,

$$hr_{d+i} = hr_d P_d + hr_i P_i$$

$$tr_{d+i} = tr_d P_d + tr_i P_i,$$

where $P_d = 0.77$ and $P_i = 0.23$, the probabilities of data and instruction references, respectively (see Section 3.2).

The configurations considered are listed below (other configurations can be similarly calculated with the previous equations). Note that a *combined* I/D cache captures *both* instructions and data, whereas *split* I+D caches consist of *two* caches: one for instructions, one for data.

• I/D cache (copyback with 4 word line)

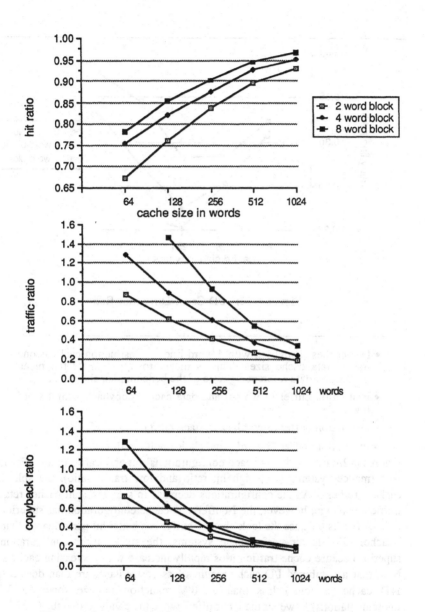

Figure 4-21: Instr/Data Cache Performance Measurements

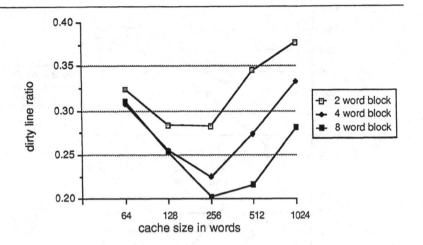

Figure 4-22: I/D Cache Dirty Line Ratio

- I+D caches (copyback with 4 word line) — instruction cache is one fourth data cache size. This is meant to approximate the mean instruction/data referencing ratio of the benchmarks, about 1:3.
- instruction buffer (3 words) and data cache (copyback with 4 word line)
- instruction buffer (3 words) and stack buffer
- instruction buffer (3 words) and choice point buffer

Figures 4-23 and 4-24 show each configurations' hit and traffic ratios. For high performance systems (i.e., high hit ratio and low traffic ratio), the split I+D caches are best. As the configurations decrease in size, the split caches retain a traffic advantage; however, the I-buffer + D-cache configuration has superior hit ratios. This is because the look-ahead I-buffer has better hit performance than an I-cache. For lower performance systems, the stack buffer configuration is superior because cache traffic ratios rapidly increase with decreasing cache size. Note that a combined I/D cache requires less costly hardware than does a split I+D cache (although less than a 10% reduction in size for most VLSI implementations) however the latter offers twice the bandwidth to the CPU.

The superiority of the split I+D caches over a combined I/D cache may not be expected because for traditional architectures large caches display the opposite behavior [75]. The result is not surprising, however, in the context of Prolog

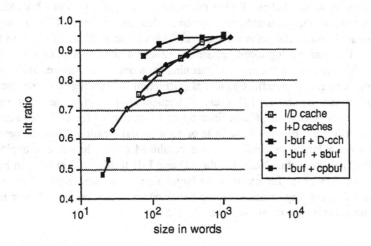

Figure 4-23: Configuration Hit Ratios

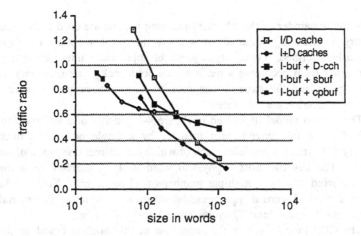

Figure 4-24: Configuration Traffic Ratios

executing on small caches. Prolog programs do not display as much locality as procedural languages, as indicated by the modest performance of the instruction caches analyzed in the previous section. This can be attributed to lack of tight loops. The long Prolog loops appear as sequential code to a small cache (note that within the loop, there may be branching from one run to another until the top of loop is re-encountered). Sequential instruction referencing has a devastating effect on the combined I/D cache. Sequential instruction fetching causes continuous replacement of data lines by code because of the LRU replacement policy. Yet the code lines have little or no temporal locality. Thus the program takes over a larger percentage of the combined cache than it can exploit as efficiently as the data. Note that the I/D and I+D traffic ratio curves, in Figure 4-24, possibly cross for cache sizes larger than those measured. This would indicate that for large caches Prolog behavior was conventional, similar to the traditional languages measured by Smith [75].

4.5. Main Memory Design

In the remainder of this chapter, queueing models are used to determine the memory interleaving required to support the local memory configurations previously described. This analysis gives the appropriate interleaving to prevent the memory from becoming a performance bottleneck. The necessary memory queue length and the expected degradation of processor performance due to memory contention are calculated.

The system model illustrated in Figure 4-1 consists of a uniprocessor CPU attached to an interleaved main memory by a single bus. The interleaved memory consists of m modules, each of which can deliver one *physical word* per access. The bus transmits a physical word in T_{bus}, the *bus cycle time*. A physical word can be a multiple number of 32-bit words. Each module can deliver a physical word in T_a cycles, the *memory access time*. The modules can be reaccessed after at least T_c cycles, the *memory cycle time*.

The CPU model used in the remainder of this book is based on the PLM [21, 20], a WAM instruction set processor. Relevant aspects of the PLM (not to be confused with the PLM benchmark) are reviewed below. For a complete description of the PLM, see Dobry [23]. Differences between the CPU model used here and the actual PLM are due to assumptions regarding timing and the memory design. The PLM timing equations described by Dobry [21] have been augmented here with timings for built-ins, derived by Mulder [54]. To the first order, the two models have approximately the same execution performance, assuming a one cycle main memory. The queueing models presented in this section can be used to estimate the performance of other types of processors, e.g., PSI-II and SPUR. These processors can be modeled by approximating the queueing model parameters relative to the PLM. Local data memory behavior for these models can be assumed to be the same. Local instruction memory behavior might be derived, for instance, from the data presented by Borriello et. al. [8].

The PLM memory design is not of concern here because the memory models previously introduced, e.g., an I/D cache, are used instead. A queueing model is developed in anticipation of its essential role in analyzing multiprocessor performance (Section 5.4.1). The model is also used to analyze simple uniprocessors because *time* is reintroduced, permitting the calculation of statistics, such as *performance degradation* and *bandwidth efficiency*, not previously obtainable with the simple model of previous sections. Because read and write requests are issued independently of service time, the requests can freely contend for the memory modules of an interleaved memory. In addition, a heuristic is added to the queueing model to approximate the effect of a read miss stalling the CPU until the target word is delivered. This heuristic is described in greater detail in Section 4.5.3.

In the next section, the general queueing models are introduced. From these general models, models of interest can be easily derived. Two such main memory queueing models are presented in the following sections. The first assumes a local memory which is a traditional I/D copyback cache. The second assumes a local memory which is a stack and instruction buffer configuration.

4.5.1. General Queueing Model

Two general queueing models are introduced in this section: an *open* model and a *closed* or *asymptotic* model. The open model, although unrealistic because its arrival and service rates are independent, is useful for motivating the closed model. The closed model is more realistic because its arrival and service rates are equal, i.e., it is in the steady-state.

The open queueing model consists of a CPU which generates requests independently of a memory which services the requests. The request rate is λ and the service rate is μ. The ratio λ/μ, called the occupancy, ρ, must be significantly less than one for the open queue model to be accurate.

Analytical solutions exist for certain Markovian processes, e.g., Poisson arrival times and exponential service times. The M/D/1 model assumes a

Poisson arrival distribution (M for Markovian) and a server (1 for single) with a constant service time (D for deterministic). Arrivals are queued in an infinite size buffer and served on a first-in first-out (FIFO) basis. The M/D/1 model corresponds to a single CPU issuing requests as a Poisson process and an interleaved memory system of n modules, each of which has a constant cycle time, T_c, and a queue for waiting requests. The single server in this model is a single memory module, the assumption being that each module in the system will act accordingly.

There are two basic statistics of interest for designing an interleaved memory. Q' is the expected number of requests queued per module not including the one in service (Q is the expected number of requests queued per module). T'_w is the expected time waiting in queue not including the time spent in the server. Solutions for these statistics are [43, p.188-191]:

$$Q' = \rho^2/2(1-\rho) \tag{4.1}$$

$$Q = \rho + \rho^2/2(1-\rho) = \rho + Q' \tag{4.2}$$

$$T'_w = (1/\lambda)^*\rho^2/2(1-\rho) = Q'/\lambda. \tag{4.3}$$

The design of the interleaved memory has been reduced to a problem of accurately determining λ and μ. The accuracy of determining these rates varies with the complexity of the model. As outlined in the previous chapter, a local memory between the CPU and main memory will filter the requests. In addition, a local memory with a complex replacement scheme, possibly based on explicit control by instructions, will add its own requests. These two effects alter the arrival rate. When various sized objects are transmitted between the local memory and main memory, the service rate is altered.

The degree of memory interleaving is determined by first calculating the processor's *peak sustainable memory request rate*, λ_p. The memory is designed around a *peak* rate because at burst speeds, the memory should not slow down the processor. A *sustained* peak rate is used to avoid overdesigning the memory; however, the definition of "sustained" is difficult to pinpoint. For scientific code, often a "typical" inner-loop, e.g., matrix multiply, is used to represent the peak sustainable rate. The analogous Prolog artificial benchmark is determinate `append/3` (see Figure 2-2). The benchmark `append/3`, however, does not use the stack and thus does not generate a peak request rate. Ideally, an artificial burst benchmark is not what is desired — a measurement of the bursty portions of a large benchmark is more realistic.

To measure λ_p the PLM timing model [21] is used. The PLM timing equations assume a one cycle memory, i.e., that read requests are serviced in one cycle. This assumption is legitimate for peak request rate calculations. Although

	CHAT	PLM	QC1	ILI
cycles	4120845	4530539	4840096	2127167
LI	47677	54694	42489	23789
KLIPS†	116	121	88	112

† assuming 100 nsec cycle

Table 4-1: PLM Timings

an instruction may need to wait for a read request to be serviced, counting the request as a single cycle gives a pessimistic peak rate, for a conservative memory design. Table 4-1 shows the PLM cycles and number of logical inferences (LI) for the benchmarks studied. A logical inference is calculated as a user-defined or built-in procedure call. Performance in terms of thousands of logical inferences per second (KLIPS) is given, assuming a 100 nsec cycle. Note that to achieve one application MLIPS performance with PLMs, about 8-10 processors are necessary. Each processor runs at about 100 KLIPS or 1.5 MIPS.

The PLM timing equations, augmented with timings derived for built-ins [54], were combined with mean reference counts per instruction, to give the mean request rate per instruction. This method is accurate because for a given instruction, cycles per instruction and references per instruction are both calculated as averages over the benchmarks. Thus the ratio, corresponding to the request rate, is independent of the mean, i.e., is a valid peak rate. The unknown factor is how the instructions combine into a burst rate. To calculate this, a moving windowed average of the rate is calculated with varying window sizes. The maximum is calculated to get an approximation of the sustained peak rate. Of course, window size affects the calculated rate. A window of one instruction is an upper bound. An infinite window size indicates an average rate for the entire program, a lower bound. Figure 4-25 shows the mean (over the benchmarks) peak sustainable memory request rate as a function of window size. $\lambda_p = 0.6$ words/cycle was chosen for the calculations of this chapter. For a large window, $\lambda_{base} = 0.46$ words/cycle, corresponding to the average request rate. Note that the CPU issues word requests, although the main memory delivers only physical words.

Again with the statistics from Section 3.2,

$$\lambda_p = \lambda_i + \lambda_d$$

$$\lambda_i = \lambda_p * v_i/v = 0.6*0.23 = 0.138 \text{ words/cycle}$$

$$\lambda_d = \lambda_p * v_d/v = 0.6*0.77 = 0.462 \text{ words/cycle,}$$

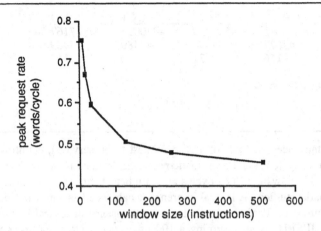

Figure 4-25: Mean Peak Sustainable Request Arrival Rate

where λ_i and λ_d are the instruction word and data word request rates, respectively. In this and subsequent queueing models, the *average* (over the benchmarks) statistics presented in Chapters 3 and 4 are used as input parameters. Several of these statistics have high variances with respect to the benchmarks and/or the WAM instructions. It should be noted that these variances reduce the accuracy of the queueing model results.

Assuming a simple model of a uniprocessor and main memory, the memory interleaving (number of modules) and module queue size can be calculated with the Flores model [28]. This gives a conservative approximation and sanity check for later calculations using more complex models. The Flores model assumes that the processor request stream splits evenly across the m memory modules,

$$\lambda = \lambda_p/m$$

$$\mu = 1/T_c$$

$$\rho = \lambda/\mu = \lambda_p T_c/m.$$

For ease of addressing a module, m is usually chosen to be a power of two, i.e., $m = 2^k$ for some integer k. With these parameters, Q' and T'_w can be calculated with Equations (4.1) and (4.3).

The *asymptotic* queueing model [28], is now described. This model permits more accurate formulations of the statistics of interest. It will also be shown how these and additional statistics, such as bandwidth efficiency, can be expressed in terms of the open model occupancy and the asymptotic model occupancy, helping the intuition. The asymptotic model represents a *closed* or *steady-state* queueing system, i.e., where the arrival and service (departure) rates are equal. This model more accurately approximates a real system, where, in contrast to the previous open queueing system, the occupancy, ρ, cannot approach arbitrarily close to one. Consider a memory system of m modules. The *offered bandwidth*, B_o, is defined as the average number of customers (requests) arriving (in the steady state) during one memory cycle, T_c. Note that these "arrivals" may be from the memory queue.

$$B_o = \lambda_p T_c.$$

Assuming uniform distribution of requests over modules, by the steady-state assumption, the average number of requests at each module will then be

$$Q = B_o/m = \lambda_p T_c/m = (\lambda_p/m)T_c = \lambda/\mu = \rho.$$

With the M/D/1 solution (Equation (4.2)),

$$Q = \rho_a + \rho_a^2/2(1-\rho_a),$$

where ρ_a is the *asymptotic occupancy*. Equating these two solutions and solving for ρ_a,

$$\rho_a = 1 + \rho - (\rho^2 + 1)^{1/2}, \qquad\qquad 0 \leq \rho_a \leq 1.$$

The *achieved bandwidth*, B_a, is defined as the average number of requests serviced each memory cycle. Note that since the model is in the steady state, B_a is also the *outside* arrival rate, i.e., the average number of requests arriving from the CPU each memory cycle. B_a is also the average number of modules busy during the memory cycle,

$$B_a = m\rho_a.$$

The *bandwidth efficiency*, ξ, is defined as the ratio of achieved to offered bandwidth,

$$\xi = B_a/B_o = m\rho_a/\lambda_p T_c = \rho_a/\rho, \qquad\qquad 0 \leq \xi \leq 1. \qquad\qquad (4.4)$$

Thus the bandwidth efficiency[12] can be easily calculated as the ratio of the asymptotic occupancy to the occupancy of the open queueing model. The efficiency is the *fraction of the bandwidth required by the system, supplied by the memory*.

---

[12]The limits on ξ are derived as follows. $\xi = \rho_a/\rho \geq 0$ is trivially true because $\rho, \rho_a \geq 0$. Also, $\rho \geq 0 \Leftrightarrow (1 + \rho)^{1/2} \geq 1 \Leftrightarrow (1 + \rho)^{1/2} \geq 1 + \rho - \rho \Leftrightarrow 1 + \rho - (1 + \rho)^{1/2} \leq \rho \Leftrightarrow \rho_a \leq \rho \Leftrightarrow \xi = \rho_a/\rho \leq 1$.

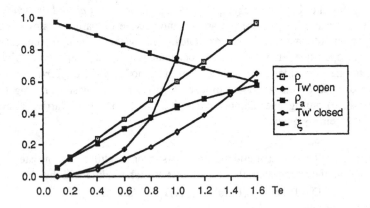

Figure 4-26: Flores Model ($\lambda_p = 0.6$)

Consider the steady state behavior of the system at a microscopic level. Assume that $(B_o - B_a)$ customers are enqueued, waiting for service at the start of a memory cycle, T_c. Over the memory cycle, B_a new customers arrive from the CPU, giving B_o total requests. B_a customers are serviced, leaving a different $(B_o - B_a)$ customers waiting. Thus in the steady state, $(B_o - B_a)$ customers are always waiting,

$$Q' = (B_o - B_a)/m = B_o/m - B_a/m = \rho - \rho_a$$

$$T'_w = Q'/\lambda_p = (\rho - \rho_a)/\lambda_p.$$

Note that both the open and closed models can be formulated in terms of the *effective memory cycle time*, $T_e = T_c/m$. T_e represents using the interleaved modules in a pipelined fashion. Therefore, in these simple models, performance can be improved by either decreasing the memory cycle time or increasing the number of modules, with equal effectiveness. Note that in a real system, because of other constraints, performance cannot be improved indefinitely by increasing the number of modules. Figure 4-26 compares the open and closed queueing models. The occupancies, expected waiting times, and bandwidth efficiency are plotted as functions of T_e.

For lightly loaded systems, both models give similar results. As the system organization degrades with increasing T_e, the open model saturates (ρ approaches one), but the closed model does not. The closed model stays saturation by *achieving* less bandwidth than the open model — this is indicated by the decreasing bandwidth efficiency, ξ, with increasing T_e. The open model *guarantees* delivery of bandwidth equal to the arrival rate of λ_p words/cycle, the *offered bandwidth*. To achieve this under saturated conditions, it requires long queues and delays. The closed model is self-regulatory in the sense that it cannot deliver impossibly high bandwidths with an inferior system (high T_e). It achieves less bandwidth, B_a, with shorter queues and delays. The closed model is considered more realistic precisely for this reason — a real system cannot tolerate excessive delays necessary to achieve high bandwidth, and will issue memory requests at a lower rate as delays cause feedback. The closed model is used throughout the remainder of the book.

4.5.2. Memory Bus Model

A memory bus can also be modeled, as an independent system resource, with the Flores model:

$$\lambda_{bus} = \lambda_p$$

$$\mu_{bus} = 1/T_{bus}$$

$$\rho_{bus} = \lambda_{bus}/\mu_{bus}.$$

The asymptotic model is derived as in the previous section with m = 1,

$$B_o = \lambda_{bus}T_{bus} = \rho_{bus}$$

$$B_a = m\rho_a = \rho_a = 1 + \rho_{bus} - (\rho_{bus}^2 + 1)^{1/2}$$

$$\xi_{bus} = \rho_a/\rho_{bus}.$$

Unless efficiency is high, i.e., occupancy is low, the bus will bottleneck the memory system, no matter what degree of interleaving is provided. As seen from the equations, a fast enough bus will avoid this problem. For local memory models transferring blocks an alternative is to increase the width of the bus, up to block size.

4.5.3. Copyback I/D Cache System

The model presented here, based on that given by Flynn [28], is a uniprocessor attached to a copyback cache (Section 4.2.4). The copyback cache uses write-allocate strategy wherein both read and write misses cause fetching of the target. The cache is line (block) oriented, i.e., all transfers to/from main memory are line transfers. The cache fetches a line on demand with fetch-bypass and wrap-around load. Fetch-bypass delivers the target line directly to the processor from memory while the cache is concurrently loaded. Wrap-around load delivers the target word within the line directly to the processor. Buffers are assumed, to allow simultaneous transfer of a dirty line from the cache and the target line from memory.

Transferring a line to/from the cache involves a delay, T_{line}, defined as

$$T_{line} = \max(T_a + (L-1)T_{bus}, T_c),$$

where L is the line size in units of buswidths, and T_{bus} is a single bus transfer time. The max is used to ensure that service cannot complete until after one memory cycle. The T_a term represents waiting for the target word within the line, and the $(L-1)T_{bus}$ term represents transferring the remaining portion of the line in burst mode (pipelined) fashion. The major assumption being made here is that the memory interleaving factor, m, is greater than or equal to L. For the uniprocessor model, there is no advantage to making m greater than L, because the extra modules cannot decrease T_{line}.

The cache request rate is approximated with two streams: λ_1 and λ_2. The first stream represents requests that do not stall the processor. The second stream represents requests that do stall the processor.

$$\lambda_1 = \lambda_w * MR_w + \lambda_p * MR * DR$$

$$\lambda_2 = \lambda_r * MR_r$$

$$T_1 = T_{line}$$

$$T_2 = T_{line} - T_{dead}$$

$$T_{dead} \approx T_a$$

These two streams are combined with an M/G/1 queueing model:

$$\lambda = \lambda_1 + \lambda_2 \tag{4.5}$$

$$T = (\lambda_1/\lambda)T_1 + (\lambda_2/\lambda)T_2 \tag{4.6}$$

$$\mu = 1/T \tag{4.7}$$

$$\rho = \lambda/\mu = \lambda_1 T_1 + \lambda_2 T_2. \tag{4.8}$$

In the above equations, MR is the miss ratio of the local memory, split into MR_r, the read miss ratio and MR_w, the write miss ratio. DR, the dirty line ratio, is the ratio of dirty to clean lines replaced. Values of these statistics are given earlier in this chapter (Figures 4-22 and 4-23). These values, with corresponding line and cache sizes, are used as input parameters to the queueing models. The input request stream, λ_p, is split into λ_r, the read miss requests, and λ_w, the write miss requests. I/O is not modeled in this or subsequent formulations, although it can be easily be included [28].

The T_{dead} term is a heuristic which indicates that requests will not arrive at the memory while the processor is waiting for the target word of a read miss, i.e., during the T_a delay. In this and subsequent models, T_{dead} is thus approximated as T_a. Consider the arrival of requests on a time line. A gap appears during the T_a delay, when no arrivals will occur. However, the simple queueing models used assume independent arrival and service rates. *The effect of a decreased arrival rate is approximated by increasing the service rate.* Note that although write-allocation is assumed, it is also assumed that the CPU need not wait for a write miss request to be serviced.

An M/G/1 asymptotic model [28] is similar to the M/D/1 asymptotic model of the previous section. Consider a memory system of m modules as a single server. By the steady-state assumption, the average queue size is

$$Q = \lambda T = \lambda_1 T_1 + \lambda_2 T_2 = \rho, \qquad 0 \le Q, \rho \le 1.$$

Using the Pollaczek-Khinchine solution [43, p.187],

$$Q = \rho_a + \rho_a^2 (1+C^2)/2(1-\rho_a),$$

where ρ_a is the asymptotic occupancy. Solving,

$$\rho_a = (1 + \rho - (\rho^2 + 2C^2\rho + 1)^{1/2})/(1-C^2). \tag{4.9}$$

The statistics of interest, T'_w and Q', are derived from the asymptotic occupancy, using the standard M/G/1 solutions,

$$Q' = \rho_a^2 (1+C^2)/2(1-\rho_a) \tag{4.10}$$

$$T'_w = Q'/\lambda, \tag{4.11}$$

where C^2, the coefficient of variation, is

$$C^2 = (\lambda_1/\lambda)(1-T_1/T)^2 + (\lambda_2/\lambda)(1-T_2/T)^2, \quad 0 \le C^2 \le 1.$$

The memory bandwidth efficiency, ξ_{mem}, is derived in a manner similar to Equation (4.4),

$$\xi_{mem} = \rho_a/\rho. \tag{4.12}$$

The degradation of uniprocessor performance due to main memory contention is now calculated. To simplify the equations, processor performance is measured in units of cycles per instruction (the inverse of the conventional definition). Degraded *typical* performance is measured rather than degraded peak performance. Recall from Figure 4-25 that the average memory request rate is $\lambda_{base} = 0.46$ words/cycle. Recall from Section 3.2 that the average request rate per instruction is $\upsilon = 3.0$ words/instr. Therefore the average processor performance, P_{base}, is

$$P_{base} = \upsilon/\lambda_{base} = (3.0 \text{ ref/instr})/(0.46 \text{ ref/cycle})$$

$$= 6.5 \text{ cycles/instr.}$$

For a 100 nsec cycle PLM, this corresponds to an execution rate of about 1.5 MIPS. The performance of a processor assuming no misses, $P_{no\text{-}miss}$, is now calculated.

$$P_{no\text{-}miss} = P_{base} + P_{branch},$$

where P_{branch} is the branch penalty in cycles/instr,

$$P_{branch} = Pr(uncond)T_{uncond} + Pr(cond)T_{cond} + Pr(micro)T_{micro}.$$

Unconditional branches are instructions such as `call`, `execute`, and `try`. Conditional branches are instructions such as `switch_constant` and `switch_term`. The `fail` operation and `escape` instructions are categorized as *micro* branches, because although they do not appear in the image architecture, they may still evoke a penalty, depending on implementation. From Section 4.3.1, Pr(branch)=0.17 on average. CHAT presents statistics close to the mean and is therefore used to estimate P_{branch}. For CHAT, Pr(uncond)=0.11, Pr(cond)=0.04 and Pr(micro)=0.04. Assume that T_{uncond}=1 cycle, T_{cond}=2 cycles, and T_{micro}=1 cycle. Therefore, assuming no cache misses,

$$P_{branch} = 0.11*1 + 0.04*2 + 0.04*1 = 0.23 \text{ cycles/instr}$$

$$P_{no\text{-}miss} = 6.5 + 0.23 = 6.73 \text{ cycles/instr.}$$

Actual processor performance, P_{actual}, accounts for misses.

$$P_{actual} = P_{no\text{-}miss} + P_{miss},$$

where P_{miss}, the miss penalty in cycles/instr, is

$$P_{miss} = T_{access}*\upsilon_r*MR_r.$$

Recall from Section 3.2 that the average read request rate per instruction is $\upsilon_r = 1.6$ words/instr. When calculating the miss penalty, only read misses are considered because of the previous assumption that only read misses stall the processor. The expected miss delay, T_{access}, is

$$T_{access} = T_a + T'_w,$$

where T_a is the memory access time and T'_w is the previously defined expected waiting time. Degradation, D, is the fraction of ideal processor performance (assuming an infinite local memory) lost due to local memory misses in an actual processor (with a finite local memory). In the following definition of D, recall that performance is defined inversely to standard definitions.

$$D = (P_{actual} - P_{no\text{-}miss})/P_{actual}, \qquad 0 \le D \le 1. \qquad (4.13)$$

A bus model for this system is derived as in Section 4.5.2, with

$$\lambda_{bus} = \lambda_p * MR * (1+DR) * L.$$

This bus model assumes that addresses issued for read requests do not require a separate bus cycle. The bus bandwidth efficiency, ξ_{bus}, is the fraction of the bandwidth required by shared memory and the processing elements, supplied by a single shared bus. Recall that the bandwidth efficiency, ξ_{mem}, is the fraction of the bandwidth required by the processing elements, supplied by the shared memory, assuming an ideal bus, i.e., $\xi_{bus} = 1$. These statistics are related to PE performance because reduction in bandwidth efficiency implies reduction in the bandwidth offered, which is approximately proportional to the rate at which the PEs execute instructions. The efficiency statistics are *not* combined with performance degradation, D, so that the effects can be viewed separately.

Figures 4-27 and 4-28 show the queueing model measurements for a selection of the I/D caches analyzed in Section 4.3.2. Shown are bus bandwidth efficiency, main memory bandwidth efficiency, and percent performance degradation, plotted as functions of cache size. Figure 4-27 assumes a two word bus, Figure 4-28 a one word bus. Sufficient interleaving to transmit cache lines in a single burst ($m \ge$ line-size/buswidth) is assumed throughout. Other implementation assumptions used are $T_{bus}=1$ cycle, $T_a=3$ cycles, and $T_c=5$ cycles.

Recall from the previous queueing model descriptions that main memory efficiency and processor degradation are modeled together, independently from bus efficiency. The decoupled models allow separate views of bus and interleaved memory performance. The main memory efficiency and processor degradation models assume that the bus achieves the full bandwidth supplied by the processor.

The results from Figure 4-27 indicate that with sufficient interleaving (implicit in the model) and enough bus capacity (speed and/or bus width), large block sizes produce the least performance degradation and achieve the most memory bandwidth. For a given cache size, as block size decreases these metrics degrade slowly at first, then rapidly. The queueing model favors large blocks as long as the cache is large enough to generate correspondingly low miss ratios. Miss ratios fail to decrease significantly with increasing block size, for a certain minimal cache size (see Figure 4-10). In these benchmarks, this happens for a 64 word cache.

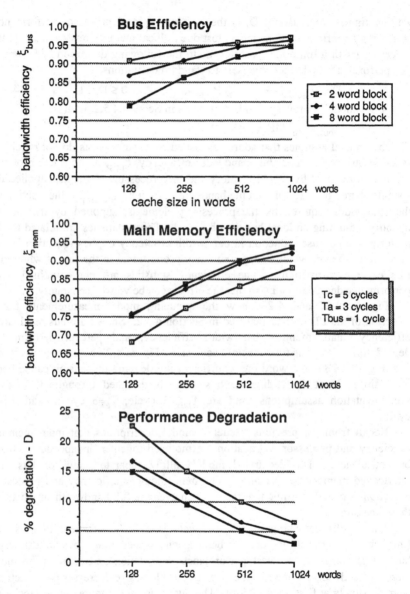

Figure 4-27:   Copyback I/D Cache Queueing Model: 2 Word Bus

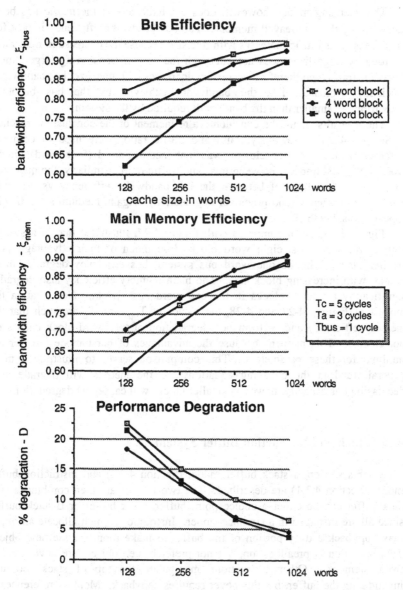

Figure 4-28: Copyback I/D Cache Queueing Model: 1 Word Bus

The queueing model, however, does not indicate that the *traffic* has been decreased by the interleaved memory. The bus bandwidth efficiency is best for small lines. Bus traffic increases with line size because the decrease in miss ratio afforded by large lines does not outweigh the cost of transferring larger lines. Since bus traffic and therefore occupancy increases with line size, bus bandwidth efficiency decreases, i.e., the bandwidth achieved by the bus becomes proportionally smaller than the bandwidth required by the system.

These results should be considered a refinement of the conclusions reached in Section 4.2.4. Previously, miss and traffic ratios were used to compare different caches. The conclusion was that medium sized (four word) blocks produce the best tradeoff between miss and traffic ratio. Similarly, the queueing model presents a tradeoff between the bus bandwidth efficiency vs. memory bandwidth efficiency (and processor degradation). Again, medium sized blocks appear to display the best characteristics.

Figure 4-28, when compared with Figure 4-27, illustrates that in a system with a one word bus, eight word blocks lose much of their advantage over smaller blocks. In the one word bus system, bus efficiency degrades more rapidly with increasing block size. The main memory efficiency also degrades significantly for large blocks in the one word bus system. Note that in the models of Figures 4-27 and 4-28, the values of T_{bus} and T_c are such that the memory efficiency and performance degradation of two word block caches do not change. This happens because the advantages of burst mode transfer are minimal for these parameters. This comparison serves to illustrate a more general trend in the queueing equations: all the metrics will degrade with decreasing bus capacity; however, smaller blocks will cause *less* degradation.

4.5.4. Stack and Instruction Buffer System

In this section, a stack buffer model (Section 4.2.2) and instruction buffer model (Section 4.3.1) are described. The two models are then combined. The data buffer can be either a choice point buffer, stack buffer or E-stack buffer, since all are managed in a similar manner. Instructions which allocate an object may copyback a dirty portion of the buffer to make room for the new object. This operation is preallocation, but not prefetch, i.e., objects are never read in from memory. Other instructions manipulate the top of stack, possibly invalidating the buffer, but this never requires copyback. Memory references to the valid portion of the buffer are serviced from the buffer, whereas other references are serviced from memory. However, buffer misses never imply replacement or copyback.

A stack buffer model similar to that of a write-through cache [28] is used. Management is modeled with three arrival rates: read misses λ_{rmiss}, write misses λ_{wmiss}, and copyback requests λ_{copy}. Misses reference a single word. Preallocation instructions copyback a *variable* sized block. Write misses and copyback requests are combined into a single stream, λ_1, with a service time T_1. The effect of memory interleaving is modeled by reducing the λ_1 arrival rate by the interleaving factor, m. The valid range of m in the model is constrained by the number of outstanding write misses and copybacks that the processor can sustain. In the previous cache model, m does not appear explicitly, and is inherently constrained to retain validity. Read misses form a separate stream, λ_2, with service time T_2. These arrival rates and service times can be combined with an M/G/1 model (Equations (4.5)-(4.8)):

$$\lambda_1 = (\lambda_{wmiss} + L*\lambda_{copy})/m$$

$$\lambda_2 = \lambda_{rmiss}$$

$$T_1 = T_c$$

$$T_2 = T_c - T_{dead}$$

$$T_{dead} \approx T_a,$$

where

$$\lambda_{miss} = \lambda_d*MR_d = \lambda_{rmiss} + \lambda_{wmiss}$$

$$\lambda_{copy} = \lambda_d*PR,$$

for stack buffer miss ratio, MR_d, prefetch ratio (ratio of preallocation instructions to memory references), PR, and average copyback block size (in words), L. λ_{rmiss} and λ_{wmiss} are calculated with read and write stack buffer miss ratios. Note that MR_d and L are *dependent*, whereas PR is *independent*, of buffer size. The T_{dead} term in T_2 is introduced for the same reason as in the cache model of the previous section. Recall that the T_{dead} heuristic models feedback within the queueing equations, to approximate the behavior wherein the processor stops issuing requests between issuing a data read miss and receiving the result.

This model lumps copyback in the arrival rate, treating all requests independently. L is measured in units of words (stack buffer entries), rather than *buswidths*. Buswidths would be more accurate, and somewhat lower, if the bus is wider than one word. A line oriented stack buffer would permit splitting the model into a system where a copyback service time, T_{copy}, would assume pipelined transfer of lines (as in copyback cache model). Line oriented buffers are not modeled in this book.

The calculation of λ_{copy} is made by determining the ratio of preallocation instructions (`allocate`, `try`, `try_me_else`) to memory requests. The assumption implicit in this calculation is that the preallocation instructions are infrequent, so that the peak sustainable rate is approximately the same as the mean rate over the benchmark programs.

A look-ahead instruction buffer model, independent of the previous stack buffer model, is now described. Recall that the instruction buffer has a traffic ratio greater than one. Here, a memory module is described with two arrival rates and service times corresponding to two types of events: sequential instruction execution and taken branches. All instruction references cause prefetching of new instruction words of equal size. A taken branch, however, indicates a miss in the buffer, causing the prefetching of an *entire* buffer, d buswidths in size. These arrival rates and service times are combined with an M/G/1 model:

$$\lambda_1 = \lambda_i/m$$

$$\lambda_2 = \lambda_i * MR_i$$

$$T_1 = T_c$$

$$T_2 = T_{line} = max(T_a + (d-1)T_{bus}, T_c),$$

where λ_i is the instruction word request rate and MR_i is the instruction buffer miss ratio. For instruction prefetching, T_{dead} is not appropriate in T_2 because the processor does not stall. Assumptions made above are that the instruction requests are distributed uniformly across the modules and that the buffer size, $d \le m$.

The model of a stack buffer configured with an instruction buffer can be simplified by assuming that $T_2 \approx 0$ in the stack buffer model. The streams of each are then combined with an M/G/1 model:

$$\lambda_1 = (\lambda_{wmiss} + L*\lambda_{copy} + \lambda_i)/m$$

$$\lambda_2 = \lambda_i * MR_i$$

$$T_1 = T_c$$

$$T_2 = T_{line} = max(T_a + (d-1)T_{bus}, T_c)$$

An M/G/1 asymptotic model for the stack buffer configuration is similar to that of the previous section. A bus for this system is modeled as in Section 4.5.2, with

$$\lambda_{bus} = \lambda_{miss} + L*\lambda_{copy} + \lambda_i + \lambda_i * MR_i * d.$$

Figures 4-29 and 4-30 show the stack buffer configuration queueing model measurements. Percent processor degradation and bandwidth efficiency are

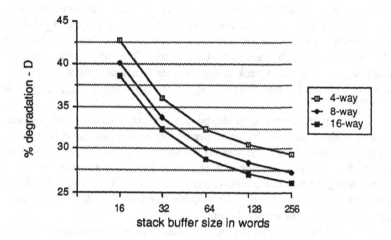

Figure 4-29: Stack Buffer Configuration: Performance Degradation

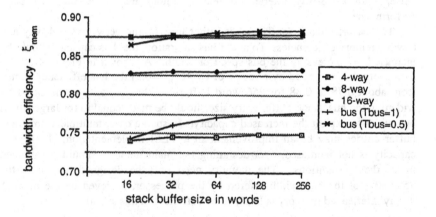

Figure 4-30: Stack Buffer Configuration: Memory Bandwidth Efficiency

plotted as functions of stack size. A set of curves is shown corresponding to different interleaving factors. It is assumed that each buffer is configured with a three word instruction buffer. A one word bus with $T_{bus}=1$ cycle, $T_c=5$ cycles, and $T_a=3$ cycles is also assumed. For stack buffers, a mean PR=0.028 and L=6.8 words have been calculated across the benchmarks. The value of PR justifies the previous assumption that a peak allocation rate is not necessary. Figure 4-30 includes two curves for bus efficiency, ξ_{bus}, corresponding to $T_{bus}=1$ cycle and $T_{bus}=0.5$ cycles.

Note that performance degradation for the stack buffer configuration is calculated with respect to the ideal performance of a processor with a local memory of unlimited size. Alternatively, degradation can be calculated with respect to the ideal performance of a processor with a *stack buffer* of unlimited size (increasing the size of the look-ahead instruction buffer will not significantly improve its performance). It is useful, however, to calibrate all degradation statistics with respect to a single baseline.

Figure 4-29 indicates that degradation decreases with increasing stack buffer size and interleaving factors. The rate of improvement decreases, however. This implies that a cost-performance optimum may be reached with mid-size buffers. The precise optimum depends on how cost increases with buffer size and interleaving factor, a function of technology. For instance, a 128-word stack buffer with an 8-way interleaved main memory may have the best cost-performance.

The bus efficiency for $T_{bus}=1$ is rather low, falling between the 4-way and 8-way memory efficiencies. To avoid bus saturation, the bus capacity should be increased, by increasing the bus speed or width. As shown in Figure 4-30, by increasing the bus speed by a factor of two ($T_{bus}=0.5$) the bus efficiency jumps from about 0.78 to 0.88 for 256 word buffers. If bus capacity is increased by widening the bus, stack buffer entry size should be made equal to (or larger than) bus width to exploit the increased capacity. In such a case, multiple word stack buffer entries may be an improvement in a VLSI implementation. If the bus capacity is not increased, over-designing the main memory should be avoided under these conditions. The memory need only be designed to handle the 75%-80% of the bandwidth offered by the processor, achieved by the bus. A 4-way interleaved memory is likely to be sufficient in this situation.

4.6. Summary

In this chapter, two-level memory hierarchies are defined for sequential Prolog architectures. The memory model consists of a fast local memory and a slower, larger interleaved main memory. Recall that in the previous chapter, architecture memory-referencing characteristics are based on the zeroth-order statistic of the number of memory references made. The local memory performance measurements presented in this chapter are based on first-order statistics such as traffic ratio. The interleaved memory performance statistics presented at the end of this chapter are based on the higher-order statistics of miss penalty, performance degradation, and bandwidth efficiency. This progression of refinement in the models allows increasingly detailed analysis of the referencing behavior of Prolog programs executing on complex hosts.

Several local memory models are presented in order of increasing performance, cost, and generality. Envisioning a single chip microprocessor, the local memories considered are small (up to 1024 32-bit words). Initially, only data referencing is considered. At the low end, a single choice point buffer as small as 12 words offers a miss ratio of 0.55 and a traffic ratio of 0.62. A stack buffer of only 64 words offers a miss ratio of 0.28 and a traffic ratio of 0.30. The stack buffer, more complex than the choice point buffer, captures both choice point and environment references. A copyback cache, capturing all types of references, does better still — a 256 word cache (with four word lines) offers a miss ratio of 0.05 and a traffic ratio of 0.23. At the high end, smart caches, which avoid transferring lines no longer in a valid storage area, reduce the cache traffic ratio by up to 30%.

Local memories for instruction references are also analyzed. Measurements of both instruction buffers and caches are presented, allowing comparison of alternative local (instruction + data) memory configurations. At the low end, the stack buffer configuration offers better memory performance than the caches because cache traffic increases rapidly with decreasing cache size. At the high end, split I+D caches display the best memory performance; however, the trend indicates that for larger caches, the combined I/D cache might achieve equal performance. Although the combined I/D cache is slightly less costly to implement in VLSI than a split I+D cache, the latter offers twice the bandwidth to the CPU.

These results clarify the discussion in Chapter 2 concerning the relationship between the traditional and register-based CIFs. As is indicated in this chapter, caches, which capture all types of references, offer greater reduction in memory traffic and higher hit ratios than stack buffers. At little extra cost, a cache-based host may implement a small, fast register set. Such hosts are expected to gain little advantage with the traditional CIF as compared to the register-based CIF (some reduction in instruction bandwidth can be expected — as much as 16% as is shown in Chapter 3). Thus the WAM, a register-based DCA, is seen to be well-suited for realistic Prolog hosts. In fact, the WAM also performs quite well on a host with a stack buffer (and register set), as is shown in this chapter. These results do not preclude the superiority of a traditional-CIF DCA for other types of hosts, e.g., a host with only a large stack buffer.

The second-level main memory and memory bus are analyzed with asymptotic M/G/1 queueing models, for alternative local memory configurations. Queueing models are beneficial primarily because they reintroduce time into the previous local memory models, allowing the calculation of second-order statistics, such as miss penalty. The queueing models are driven with a peak sustainable memory request rate corresponding to a WAM processor with an average execution rate of approximately 100 application KLIPS. This peak request rate parameter is calculated in the emulator with the PLM timings [21], assuming a 100 nsec cycle time and one cycle memory latency. In the uniprocessor organizations considered in this chapter, main memory and bus performance are characterized with statistics for performance degradation and bandwidth efficiency (the fraction of the bandwidth required by the system, supplied by the memory or bus). The main memory and bus are modeled independently to allow separate views of the system components. Alternatively, the queueing models could be coupled to produce a single metric of system performance.

Both a combined I/D cache configuration and a stack buffer + instruction buffer configuration are analyzed. For the I/D cache, memory bandwidth efficiency is maximized with large cache blocks. Bus bandwidth efficiency, however, is maximized with small cache blocks. These results support the previous first-order statistical results, indicating that medium size (four word) blocks appear to display the best tradeoff of characteristics. The selection of block size is also shown to be dependent on bus width. In general, with decreasing bus capacity, small blocks cause the performance and efficiency metrics to degrade more slowly than do large blocks.

For the stack buffer configuration, main memory bandwidth efficiency improves with increasing interleaving. In contrast to the cache configuration, where interleaving is implicitly limited by block size, the stack buffer configuration can take advantage of larger interleaving factors. This is because the stack buffer is managed by copying-back groups of stack entries. Copybacks, write misses, and instruction read requests are assumed to be uniformly distributed across the memory modules. Large interleaving factors offer the stack buffer configuration greater memory bandwidth efficiencies than the cache configuration, for approximately equal size local memories.

The bus efficiency of the stack buffer configuration is somewhat inferior to that of the cache configuration. For equal capacity buses and local memory sizes, the 256 word stack buffer configuration bus efficiency falls between the bus efficiencies for the four and eight word block cache configurations. The stack buffer configuration bus efficiency does not significantly improve with increasing local memory size, as in the cache configuration. These results can be attributed to the higher miss ratios of the stack buffer and the look-ahead instruction buffer as compared to the I/D cache miss ratio. As discussed, the stack buffer is limited by capturing only stack references, and the look-ahead instruction buffer is limited by the branch frequency. In contrast, the I/D cache captures all reference types and can also capture loops.

The performance degradation of the stack buffer configuration, calculated with respect to the same baseline as the cache configuration, is significantly higher than that of the cache configuration. The minimal achievable performance degradation is constrained primarily by the previously mentioned high miss ratio of the stack buffer configuration. For instance, with 16-way interleaving, the benchmarks measurements indicate a minimal limit of about 25% degradation. In comparison, even a 256 word I/D cache configuration (with four word blocks and one word bus, implying 4-way interleaving) can achieve about half this degradation. Large caches achieve less than 5% performance degradation.

In the next chapter, similar analysis and performance measurements are given for parallel Prolog executing on shared memory multiprocessors. The difficulties encountered in extending the models of this chapter to a multiprocessor include both memory design (e.g., how to efficiently maintain consistency in a two-level hierarchy) and memory analysis (e.g., how to accurately represent multiple processing elements within a simple queueing model).

5 Multiprocessor Memory Organizations

In this chapter, two-level memory hierarchies are defined and analyzed for the Restricted AND-Parallel Prolog (PWAM) architecture (reviewed in Section 2.3). PWAM is chosen for study in this book for several reasons. It is an extension of the Warren Abstract Machine (WAM), which allows fair comparison between sequential and parallel Prolog architectures. It is designed to execute sequential code efficiently with a modified WAM storage model. High-level measurements presented in Section 3.5 support this criterion. It is designed to execute parallel code with low communication and parallelism control overheads. Measurements are presented in this chapter which support this second criterion. The results from the RAP-Prolog benchmark measured indicate, for example, that a tightly-coupled shared memory multiprocessor with eight high-performance processing elements coupled with a 32-way interleaved memory and a high capacity bus can achieve a speed-up of 750%.

5.1. Memory Model

RAP-Prolog programs are modeled executing on a shared memory multiprocessor model. Many alternative types of multiprocessors have been designed for the execution of procedural/scientific programs [49]. These organizations offer high performance by incorporating distributed memories and complex interconnection networks. The approach taken in this book is to measure PWAM under the assumptions of a relatively simple multiprocessor model to acquire insights into the memory bandwidth requirements of PWAM. There are currently few published results concerning the execution performance or memory characteristics of parallel logic programs. Therefore little intuition

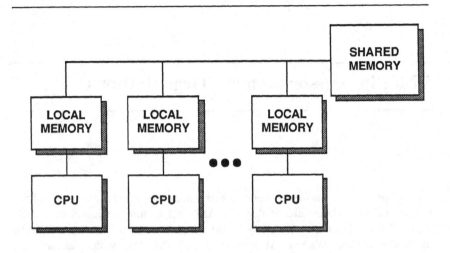

Figure 5-1: Multiprocessor Shared Memory Model

exists, as it does for procedural/scientific programs, as to the best multiprocessor configurations. The first step in this evolutionary approach was taken by Hermenegildo — an abstract shared memory with no contention was assumed for the design of PWAM [36]. The simple memory model used in this book extends Hermenegildo's model and is sufficient to indicate communication costs and the effectiveness of local memory designs. With the flexibility of the simulation and queueing models presented here alternative memory design parameters can be explored.

The multiprocessor system model considered in this book, as illustrated in Figure 5-1, consists of a shared memory connected to a set of identical processing elements (PEs), each with a private, local memory. Each PE references its own local memory, which if it misses, makes a request to shared memory. One PE cannot *directly* access another PE's local memory, nor can a PE directly *steal* a shared memory request from another PE and satisfy it. The shared memory consists of a set of identical memory modules. The modules are connected to the PEs with an interconnection network. Similar to the analysis of the last chapter, queueing models are developed to determine the performance of the interleaved shared memory and the efficiency of a single shared bus interconnection network.

A single shared bus system represents only one of several alternative multiprocessor configurations. Of course, a single bus interconnect cannot be used in a parallel system of arbitrary size; however, it is a reasonable organization for a tightly-coupled PWAM shared memory multiprocessor with a limited number of high-speed PEs. Figure 5-1 illustrates such an organization. The single bus allows all PEs to simultaneously view all memory requests and acts as an arbiter to resolve races to update locks (described in detail in later sections).

The memory referencing characteristics of PWAM are of interest to determine the cost, in terms of increased memory traffic, of exploiting parallelism. The various overheads involved are listed below.

- **CGE conditions** — To execute a *conditional graph expression* (see Section 2.3), evaluation of conditions at runtime may be necessary. This is not analyzed here.

- **control of parallelism** — Extra bookkeeping references (not present in the WAM) are necessary in PWAM to control parallelism. Measurements of this overhead are presented in Section 3.5.

- **loss of locality** — The WAM stack is a private area, yet the PWAM objects allocated to it, for the most part, are used for process management, a global function. This implies that some percentage of *sequential performance* has been sacrificed to implement the mechanics of the PWAM model. The performance loss is due to reduced memory locality, a result of mixing choice points and environments with Parcall Frames and Markers. Note that the RAP-Prolog benchmark analyzed is determinate, so that no Markers are used. Therefore locality measurements presented include only the effects of Parcall Frames.

- **coherency overheads** — To solve the consistency problem in certain multiprocessor organizations, overhead traffic is generated.

PWAM (and its relative, the WAM), is an abstract model *above the level of the memory organization*. In other words, specifications for caches and other hardware organizations are *not* included in the architecture. A problem of maintaining consistency among the local memories arises when mapping the architecture onto a two-level memory hierarchy. PWAM avoids copying of passed arguments (i.e., copying at the architecture level) by having a child process access its arguments nonlocally from a parent process. This method of "on demand" access is in a sense optimal because no overheads are invoked for portions of passed arguments that are not used. However, a two-level shared memory hierarchy causes nonlocal-access consistency problems. These can only be solved by copying *at the memory organization level*. This problem implies that the advantages of avoiding argument copying will be lessened because of the extra memory traffic generated when retaining consistency.

Many of the local memory designs presented in the previous chapter cannot be used within the shared memory model because these local memories cause consistency problems. In the next section the consistency problem is defined in detail. Coherent local memory models are described and measurements of their efficiencies are presented.

5.2. The Consistency Problem

The *consistency* or *coherency* problem refers to the management of local memories in a multiprocessor system, ensuring that each processor sees a consistent view of the virtual address space. The consistency problem is composed of two parts: keeping the shared memory consistent with a local memory, and keeping the local memories consistent with each other. Rather than give a general description of the consistency problem (see Censier [15] for instance), a description specific to PWAM is given in this section.

PWAM can be considered a *work driven* paradigm (c.f., process driven paradigm), where parallel call goals are stacked (in the Goal Stack) by a parent process. An idle processor can access one of these goals and initiate a child process. The consistency problem is best illustrated by considering the simple case of two processors. Assume the parent and child processes reside on different processors. The child process references argument structures in the stack and heap of the parent process. A structure consists of ground terms and unbound variables. For instance, if the goal contained an argument instantiated to the structure $f(a, Z)$, the ground terms are the structure $f/2$ and the constant $a/0$. The unbound variable is Z. When local memories exist, the following problems can occur:

1. If the local memories are copyback managed, the passed structure may exist (in most recent form) in the parent processor's local memory, but not in shared memory. Since the child processor cannot direct access the parent processor's local memory, there is a consistency problem.

2. Unbound variables of a passed structure are no longer valid in the parent processor once the parallel call is entered. The variables won't be referenced until after the parallel call is exited; however, at this point, the variables are not guaranteed to be up-to-date (the child process may bind them).

3. If the local memories are copyback managed, the solutions (bindings for previously unbound variables in the passed arguments) produced by the child process may exist (in most recent form) in the child processor's local memory, but not in shared memory. This consistency problem is symmetrical to 1.

4. Unbound variables in the passed structures are no longer valid in the child processor after the child process succeeds, if subsequent processors bind them. This consistency problem is symmetrical to 2.

As is apparent from the above description, consistency need be ensured only at process invocation and completion, i.e., *process boundaries*. While a process is running, it is guaranteed, by PWAM, not to modify shared data, and therefore consistency need not be ensured. For instance, a standard local memory could be made consistent at these process boundaries by invoking a software manager which operated locally (making worst case assumptions concerning which data object will be shared *after* the process boundary is crossed). It is more efficient, however, to ensure consistency incrementally, for each memory reference, with coherent local memories. Historically, the first such coherent caches proposed used a write-through strategy for all writes [32]. A write to a block that is shared among the caches causes invalidation of all remote copies. This is considered the least costly and lowest performance solution.

Cache coherency protocols recently proposed in the literature, although designed primarily for scientific multiprocessors, can also be used for implementing a PWAM multiprocessor. A family of *fully distributed broadcast cache synchronization schemes* is described by Bitar [6] and measured by Archibald [3]. Two main variations of broadcast cache protocols are analyzed here. Both are identical except for how they handle a write to a block that is possibly shared among the caches. The first scheme ("write-in") involves writing into the local cache only, and invalidating shared (remote) copies. The second scheme ("write-through") involves writing-through to remote copies (and shared memory), i.e., shared copies are updated. These are high cost, high performance solutions. Traditional write-through cache schemes should not be confused with the write-through broadcast scheme. For traditional write-through caches shared memory is updated for all writes. The write-through broadcast scheme indicates that only "possibly shared" blocks (as indicated by the blocks' status) are written-through. This broadcast scheme implies that dirty blocks may exist which need to be copied back to memory upon replacement.

Prolog architectures have several advantages over traditional architectures which should alleviate the complexity and cost associated with broadcast caches, if properly exploited. A variation of the proposed write-through broadcast caches and traditional write-through caches, called a *partial write-through* or *hybrid* cache, is analyzed as an example of this type of solution. The hybrid cache is a compromise between the simplicity/inefficiency of a traditional write-through cache, and the complexity/efficiency of a write-through broadcast cache. The hybrid cache, described in detail in a later section, is simpler than the broadcast model in one major respect: blocks do not require an *access status* (such as *private* or *shared*). The proposed broadcast schemes use the status to determine if a write-through is needed. The hybrid cache writes-through references *by static type*, not by dynamic status.

5.2.1. Broadcast Cache Coherency

Recently proposed coherent caches are based on copyback caches with the attribute that shared memory need not be consistent at all times with the local memories. The local memories must still be consistent among themselves. In this book, these schemes are collectively called *broadcast* cache models. An abstract model is developed here encompassing a family of fully distributed broadcast caches, as described by Bitar [6]. The model abstracts the traffic behavior of the various individual protocols, without specifying management detail. The model assumes that each local cache line has an *access status*. Most proposed statuses include the concepts of *private* (the line is resident only locally) and *shared* (the line is resident locally and possibly resident remotely). Line status is used by a particular protocol to determine how to manage read and write requests. There are many design options available in these protocols, but only one is a major concern here: the treatment of a write to a possibly shared line. There are basically two ways to do this write: *write-through* and *write-in*. In the following discussion, a write-allocation policy is assumed. Recall that write-allocation fetches the target of a write miss into the cache.

A write-through strategy updates remote copies, and possibly shared memory. During a write to a shared line, the processor first arbitrates for the bus. After getting control of the bus, it places the address and the value on the bus (this is known in the literature as a *write-broadcast*). Other caches communicate back if they had copies. If there are no remote hits, the cache changes the status of the block from shared to private, otherwise the status remains shared. Assuming that handshaking is not needed, the action requires only a minimal bus transaction cycle.

In its most general form, a write-through synchronization policy need not update shared memory. In some systems, it may be advantageous to avoid the update, e.g., if the bus cannot be used to simultaneously write to both remote caches and shared memory, or if the shared memory is very much slower than the caches. For instance, the Dragon computer does *not* update shared memory [3]. In this book, hardware is assumed that benefits from simultaneous update of shared memory. In most systems, the status of a line cannot indicate, with absolute certainty, if a line is shared because natural replacement may independently remove all remote copies. In this case, the write-through policy will accomplish only an update of shared memory.

A *write-in*, *write-back* or *copyback* strategy is based on the restriction that to write a line, the line must be privately cached by the writer. During a write to a shared line, the processor first arbitrates for the bus. After getting control of the bus, it places the address and an invalidation command on the bus. The line is then updated locally and marked private. Shared copies can simply be invalidated, and need not be copied back, because they cannot be dirty. Private lines may be dirty, and require copyback either on request from another cache or by natural replacement. The write-through scheme can *also* produce dirty lines, depending on the policy concerning writes to non-shared lines. For example, the Firefly computer uses write-broadcast on shared lines and write-in on non-shared lines [3].

5.2.2. Locking in Broadcast Caches

An interesting operation to analyze for the two broadcast schemes is the use of *locks* to protect data structures from two or more processors racing to update. Locks are frequently used, in PWAM and other architectures, to protect process management structures. The following discussion [7] serves two purposes. Its first purpose is to indicate that the two coherency protocols implement locks efficiently, i.e., without generating excessive memory traffic. Its second purpose is to compare the efficiency with which the two protocols implement locks.

A lock is a single location which one of several processes can *set* (e.g., to one). The locked-out processes continue to read the lock, waiting for the lock to be released (e.g., to zero). This type of read loop is called a *busy wait*. When the lock is released, the waiters race to set the lock for themselves. Each busy wait loop surrounds a *read-modify-write* operation intended to set the lock. The read-modify-write operation is an *atomic* action, i.e., it commands the bus for the duration of its execution. Thus only one read-modify-write can be executing in the entire system at any one time. If several busy wait loops are entered concurrently, more than one read-modify-write may be *attempted*, but only one will get control of the bus. The others will be aborted and retried. For write-through, a successful read-modify-write (i.e., one that passes the read test) issues a write on the bus. For write-in, a successful read-modify-write issues an invalidation command on the bus. An unsuccessful read-modify-write releases the bus immediately.

A processor busy waiting for a lock continually reads a copy of the lock (with a value of one) in its cache. For the write-through policy, when the lock is unlocked by another processor, the zero is written to all caches having a copy of the block. A waiting processor then reads the zero during its next busy wait iteration, and initiates a read-modify-write in an attempt to set the lock. Races between concurrent attempts to set the lock are naturally resolved because the read-modify-write operation is atomic, commanding the bus for the duration of the action. The winner's read-modify-write checks that the lock still has a zero value (which it does) and sets the lock to one, writing through to all caches having a copy of the block. Subsequently, a processor which already issued a read-modify-write, checks the set lock in the read part of the read-modify-write and aborts its action. The processor then resumes busy waiting. A waiting processor which did not yet issue a read-modify-write, avoids issuing one because it reads the set lock in its cache.

For the write-in policy, when the lock is unlocked by a processor, the block is invalidated in all remote caches having a copy of the block. A waiting processor then takes a cache miss for the lock read request made during its next busy wait iteration. The cache block is fetched and the busy wait loop continues as before. If the value is zero, the waiting processor initiates a read-modify-write in an attempt to set the lock. Again, races are resolved by virtue of read-modify-write's atomicity. If the read-modify-write read value is one, the waiting processor resumes looping. Note that it is important in this scheme that upon a miss, a cache enter the target address in its address translation directory, in anticipation of a possible invalidation of the target *before* the miss is serviced.

The cost complexity and performance of busy wait under assumptions of the two policies appears to be equal because waiting processors need not reference shared memory within their busy wait loops. The write-in policy is slightly less efficient than the write-through policy because all waiting processors must service cache misses when the lock is released. For the PWAM model, this overhead is not significant because multiple processors rarely wait for the same lock. Recall, from Section 3.5, that busy waiting is used in the PWAM model by parent processes which are waiting for *all* their parallel goals to complete. The alternative policy, of switching out a waiting parent process for a runnable process, was not modeled because it would be less efficient for the simple benchmark measured.

5.2.3. Hybrid Cache Coherency

A new proposal for a coherent cache scheme targeted for RAP-Prolog is described in this section. The objective of this scheme is to combine the simplicity and low cost of a traditional write-through cache, with the efficiency of a write-through broadcast cache. The proposed cache is called a *hybrid* or *partial write-through* cache, because certain types of data are written-through and others are copied back. The basic idea is that shared memory is kept consistent with the caches by writing-through a certain subset of all write references, and that cache-to-cache consistency is kept by write-broadcasting a certain subset of all written-through references. The hybrid cache protocol and its motivations are developed in detail in the remainder of this section.

As summarized in Table 2-7 (Section 2.3), objects in the PWAM storage model can be categorized as local and global. Within a given process's storage segment, local objects can only be referenced locally, i.e., by that process. Global objects, however, can be referenced both locally and globally, i.e., by other processes (possibly running on other processors). Thus writes can be categorized as both local and global. Whether a write reference issued by some PWAM instruction is local or global, is known statically because the instructions manipulate the storage model in a regular and highly structured manner. The host therefore can easily determine which write references are local and which are global.

To keep shared memory consistent with the caches, the following policy is used. Local references are copyback managed by the hybrid cache. Global references, except for communication references (Goal Stack and Message Buffer references), are write-through managed. It has been determined here that the communication references have little locality, so that making them non-cacheable does not significantly affect memory traffic. The capability of the hybrid cache to copyback, write-through or bypass the cache for individual references is similar to that of the Clipper machine [25] (although the consistency protocol is *not* similar to that of Clipper). In the Clipper architecture each virtual memory page is marked as copyback (write-in), write-through, or non-cacheable. The hybrid cache model allows each individual reference, as marked by the host, to be similarly treated.

Write-broadcast is used to guarantee cache-to-cache consistency; however, unlike previously proposed write-broadcast schemes, no access status is kept for each cache line, thus reducing complexity and cost. Various access status protocols were developed over the past years with the primary goal of reducing consistency traffic. The hybrid cache reduces consistency traffic by write-broadcasting only a small subset of all write references. This reduction in traffic, without status, is possible because of some sympathetic attributes of Prolog and RAP-Prolog, as described below.

The traditional problem of multiple, concurrent writers for a shared line is greatly reduced by RAP-Prolog. Two processes can safely write to their own copy of a shared line, each updating the other. The writes are guaranteed by RAP-Prolog to update different words within the same line. Races can still occur, however, at the level of process management. To prevent this, locks are still needed to protect process management data structures.

Prolog can be viewed as a single assignment language because within a clause containing only determinate goals, logical variables can be bound only once. In clauses with nondeterminate goals, logical variables may be bound and then rebound due to backtracking. Writes are comprised of:

- structure creation writes (creating structure on the top of the heap)
- binding writes (binding a previously unbound variable)
- unbinding writes (during detrailing upon failure)
- bookkeeping writes (e.g., creating choice points)
- process management writes (e.g., signaling the completion of a process)

In PWAM, a processor need only broadcast a *subset* of those global writes that are written-through: (un)binding writes (i.e., both bindings and unbindings), and global Parcall frame writes. Communication writes (to Goal Stack and Message Buffer) need not be broadcast because they are chosen to be non-cacheable. Heap writes during structure creation (on the top of the heap) need not be broadcast because newly created structure cannot be shared. Note that this optimization is akin to filtering methods first proposed by Censier [15].

It should be stressed that in the proposed broadcast schemes of the previous section, invalidates or writes-throughs are performed only if the line's access status indicates to do so. This greatly reduces the amount of traffic, but implies that shared memory and local memories are not necessarily consistent at all times. Therefore, a read miss may have to be serviced from another local memory. An underlying tenet of the hybrid cache scheme is to avoid this complexity by keeping shared memory consistent with local memory. The cost of this is the traffic required to write-through a subset of the processor write requests. As discussed above, to maintain consistency between local memories requires broadcasting a subset of the write-throughs.

writes	CHAT	PLM	QC1	ILI
trails	51082	14156	22685	4599
bindings	77478	29616	45602	12963
unbindings	49279	8213	9466	3512
heap+perms	192245	147676	160226	83694
writes	700422	717946	647358	300950
1-trails/bindings	0.34	0.52	0.50	0.64
1-(heap+perms)/writes	0.73	0.79	0.75	0.72
1-(un)bindings/(heap+perms)	0.34	0.74	0.66	0.80

Table 5-1: WAM Binding Statistics

The optimization of broadcasting only a subset of write-throughs is beneficial only if broadcasts have a significant cost. Otherwise, requests selected for write-through to shared memory are simultaneously broadcast. Since the caches spy on the shared memory bus, a broadcast itself does not cost more than a write request. However, each cache must check a broadcast address. If the cache address translation directory does not have a dedicated port for this check, unnecessary broadcasts incur overheads.

Table 5-1 shows the WAM binding statistics. The binding operation is combined with a trail test, necessary to implement backtracking. The number of trail writes is therefore less than (or equal to) the number of binding writes. During failure, an unbinding occurs for each trailed binding, with the following exceptions. As described in Section 3.4, an "inverse trail test" is used to reduce the number of unbindings. In addition, if choice points remain after the program completes, trailed bindings may remain (that were never unbound). Also shown are the number of writes to the heap and to permanent variables (heap+perms), i.e., the number of write-throughs. Lastly, the total number of writes is given.

Three efficiency statistics are presented in Table 5-1, calculated from the ratio of trailed bindings (trails) to bindings, write-throughs (heap+perms) to writes, and (un)bindings to write-throughs. The first statistic indicates the efficiency of the trail test. Notice that CHAT is least efficient, requiring the most trails, a result of its nondeterminacy.

The second statistic approximates the write-through efficiency in the hybrid cache, although PWAM will be less efficient because of additional global references. About 25% of all writes (and 12% of all data references) require write-through. For traditional sequential architectures, similar optimizations can be used to reduce write traffic for maintaining consistency. Mulder [55] reports that approximately 25% of data references in typical Pascal programs are to potentially shared objects and that 25% of data references are writes. Therefore about 6% of all data references require write-through.

The third statistic approximates the broadcast efficiency. From 20% to 66% of the write-throughs require broadcast. Again, CHAT is least efficient. Note that in the simulation results presented in Section 5.3, the model assumes that shared memory update and write-broadcast proceed concurrently. Thus the previous optimization of broadcasting only a subset of write-throughs is not needed in the simulator because no additional overheads are incurred for broadcasts (e.g., contention for cache directory access, as previously mentioned).

5.3. Coherent Cache Measurements

The various solutions to the consistency problem for RAP-Prolog executing on a shared memory multiprocessor with local memories are discussed in the previous section. These coherent local memory designs include:

- traditional write-through cache
- write-in broadcast cache (invalidates remote copies on write)
- write-through broadcast cache (updates remote copies on write)
- hybrid cache

Efficiency measurements of the above designs are now presented and analyzed. The models were simulated executing the Sderiv benchmark presented in Section 3.5. Recall that Sderiv is a synthetic version of Warren's symbolic differentiation benchmark. It is hypothesized that the Sderiv behavior under these models resembles that of larger benchmarks. If this is true, conclusions drawn in this section can be extrapolated to RAP-Prolog programs in general. The Sderiv benchmark accurately models parallel programs that do not require the expensive evaluation of CGE conditions at runtime. The benchmark represents programs wherein parallel goals do not manipulate a large number of terms passed by the parent. Conversely, the Sderiv benchmark does not accurately model programs with frequent evaluation of complex CGEs and extensive unification of passed structures. The Sderiv experiments allow, at the very least, comparisons between alternative coherent memory designs.

Consider the evidence that shows that Sderiv behavior resembles that of larger benchmarks. In Section 3.5 it is shown that sequential Sderiv displays the referencing characteristics of the large WAM benchmarks. The local memory characteristics of sequential Sderiv and the large WAM benchmarks are compared in Figures 5-2 and 5-3. These figures show the performance of a four word line data cache (throughout this chapter, only four word line, write-allocate data caches are considered — in general, two word lines offer slightly lower traffic). For these copyback data caches, Table 5-2 gives the number of standard deviations the hit and traffic ratios of Sderiv are from the mean statistics of the large WAM benchmarks. The Sderiv benchmark fits rather well, conservatively biased to lower hit ratios and higher traffic ratios. Again, one cannot confidently extrapolate the parallel behavior of the large benchmarks from Sderiv alone. A close fit ensures that the programs exercise the sequential storage model (the foundation of the PWAM storage model) in a reasonable, typical way.

All of the coherent cache models are simulated with the same parameterized multiprocessor cache simulator. As in the copyback cache simulator, each private cache is categorized by a number of blocks of a given size (in words).

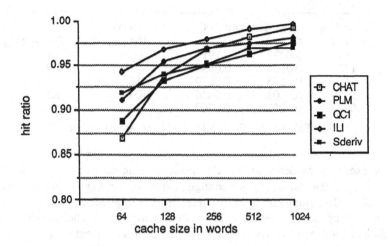

Figure 5-2: Sderiv Fit: D-Cache (4 word line) Hit Ratio

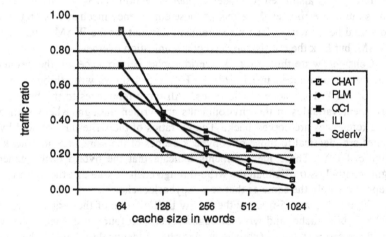

Figure 5-3: Sderiv Fit: D-Cache (4 word line) Traffic Ratio

cache size (words)	large benchmarks σ_{hr}	σ_{tr}	Sderiv $(hr\text{-}E_{hr})/\sigma_{hr}$	$(tr\text{-}E_{tr})/\sigma_{tr}$
64	0.0272	0.191	-0.04	0.4
128	0.0134	0.0886	-0.6	1.0
256	0.0103	0.0549	-1.2	1.7
512	0.0103	0.0626	-0.6	1.1
1024	0.0082	0.0569	-1.6	2.0

Table 5-2: Fit of Sderiv to Large Benchmarks

Each cache is modeled as a fully associative memory with perfect LRU replacement. The simulator is reconfigurable to support the various consistency protocols. The simulator processes trace records sequentially, using the cache corresponding to the record's processor identifier. Cache consistency is maintained for each reference. The simulator models a system with no cache-to-cache transfer capability. Therefore in the broadcast models, if the most up-to-date version of a miss target is held by a remote cache, the line is first copied back to memory, and then transferred to the requesting cache.

A modified copyback cache simulator (derived from the DELCACHE program [2]) is also used to model *sequential* hybrid and write-through caches. This simulator estimates the effect of these consistency mechanisms on the large sequential benchmarks. The measurements account for the WAM component of PWAM, but lack the consistency and communication overheads.

Consider write-through and hybrid cache performance of the sequential benchmarks introduced in Chapter 3. Figure 5-4 shows write-through, hybrid, and copyback data cache traffic ratios. All write references to the heap and to permanent variables in the environments are written-through, whereas all other write references are copied back. The hit ratios of the write-through and hybrid caches are identical to those of copyback caches of the same size and block size (Figure 4-10). These measurements indicate that the hybrid cache generates significantly less traffic than the write-through cache. Note that the hybrid traffic is approximately the same as that of a copyback cache.

Figures 5-5 and 5-6 show the Sderiv traffic ratios of the write-in broadcast cache, hybrid cache, and write-through cache, with four word lines. The write-broadcast cache statistics (not shown) are almost identical to those of the write-in broadcast cache. This indicates that communication traffic is very low (as is apparent from Table 3-17).

Figure 5-5 shows families of curves corresponding to numbers of PEs, plotted as a function of *total* local memory size (i.e., the sum of the individual PE cache sizes). Figure 5-6 redisplays this data, showing families of curves

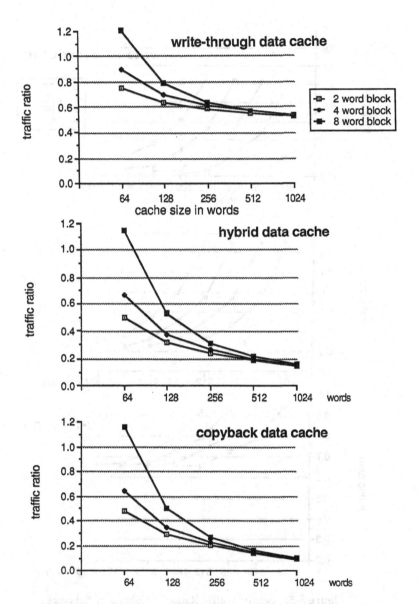

Figure 5-4: Data Cache Traffic Ratios: Sequential Benchmarks

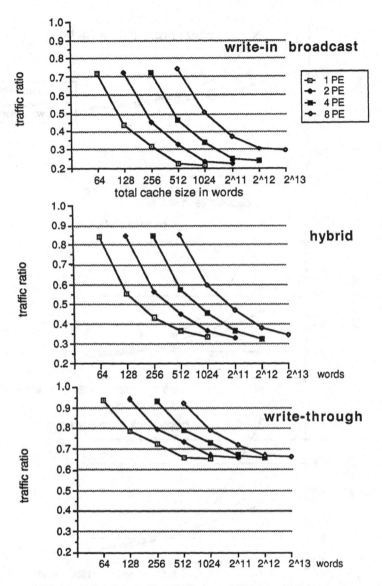

Figure 5-5: Sderiv Traffic Ratios of Coherency Schemes
for Varying #s of PEs

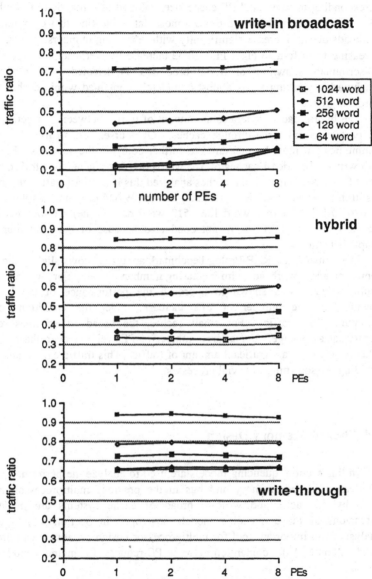

Figure 5-6: Sderiv Traffic Ratios of Coherency Schemes
for Various Cache Sizes

corresponding to individual PE cache sizes, plotted as a function of numbers of PEs. The curves in Figure 5-6 are almost flat, indicating that communication overheads do not increase significantly with increasing numbers of PEs. When increasing from four to eight PEs, some increase in overhead, corresponding to indiscriminate spawning of trivial processes, is detected. In addition, the benchmark's working set is almost completely contained within caches of 512 words or greater.

The hybrid cache generates an amount of traffic between that generated by the broadcast and write-through caches. Of course, benchmarks doing more communication must be measured to further compare the schemes. Eight PEs with write-in broadcast caches of 512 words or greater generate a traffic ratio of about 0.30. Although for the caches analyzed this is the least traffic generated, it is still high (recall, from Section 4.2.4, that the WAM programs display a traffic ratio of 0.16 for a four word line, 512 word data cache). Experiments with greater numbers of PEs were not conducted because of the limitation of the simple benchmark.

In summary, the RAP-Prolog benchmark analyzed shows slightly increasing communication overheads with increasing numbers of PEs. For large caches, the hybrid scheme was shown to approach the performance of the broadcast schemes, as the number of PEs increase, under the conditions of low communication traffic. For small caches, the broadcast schemes retain a significant advantage. For a large number of PEs (eight), even the best cache scheme generates a significant amount of traffic. This traffic can be reduced by avoiding the spawning of trivial processes.

5.4. Shared Memory Design

In this section, queueing models are used to analyze the performance of the interleaved shared memory and bus in the previous multiprocessor systems. Both hybrid cache and write-in broadcast cache systems are modeled as extensions of those queueing models developed in Section 4.5. Queueing analysis is an important tool for multiprocessor design because it can provide a valid estimate of the contention between PE requests for memory modules and the bus.

5.4.1. Shared Memory and Bus Queueing Models

The shared memory model considered here consists of simple memory modules of the type described in Section 4.5. Recall that each module can deliver a physical word in T_a cycles and that the module can be reaccessed after at least T_c cycles. This type of memory module does not offer as high performance as, for instance, a memory *bank*, which is itself interleaved. Higher performance models may include a two-level local memory for each processing element. These local memories may be transparent to the architecture, i.e., are paged out to a very large shared memory. Another option is to page the second level local memories directly to disk, dedicating one local memory to hold shared data.

For most applications, a shared memory multiprocessor without local memories is of little interest because memory traffic is excessive. In a uniprocessor model (Section 4.5.3), a single processor makes requests (i.e., customers) of an interleaved memory (i.e., server). This memory can be modeled as a single server even though it is interleaved, because of two approximations. First, the arrival rate of individual (word) requests is scaled by the inverse of the interleaving factor. Second, the service time to transfer a block (on a miss or copyback) is calculated assuming a burst mode transfer. The effect of waiting for a local memory miss, when no further customers can arrive, is approximated by decreasing the service time by T_{dead}.

A key point in the uniprocessor main memory model is that the processor must wait for a read miss to be serviced, i.e., the processor stalls. In a multiprocessor, however, although a given PE stalls for a read miss, other PEs may not be stalled. One method of modeling this is with a multiple server. A simpler method is to use a single server model, as in the uniprocessor case, with a scaled T_{dead} heuristic. Again, misses are approximated as occurring uniformly across the memory modules. For a block size of L buswidths and interleaving factor m, the maximum number of concurrently serviced miss requests is m/L. A single server can be used by scaling the miss request (block) arrival rate by the inverse of m/L. Abstractly, the model views the system from a single set of L modules that together service line requests.

In the previous sections, various local memories compatible with PWAM are introduced. Certain types of local memories are discussed which have no consistency problems. These include a choice point buffer, instruction buffer, and instruction cache. In addition, local memories which *guaranteed* consistency via special protocols are analyzed: a traditional write-through cache, write-in and write-through broadcast caches, and hybrid caches. In the next sections two main memory models are presented: a system with local hybrid caches and a system with local write-in broadcast caches. Both types of caches use write-allocation policies.

Hybrid Cache System

The details of the hybrid cache simulations, presented in Section 5.3, are first reviewed. Communication references (Goal Stack and Message Buffer references) are assumed to be non-cacheable and are thus accounted for in a higher miss ratio. Other global write references are written-through. (Un)binding writes and global Parcall frame writes are broadcast. Writes to shared lines cause remote copies to be updated.

A review is now given of an open M/G/1 model for a pure write-through I/D cache [28], from which the hybrid model is derived. On a miss, a write-through cache fetches a line (assuming write-allocate), but does not copyback the replaced line, because it cannot be dirty. The arrival rates of misses and write-throughs are modeled as independent Poisson processes, with independent service times. The effect of interleaved memory is incorporated into the write-through arrival rate, λ_1, the miss arrival rate, λ_2, and the miss service time, T_2. For calculation of λ_1 and λ_2, it is assumed that the write-throughs and misses, respectively, are uniformly distributed across the memory modules. For calculation of T_2, it is assumed that the line size, L, is less than or equal to the number of memory modules, m. The model here assumes multiple processing elements (PEs), hence the factor of n, the number of PEs, in the arrival rates.

$$\lambda_1 = n * \lambda_{wt}/m$$

$$\lambda_2 = n * \lambda_{miss} * L/m$$

$$T_1 = T_c$$

$$T_2 = T_{line} = \max(T_a + (L-1)T_{bus}, T_c)$$

where

$$\lambda_{miss} = MR * \lambda_p$$

$$\lambda_{wt} = WT * \lambda_p.$$

Recall that λ_p is the PE request rate and MR is the PE miss ratio. WT is the write-through ratio. Processor stalling is not modeled above; however, stalling is incorporated into the hybrid model below with T_{dead}. Several other points should first be noted. This model views the system from a group of L modules, assuming the interconnection network does not degrade the system bandwidth (a bus is modeled independently, later in this section). The arrival rate of line misses are scaled, assuming multiple misses can be serviced concurrently and that misses are uniformly distributed across the modules. As a result, the detrimental effect (that of increasing memory traffic) caused by increasing n can be removed by increasing m.

In comparison to a pure write-through cache, a hybrid cache contains both copyback lines and write-through lines. Copyback lines may be dirty, in which case they must be copied back during replacement. Write-through lines are never dirty because writes to them are written through. The hybrid cache queueing model presented here assumes that all types of references are cached, in order to simplify the equations. The measurements presented in this section, however, were generated assuming that communication references are *not* cached. Instructions are captured in a separate I-cache, assumed to have the same line size as the data cache. The previous M/G/1 write-through cache model is extended for the hybrid by splitting λ_2 into two streams: λ_{2a} and λ_{2b}. The λ_{2a} stream approximates miss requests that stall the issuing processor until the requests have been serviced. The λ_{2b} stream approximates miss requests that do *not* stall the issuing processor.

$$\lambda_{2a} = n*\lambda_{stall}*L/m$$

$$\lambda_{2b} = n*\lambda_{nostall}*L/m$$

$$T_{2a} = \max(T_a+(L-1)T_{bus},T_c) - \alpha T_{dead}$$

$$T_{2b} = \max(T_a+(L-1)T_{bus},T_c)$$

where

$$\lambda_{stall} = MR_r*\lambda_r$$

$$\lambda_{nostall} = MR_w*\lambda_w + MR*\lambda_p*DR.$$

In the above equations, MR is the miss ratio of a PE, split into MR_r, the read miss ratio and MR_w, the write miss ratio. The input request stream, λ_p, is split into λ_r, the read miss requests, and λ_w, the write miss requests. Note that DR, the dirty line ratio, is lower than in the copyback cache. Also, WT, the write-through ratio, is lower than in the pure write-through cache. Both DR and WT are measured with the hybrid cache simulator. Miss ratio, uneffected by write strategy, is identical for both the hybrid and copyback caches.

The T_{dead} heuristic, used to model processor stalling as in Section 4.5.3, includes a scale factor, α, in the multiprocessor model. α reflects the fact that not all PEs are stalled during a given read miss request. $\alpha = 1$ represents all PEs stalling and $\alpha = 1/n$ represents only the given PE stalling. In general α falls between these two values:

$$\alpha = (1 + E(\# \text{ additional PEs stalled at any time}))/n.$$

The expected number of additional PEs stalled at any time is calculated with a binomial distribution in Pr(stall), the probability that a PE is stalled. Therefore

$$\alpha = (1 + (n-1)\text{Pr(stall)})/n.$$

Pr(stall), estimated assuming no miss penalty, ranges from about 0.05 to 0.10 for the cache sizes considered in the next sections. α ranges from about 0.5 to 0.2 for two to eight PEs. In other words, α reduces the effect of T_{dead} for large numbers of PEs. In fact, for large numbers of PEs, the results presented here are approximately the same as those calculated assuming no stalls, i.e., $\alpha = 0$.

An asymptotic M/G/1 model is derived for three arrival streams in a manner similar to that of Section 4.5.3 (Equations (4.5) - (4.12)). Recall that the shared memory bandwidth efficiency, ξ_{mem}, is defined as

$$\xi_{mem} = \rho_a/\rho,$$

where ρ is the open queue occupancy and ρ_a is the asymptotic occupancy. Recall that processor performance degradation is defined (Equation (4.13)) as

$$D = (P_{actual} - P_{no\text{-}miss})/P_{actual}, \qquad 0 \leq D \leq 1$$

where $P_{no\text{-}miss}$ is the PE performance (in cycles/instr) assuming no local memory misses and P_{actual} is the PE performance accounting for local memory read misses which stall the processor.

A single bus is chosen for the multiprocessor model considered in this book because it is required by the coherent cache protocols studied for implementing locking. The bus model is simple and can be extended by adjusting the bus cycle time, T_{bus}. For instance, a faster bus can be modeled by decreasing T_{bus}. Of course, a single bus interconnect cannot be used in a parallel system of arbitrary size; however, it is a reasonable organization for a tightly-coupled PWAM shared memory multiprocessor with a limited number of high-speed PEs, as is modeled here.

In contrast to shared memory queueing model, the bus arrival rate cannot be scaled by the number of modules, so that the detrimental effect (that of increasing memory traffic) caused by increasing numbers of PEs cannot be alleviated. In other words, a single bus is burdened by the total system traffic. If the bus is not extremely fast ($T_{bus}/T_c \ll 1$), it becomes saturated by a few PEs. In the measurements presented in the next section, $T_{bus}/T_c = 0.2$ is initially chosen. Later measurements of bus efficiency are presented relaxing this assumption. The standard asymptotic model is derived as in Section 4.5.2, with

$$\lambda_{bus} = m(\lambda_1 + \lambda_{2a} + \lambda_{2b}).$$

Note that since the simulator assumes that broadcasts and write-throughs occur simultaneously, coherency traffic is hidden in λ_{wt} (a component of λ_1).

Broadcast Cache System

A shared memory queueing model for a write-in broadcast cache system is described here in terms of modifications to the hybrid cache model of the previous section. The two queueing models are similar with the following exceptions. Recall from Section 5.2.1 that write-in broadcast caches do not generate write-through traffic, but retain consistency rather by issuing line invalidations. Invalidation traffic, λ_{inv}, is not included in the shared memory queueing model because it is directed from one PE to another, not to shared memory. Unlike the hybrid cache, the write-in broadcast cache generates an additional stream of forceback traffic due to the invalidation of dirty lines. Note that a forceback does not stall the associated processor. The M/G/1 shared memory queueing model for the write-in broadcast system is the hybrid model with the λ_1 stream (for write-throughs) removed. In addition, the definition of $\lambda_{nostall}$ is appended with forceback traffic,

$$\lambda_{nostall} = MR_w * \lambda_w + MR * \lambda_p * (DR+FB).$$

Definitions of all parameters in this model are the broadcast cache equivalents of the corresponding parameters in the hybrid model. FB, the forceback ratio, is the ratio of forcebacks to shared memory requests. Note that forcebacks are essentially premature copybacks. The dirty line ratio, DR, of a write-in broadcast cache is significantly greater than that of the hybrid cache because the broadcast caches do not write-through and therefore collect a large percentage of dirty lines. The miss ratios of the broadcast and hybrid caches are identical.

The bus queueing model for the write-in broadcast cache system is the standard asymptotic model of Section 4.5.2 with

$$\lambda_{bus} = m(\lambda_1 + \lambda_{2a} + \lambda_{2b}),$$

where λ_{2a} and λ_{2b} are as previously defined and

$$\lambda_1 = n * \lambda_{inv}/m.$$

5.4.2. Measurements

Performance measurements of the shared memory and bus queueing models are now presented. Assumed throughout is a local instruction cache of one fourth the size of the data cache, with equal line size. Also assumed are L = 4 words, T_a = 3 cycles, and T_c = 5 cycles. Initially, a two word bus is assumed with T_{bus} = 1 cycle.

Figures 5-7 and 5-8 show the statistics for 16-way and 32-way interleaved shared memories, respectively. The bus bandwidth efficiency, shared memory

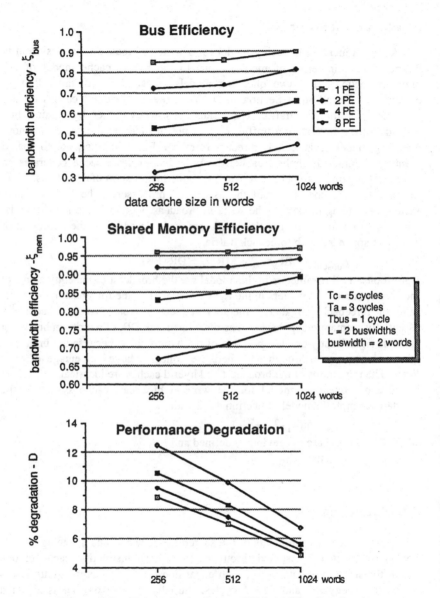

Figure 5-7: Hybrid Cache System With 16-Way Interleaving

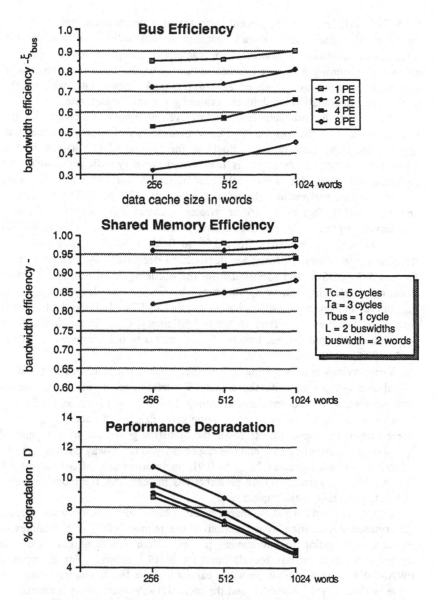

Figure 5-8: Hybrid Cache System With 32-Way Interleaving

bandwidth efficiency, and percent performance degradation are given as functions of cache size. Recall that the shared memory efficiency and performance degradation statistics are calculated independently of the bus efficiency, assuming a perfect interconnection network. Also recall that these efficiency statistics are calculated assuming a peak request rate, whereas the performance degradation is calculated assuming a typical request rate.

The primary hybrid cache result is that even with very few processors, the bus saturates. As the number of PEs increases, bus efficiency decreases at approximately the same rate, i.e., doubling the number of PEs halves the bus efficiency. A secondary result is that shared memory efficiency, assuming sufficient bus bandwidth, is reasonable, falling to 67% for 8 PEs with 256 word caches. Percent performance degradation is less than 7% for 1024 word caches and interleaving factors of 16 or greater. Increasing 16-way to 32-way interleaving significantly improves memory efficiency. For 8 PEs with 1024 word caches, ξ_{mem} increases from 0.77 to 0.88, a 14% improvement. As interleaving increases, performance degradation decreases. As can be seen in Figures 5-7 and 5-8, and surmised from the queueing equations, the effect of doubling interleaving can be approximated by simply relabeling the ξ_{mem} and ξ_{bus} curves in Figure 5-7 with twice the number of PEs. Halving the bus cycle time, T_{bus}, has the same effect on the bus efficiency, ξ_{bus}. For example, for 8 PEs with 1024 word caches, halving T_{bus} from 1.0 to 0.5, increases ξ_{bus} from 0.45 to 0.65, a 44% improvement.

The previous results assume a sustained peak burst reference rate. If an arrival rate compatible with the actual PE performance is used, the metrics improve somewhat. For instance, assuming λ_p = 0.46 words/cycle, 8 PEs with 1024 word caches and 16-way interleaving gives ξ_{bus} = 0.52 and ξ_{mem} = 0.82. These constitute improvements (over the statistics generated with a peak of λ_p = 0.6 words/cycle) of 15% and 6% respectively. For 32-way interleaving, the reduced input rate increases ξ_{mem} to 0.91, an improvement of only about 3% over a peak rate system. These perturbations indicate that the model is stable around the sustained peak request rate.

Figures 5-9 and 5-10 show shared memory bandwidth efficiency and percent performance degradation as a function of the number of PEs for families of curves corresponding to interleaving factors. Note that these curves do not represent realistic models for all numbers of PEs shown. For example, a PWAM/WAM uniprocessor probably cannot sustain 16 simultaneous memory requests (line = two buswidths) and therefore 32-way interleaving is unrealistic. For 8 PEs, 32-way interleaving corresponds to about two outstanding memory requests per PE, a reasonable assumption. These limitations do *not* suggest that a tightly-coupled multiprocessor need not implement a highly interleaved memory.

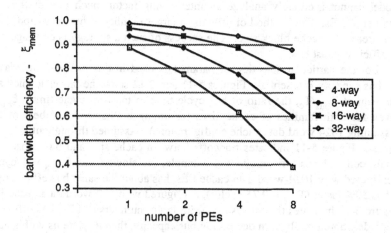

Figure 5-9: Memory Efficiency: 1024 Word Hybrid Cache System

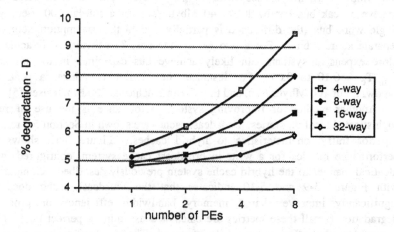

Figure 5-10: Percent Performance Degradation:
1024 Word Hybrid Cache System

The limitations are only in the *interpretation* of the queueing model results — the model cannot accurately analyze an interleaving factor much greater than the number of PEs. One method of utilizing a larger number of memory modules is to increase the cache block size. The success of such a strategy is contingent on a sufficiently fast bus.

For the particular selection of parameters used in this example, increasing the bus capacity is essential. Figures 5-11 and 5-12 show the bus efficiency as a function of T_{bus}/T_c, the ratio of bus cycle time to memory cycle time. ξ_{bus} is given for both families of cache sizes (assuming 8 PEs) and numbers of PEs (assuming 1024 word data cache configurations). Assumed throughout is $T_c = 5$ cycles. Figure 5-11 indicates tradeoffs between cache size and bus capacity to retain constant bus efficiency. For example, the slowest bus ($T_{bus} = 1$ cycle), configured with 1024-word data cache PEs, has about the same bus efficiency as a bus 50% faster ($T_{bus} = 0.75$ cycles), configured with 512-word data cache PEs. Figure 5-12 indicates that in systems with larger numbers of PEs, bus efficiency degrades more rapidly with decreasing bus capacity, than in systems with smaller numbers of PEs.

The slowest bus presented is representative of current, conservative technology assumptions. The current generation Sequent achieves a peak bus bandwidth of 32 Mbytes/sec, with $T_{bus}/T_c \approx 0.1$. The buses modeled here achieve a peak bus bandwidth of 40 Mbytes/sec for a similar 100 nsec cycle single word bus (the difference is partially due to the assumption here of a separate address bus). For a two word wide bus, 80 Mbytes/sec is achieved. More expensive systems can likely achieve bus capacities in the range of $T_{bus}/T_c = 0.10$ to 0.05. For instance, the Pyramid achieves a peak bus bandwidth of 100 Mbytes/sec, and the Cydra-5 achieves 200 Mbytes/sec [5].

Another method of improving system performance is the use of more sophisticated local memories. Broadcast caches are shown in Section 5.3 to have superior traffic characteristics to hybrid caches. Figure 5-13 shows the performance metrics for a write-in broadcast cache system, configured in an identical manner to the hybrid cache system previously described. Comparison with Figures 5-9 and 5-10 indicates that the broadcast cache does not significantly improve shared memory bandwidth efficiency or processor degradation (recall these metrics are calculated assuming a perfect bus). Note however that bus efficiency is vastly improved. The broadcast cache reduces the bus traffic by removing the write-through traffic of the hybrid cache. Interestingly, the write-through traffic loads the bus to a significantly greater degree than it loads the shared memory.

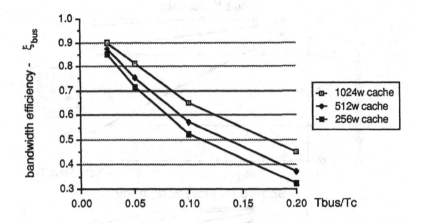

Figure 5-11:   Bus Efficiency: Hybrid Cache System
(8 PEs/2 word bus)

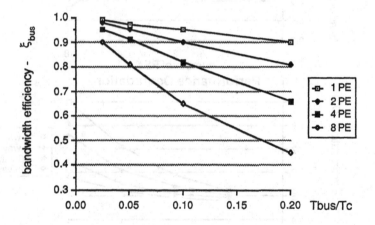

Figure 5-12:   Bus Efficiency: 1024 Word Hybrid Cache System
(2 word bus)

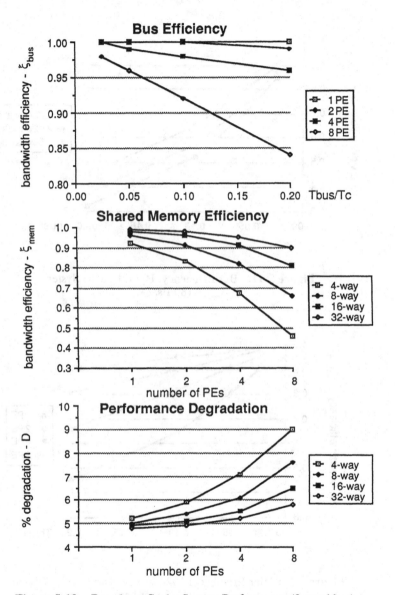

Figure 5-13:   Broadcast Cache System Performance (2 word bus)

5.5. Summary

In this chapter, two-level memory hierarchies are defined and analyzed for a parallel Prolog architecture. Specifically, the memory performance of the Restricted-AND Parallel Prolog (PWAM) architecture, executing on a tightly-coupled, shared memory multiprocessor, is analyzed. Shared memory multiprocessor consistency problems for PWAM are solved in a variety of ways — measurements of the memory performance of broadcast, hybrid, and write-through coherent cache schemes are presented. The hybrid cache, a new combination of write-through and write-broadcast cache designs, takes advantage of RAP-Prolog attributes to guarantee consistency with moderately low overheads and inexpensive hardware. The PWAM memory performance measurements presented here and in Chapter 3 support the PWAM design tenets — the PWAM displays low communication overheads and efficient sequential execution.

Queueing models for the multiprocessor's shared memory and shared bus are developed from the M/G/1 models of the previous chapter. Measurements are presented for two split I+D cache configurations: one with a hybrid data cache and one with a broadcast data cache. The primary result of the queueing analysis is that for a multiprocessor with a small number (eight) of high-performance PEs, buses of insufficient capacity become a performance bottleneck. Consider systems with a two word bus connecting a shared memory and eight high-performance PEs, each with a 1024 word data cache and 256 word instruction cache. Assuming $T_{bus}/T_c = 0.2$ (current, conservative technology) a hybrid data cache system achieves 0.45 bus bandwidth efficiency, whereas a write-in broadcast data cache system achieves 0.84 bus efficiency. Assuming higher capacity buses, for instance $T_{bus}/T_c = 0.05$ (now emerging technology), the hybrid system achieves 0.80 bus efficiency whereas the broadcast system achieves 0.96 bus efficiency.

Measurements indicate that both hybrid cache and broadcast cache systems display approximately the same shared memory bandwidth efficiency and processor performance degradation, given buses of sufficient capacity. For the system configurations considered immediately above with 32-way interleaving, both the hybrid cache and broadcast cache systems exhibit about 6% performance degradation (6.5% for 16-way interleaving). These results show that an interleaved shared memory can successfully reduce the miss penalty seen by an individual PE. Given an advanced bus with bandwidth efficient close to one, these performance degradations translate into speed-ups of about 750% for an eight PE system.

6 Conclusions and Future Research

6.1. Conclusions

This book synthesizes logic programming architecture design with the lessons learned from procedural programming architecture design and memory organization. The field of logic programming machine design is new. At the time of the completion of this book, as few as two Prolog machines had the ability to execute the benchmarks measured here. It is therefore not surprising that little has been published in the area of logic programming machine performance. This book helps fill this large gap, but much additional research is needed because the supply of questions is seemingly endless. The vast store of knowledge and folklore available about procedural language architectures and machines is absent for logic programming languages. Therefore, results that are similar for the two paradigms are just as interesting as results unique to logic programming.

One of the contributions of this book is the extension of the principles of canonical machine architectures [27], first developed for FORTRAN, to Prolog. The Prolog canonical interpretive forms (CIFs) efficiently model extensive use of dynamic structure creation and pointers, frequent procedure calls, and nondeterminate execution behavior. Initially a so-called traditional CIF is developed, based on a very close correspondence with Prolog. The traditional Prolog CIF assumes a host with an unlimited size stack buffer, in the tradition of procedural CIFs. Such an assumption is ill-directed for Prolog, however, where only about 75% of data references are to the stack.

A second CIF is then developed, based on a less expensive host, assuming only a register set. A two-level name space model is used, consisting of a register set and environment. The architecture places as many variables in the registers as possible, using environments only when necessary. It is shown that the traditional CIF performs far better than the register-based CIF, reducing instruction bandwidth by 15% and data bandwidth by 75% on average. The register-based CIF, however, has the potential to attain higher performance than the traditional CIF on both minimal hosts and cache-based hosts with register sets. The Warren Abstract Machine (WAM) model [96] is shown to be an actualization of a register-based CIF. Consequently, the CIF design paradigm can be viewed as an informal method of *deriving* the WAM instruction set. The WAM model is used throughout the book as a *typical* Prolog architecture, to study the memory performance of Prolog benchmarks. The selection of the WAM is beneficial because it facilities the study of a closely related Restricted AND-Parallel Prolog architecture.

The Prolog CIFs are introduced as collections of architecture attributes. Some of the attributes are more completely defined than others. In contrast to procedural CIFs, the Prolog CIF attributes could only be measured empirically. Results indicate that the most promising attributes are tight instruction encoding and ideal indexing. Realizable attributes can be constructed from these, for use in high-performance instruction sets. For instance, byte encoding of instructions and indexing on first argument are realizations of CIF attributes. It is important to develop more efficient implementations of these and other CIF attributes.

The CIFs presented are based on a single clause scope for the definition of identifiers, a result from the direct correspondence with Prolog. This definition allows simple translation from source to CIF, but does not offer optimal memory performance. An alternative approach is to relax the correspondence, increasing the size of the scope at the architecture level, e.g., to a procedure or set of procedures, at the cost of increased compilation complexity. For the traditional CIF, increasing the scope size would allow tighter encoding of identifiers, reducing the memory bandwidth requirement. For the register-based CIF, a larger scope would allow more efficient register allocation and would facilitate the translation of recursion into iteration. These are important topics for further research in logic programming language implementations.

A conventional empirical methodology is used in this book to measure the memory characteristics of the sequential and parallel logic programming architectures. This methodology consists of a compiler, an emulator, trace-driven memory simulators, and a queueing model analyzer. The contributions of this portion of the study lay not in the methodology, but rather in the results collected. At the highest level, shallow backtracking is the primary data-memory performance bottleneck of the WAM — 46% of dynamic data memory traffic is devoted to procedure control and failure, as compared to 39% for both general and specialized unification. This result was unexpected, because the WAM model is optimized for determinate programs, which do little deep backtracking.

Shallow backtracking, however, is the result of an "if-then-else" action within a procedure. Because the compiler is not sophisticated enough to frequently avoid this behavior, the full penalty (in memory traffic) for backtracking is paid. This result indicates that a simple (single) choice point buffer could effectively reduce the data bandwidth requirement. Simulation measurements presented verify this — for data references, a 12 word buffer offers a miss ratio of 0.55 and a traffic ratio of 0.62.

These results are promising, but performance is still low. Other local memories adept at reducing the memory bandwidth requirement are therefore studied. Envisioning a single chip microprocessor, the local memories considered are small (from 64 to 1024 words). A stack buffer of only 64 words offers a miss ratio of 0.28 and a traffic ratio of 0.30. The stack buffer, more complex than the choice point buffer, captures both choice point and environment references. A copyback cache, capturing all types of references, does better still — a 256 word cache (with four word lines) offers a miss ratio of 0.05 and a traffic ratio of 0.23. Smart caches, which avoid transferring lines no longer in a valid storage area, reduce the cache traffic ratio by up to 30%. The local data memories analyzed fall into three price-performance ranges. The choice point·buffer occupies the low-end, the stack buffer occupies the mid-range, and the cache occupies the high-end. Many current Prolog machines [21, 58, 57, 56] incorporate large caches to ensure high performance. For these machines, built with discrete logic, cache size was not as limiting a factor as in a VLSI implementation. Efficient cost/performance VLSI designs (e.g., for the processing element of a multiprocessor) integrate both the CPU and local memory on a single chip. The data provided here should aid these designs, where size is a critical factor.

A comparison of logic programming to procedural programming paradigms is of interest because most current logic programming languages are implemented on conventional hosts. In this book, various comparisons are drawn between Prolog, FORTRAN, and Pascal. A portion of these results are summarized in Table 6-1. The data cache traffic ratios are given for a four word line cache with write-allocation. The results indicate that Pascal, with a smaller working set than Prolog, exhibits higher locality, resulting in about half the data traffic for equal sized caches. This holds for both copyback and write-through data caches. Interestingly, both languages make about 25% of their data references to global data objects. Estimating multiprocessor broadcast traffic as writes to global (potentially shared) data, Pascal generates half the broadcast traffic of Prolog because it makes about half the number of writes.

A major conclusion of the book is that shallow backtracking contributes more to Prolog's data bandwidth requirement than any other factor. Advanced

	Prolog WAM	FORTRAN IBM/370	Pascal
v_d, data ref/instr (words)	2.32	0.524	
v_i, instr ref/instr (words)	0.679	0.837	
mean instr size (bytes)	2.6	3.35	
mean run length (instr)	6.5	16.9	
copyback data cache TR	0.10		0.05
write-thru data cache TR	0.53		0.24
% write/data traffic	47%	18%	25%
% broadcast/data traffic	12%		6%

Table 6-1: Prolog, FORTRAN, and Pascal

compilation techniques [87, 4, 90] are not discussed here, but promise to allay the problem. The effectiveness of future compiler optimizations in reducing the choice point traffic is unknown, however. Very effective compilers will alter the memory referencing characteristics presented here, placing more emphasis on heap referencing. With this trend in mind, data caches seem most appropriate for future high-performance implementations.

In the area of local instruction memory design and analysis, the results obtained are similar to those of traditional architectures. Byte encoding generates 63% of the instruction traffic of word encoding. Bit encodings save about 10% of the traffic generated by byte encoding. Look-ahead instruction buffer measurements indicate that an instruction miss ratio of 0.18 could be obtained by prefetching alone. The disadvantage of this model is the excessive traffic wasted for each taken branch. Instruction caches have the ability to reduce traffic and are therefore examined. The Prolog instruction stream exhibits less temporal locality than instruction streams of procedural languages, because loops, implemented recursively, are more spread out. This loss of locality is verified by instruction cache and combined I/D cache measurements. The I-caches perform only moderately well and combined I/D caches generate *more* traffic than split I+D caches. The split caches are advantageous because spread out loops act like sequential code in small combined caches, forcing data lines out with LRU replacement.

Prolog performance can be increased further still with parallel architectures and multiprocessor hosts. A contribution of this study in this area is the memory performance analysis of the Restricted-AND Parallel Prolog architecture (PWAM) [35] executing on a tightly-coupled shared memory multiprocessor model. Shared memory multiprocessor consistency problems for the PWAM architecture are solved in a variety of ways. Measurements of broadcast, hybrid, and write-through coherent cache schemes are presented. The hybrid cache, a new combination of write-through and write-broadcast cache designs, takes advantage of RAP-Prolog attributes to guarantee consistency with moderately low overheads and inexpensive hardware. The cache schemes analyzed fall into three price-performance ranges. Traditional write-through caches occupy the low-end, the hybrid caches occupy the mid-range, and the write-in broadcast caches occupy the high-end. The PWAM memory performance measurements presented in this book help verify the design tenets of the PWAM architecture: low communication overheads and efficient sequential execution.

The analysis of the local memories cannot be accomplished solely within the simple framework of miss and traffic ratios. This is because memory requests contend for the service of a single main memory. To lessen this damaging effect, interleaved main memories consisting of a set of single-port modules are analyzed. Analytical queueing models based on the M/G/1 model are used to estimate the performance of the memory hierarchies. Of course, the contention problem is worse for the shared memory multiprocessor model than for a uniprocessor. Measurements of these effects are presented for two families of organizations utilizing hybrid caches and write-in broadcast caches. The queueing models measure bus and shared memory bandwidth efficiency (i.e., the fraction of the bandwidth required by the system, supplied by the bus or shared memory), and processor performance degradation. A single shared bus is modeled because it is required by the coherent cache protocols studied.

The primary result of the queueing analysis is that for a multiprocessor with a small number (eight) of high-performance processing elements (PEs), buses of insufficient capacity become a performance bottleneck. Consider systems with a two word bus connecting a shared memory and eight PEs, each with a 1024 word data cache and 256 word instruction cache. Assuming $T_{bus}/T_c = 0.2$ (the ratio of the bus cycle time to the main memory module cycle time) a hybrid data cache system achieves 0.45 bus bandwidth efficiency, whereas a write-in broadcast data cache system achieves 0.84 bus efficiency. Assuming higher capacity buses, for instance $T_{bus}/T_c = 0.05$, the hybrid system achieves 0.80 bus efficiency whereas the broadcast system achieves 0.96 bus efficiency. In addition to tradeoffs between cache protocol performance and cost, cache size and bus capacity can also be traded-off.

If bus capacity is sufficient to achieve the bandwidth required by the PEs, measurements indicate that both hybrid cache and broadcast cache systems deliver about the same shared memory bandwidth efficiency and processor degradation. For the systems considered in the previous paragraph with a 32-way interleaved shared memory, both the hybrid cache and broadcast systems exhibit about 6% processor performance degradation. 16-way interleaving results in about 6.5% degradation. Thus, an interleaved shared memory can successfully reduce the miss penalty seen by an individual PE.

These results indicate that given sufficient parallelism in an application, a speed-up of about 750% can be achieved on a tightly-coupled PWAM multiprocessor with eight high-performance (e.g., 100 KLIPS on large applications) PEs. The design space investigated in this book may be considered limited — conventional shared memory designs with single bus interconnect, one-level interleaved memory, and few processing elements with small local memories. The view taken here, however, is that all types of uniprocessors will soon evolve into such systems because these limited multiprocessors offer the best cost/performance tradeoff. This book analyzes the memory design parameters for Prolog architectures. A low-cost PWAM multiprocessor achieving over one million application LIPS appears to be a realistic goal, well within current technology constraints.

6.2. Future Research

Recent comparisons of the PLM with SPUR [8] and the MC68020 [54] indicate that reduced and multi-purpose instruction-set architectures have certain advantages over the high-level WAM. These types of instruction sets allow more sophisticated compiler optimizations. A detailed study, similar to this book, of the memory characteristics of low-level Prolog instruction sets is necessary to evaluate these architectures. The effects of compiler optimizations should also be evaluated.

More precise cost and area measurements are needed for the local memories described here (e.g., Mulder's study of Pascal [55]). This would permit a more accurate accessment of the price-performance niches of the local memories. Larger benchmarks would allow larger local memories to be measured. In addition, a more thorough study of alternative designs for the zeroth memory level, i.e., the register set, should be conducted. For instance, the Pegasus chip [71] implements a single choice point buffer as a set of shadow registers — the cost (in area)/performance tradeoffs of this and similar designs (including general-purpose microprocessors, such as the AM29000 [99]) are of great interest. The traditional Prolog CIF architecture presented in Chapter 2, and its direct correspondence architectures, such as Prolog-10, may be better suited than the WAM for a host with a large stack buffer or multiple register set.

This book analyzes the memory performance of a Restricted AND-Parallel

Prolog architecture. The study of PWAM executing on a shared memory multiprocessor requires more detailed simulations of coherent caches. The shared memory and bus queueing models should be coupled for more accurate estimations of performance degradation and speed-up. Most importantly, more realistic benchmarks are required, including those with CGE conditions and nondeterminism. The efficient exploitation of other types of parallelism in logic programs is also of great importance. Extensive performance studies of other parallel Prolog architectures (e.g., Shen's study of ANLWAM [73]) are needed to evaluate their potential benefits.

Appendix A

Glossary of Notation

υ	memory references per instruction.
λ	customer arrival rate in a queueing model, measured in units of requests per machine cycle.
λ_d	sustained burst memory data request arrival rate from a processor.
λ_i	sustained burst memory instruction request arrival rate from a processor.
λ_p	sustained burst memory request arrival rate from a processor. For Prolog this arrival rate corresponds to the intense memory activity during a chain of successive failures.
μ	service rate in a queueing model, measured in units of customers (requests) per machine cycle.
ξ	bandwidth efficiency, i.e., the ratio of the achieved bandwidth to the offered (desired) bandwidth.
ρ	occupancy of the open queueing model, measured in units of Erlangs (an abstract unit). Occupancy is calculated as the (effective) arrival rate over the (effective) service rate. Represents the load on the server.
ρ_a	asymptotic occupancy, i.e., occupancy of the closed queueing model.
ANLWAM	Argonne National Laboratory OR-Parallel Prolog architecture.
B_a	achieved bandwidth in an asymptotic (closed) queueing model, measured in units of words per cycle. Also referred to as B(m,n) in the literature.
B_o	offered bandwidth in an open queueing model, measured in units of words per cycle.
B	current (top) choice point pointer in the WAM.

C^2	coefficient of variation for queueing models.
c	current choice point E-stack pointer in the split-stack architecture.
CIF	Canonical Interpretive Form.
CP	continuation pointer in the WAM — points to next instruction to be executed should the current goal succeed. This register acts like a hardware return pointer from the current procedure call.
CR	copyback ratio, defined for a copyback cache as the ratio of the number of words copied back from the cache to main memory, to the number of write requests issued by the processor.
D	processor performance degradation, defined as the fraction of ideal processor performance (assuming a local memory of unlimited size) lost due to local memory misses in an actual processor (with a finite local memory).
DCA	Direct Correspondence Architecture.
DR	dirty line ratio, defined for write-through and hybrid caches as the ratio of the number of copied back lines to the number of caches misses, i.e., the fraction of replaced lines that are dirty.
E	current environment pointer in the WAM.
H	top of heap pointer in the WAM.
HB	heap backtrack pointer in the WAM — points to where the top of heap was at the time the current choice point was created.
HPM	High-speed Prolog Machine (also called Chi).
L	cache line (block) size.
LIPS	logical inferences per second.
LRU	Least Recently Used.
MIPS	millions of instructions per second.
MR	miss ratio, defined as the fraction of references that cannot be serviced from local memory.
m	interleaving factor, i.e., number of memory modules in an interleaved memory.
n	number of processing elements in multiprocessor.
P	processor performance, measured in units of cycles per instruction.
P	current instruction pointer (program counter) in the WAM.
PLM	Programmed Logic Machine.

PSI	Personal Sequential Inference machine.
PWAM	Restricted AND-Parallel Prolog architecture (also known as WHAM!).
Q	average number of customers in system, in units of words.
Q'	average number of customers enqueued, in units of words.
RAP-Prolog	Restricted AND-Parallel Prolog.
RISC	Reduced Instruction Set Computer.
s	heap structure pointer in the WAM — points to elements of structures and lists on the heap.
SPUR	Symbolic Processing Using RISCs.
T_a	memory access time, in cycles.
T_{access}	average memory request delay, in cycles.
T_b	bus transfer time, in cycles.
T_c	memory cycle time, in cycles.
T_{dead}	heuristic used to model processor stalling due to local memory read miss.
T_e	effective memory cycle time, in cycles, calculated as T_c/m.
T'_w	average time a memory request waits for service, in cycles.
TR	top of trail pointer in the WAM.
TRO	Tail Recursion Optimization.
WAM	Warren Abstract Machine.
Xi	temporary register i in the WAM. Also referred to as Ai in the literature.
Yi	permanent variable i in the WAM, resident in the current environment.

Appendix B

Lcode Instruction Set Summary

Table B-1 lists each Lcode instruction with its sizes for both word and byte encoding schemes. Each instruction is listed alphabetically by opcode, with an instance of the assembly code. The word encoding size is given in units of words. The byte encoding size is given in units of bytes. Refer to Tick [84] for the complete Lcode semantics. Refer to Warren [96] for the WAM instruction semantics. Notes concerning Table B-1 follow.

1. Local branch instructions (i.e., branches within a procedure) are given two sizes for each encoding scheme. The first size corresponds to a short offset of one byte. The second size corresponds to a long offset of two bytes. For example, with a byte encoding, **branch** requires 3 bytes for short offsets and 4 bytes for long offsets.

2. Non-local branch targets (**call** and **execute** instructions) are encoded as a two byte offset from a segment register.

3. The index instructions **switch_constant** and **switch_structure** have sizes of 1 word or 2 bytes. This does not include the size of the hash table following the instruction. During emulation, only one hash entry reference (two reads — one for the key, one for the value) is counted in addition to the instruction fetch.

4. In general, the **trust_me_else** operand can be a local clause label. This facilitates code assertion and retraction. Since assertion/retraction of code is not implemented in the Lcode system, the **trust_me_else** instruction is always given a **fail** operand.

Table B-2 lists each Lcode instruction with associated dynamic statistics measured by averaging the statistics from the individual benchmark programs (CHAT, PLM, QC1, and ILI). Instructions not executed in any of the programs are not included in the table. The mean instruction frequency, data and instruction references per instruction (in *bytes*) and percent weight are shown. Instruction weight is calculated as the product of instruction frequency and references per instruction. All instructions have a fixed number of instruction references (except for the indexing instructions for which instruction references were not accurately measured). Notes concerning Table B-2 follow.

1. The **escape** statistics are averaged over those built-ins present in the benchmarks.

2. The *failure* statistics are averaged over *all* failures. No instruction bytes are referenced because failure is similar to a software trap.

3. The **get_constant**, **put_constant**, and **unify_constant** instructions are further categorized as **atom** or **integer**. All the statistics presented are additive, so that for instance, **get_constant** accounts for 2.046% of all instructions executed, with 1.67% of the total weight. Note that the benchmarks show a strong bias towards symbolic rather than arithmetic computation.

4. The Lcode compiler does not have the ability to generate **unify_value** instructions. Only the unoptimized form of **unify_local_value** instructions are generated. For read mode, these instructions are equivalent, and are listed as **unify_value**.

5. Copy instructions correspond to unify instructions executed in write mode.

6. In write mode, a **unify_local_value** instruction dereferences its operand and globalizes it onto the heap if necessary. The **copy_local_value** category corresponds to write mode execution of **unify_local_value** instructions that *do* require globalization.

7. The **copy_value** category corresponds not to **unify_value** instructions executed in write mode, but rather to **unify_local_value** instructions that do *not* require globalization (in this case, execution of the two forms are identical, except for the extra dereference). Note that globalization was required only about 1 in 9 times.

Table B-3 summarizes these statistics by *instruction type*, as defined in Table 2-5. The instruction types are listed in order of greatest percent weight. These statistics consider *failure*, *general unification*, and **escape** as separate instruction types. Therefore the cost of general unification is *not* counted in the head or structure matching groups. Note that the indexing weight is highly optimistic, calculated assuming perfect hashing.

opcode	assembly instance	words	bytes
add	add X1,X2,X3	1	3
add_constant	add_constant X1,X2,15	2	6
allocate	allocate 8	1	2
branch[1]	branch nil,X1,_1234	1	3/4
call[2]	call _1234	1	3
comp_x	comp <,X1,X2	1	3
comp_y	comp <,Y1,Y2	1	4
cond_x	cond var,X1	1	2
cond_y	cond var,Y1	1	3
cut	cut	1	1
cutd	cutd _1234	1	2/3
cut_strong	cut_strong	1	1
deallocate	deallocate	1	1
decrement	decrement X1,X2	1	2
divide	divide X1,X2,X3	1	3
divide_constant	divide_constant X1,X2,15	2	6
escape	escape 3	1	2
execute[2]	execute _1234	1	3
fail	fail	1	1
get_constant	get_constant X1,-44	2	6
get_list	get_list X1	1	2
get_nil	get_nil X1	1	2
get_structure	get_structure X1,f/4	2	6
get_value_x	get_value X1,X2	1	2
get_value_y	get_value Y1,X2	1	3
get_variable_x	get_variable X1,X2	1	2
get_variable_y	get_variable Y1,X2	1	3
increment	increment X1,X2	1	2
jump	jump _1234	1	2/3
mod	mod X1,X2,X3	1	3
mod_constant	mod_constant X1,X2,15	2	6
multiply	multiply X1,X2,X3	1	3
multiply_constant	multiply_const X1,X2,15	2	6
proceed	proceed	1	1

Table B-1: Lcode Instruction Set Formats (notes 1-4 in text)

opcode	assembly instance	words	bytes
put_constant	put_constant X1,-44	2	6
put_list	put_list X1	1	2
put_nil	put_nil X1	1	2
put_structure	put_structure X1,f/4	2	6
put_unsafe_int_x	put_unsafe_int X1	1	2
put_unsafe_int_y	put_unsafe_int Y1	1	2
put_unsafe_value_y	put_unsafe_value Y1,X2	1	3
put_value_x	put_value X1,X2	1	2
put_value_y	put_value Y1,X2	1	3
put_variable_x	put_variable X1,X2	1	2
put_variable_y	put_variable Y1,X2	1	3
retry	retry _1234	1	2/3
retry_me_else	retry_me_else _1234	1	2/3
stop	stop	1	1
subtract	subtract X1,X2,X3	1	3
subtract_constant	subtract_const X1,X2,15	2	6
switch_constant[3]	switch_constant 8	1+2	2+8
switch_structure[3]	switch_structure 8	1+2	2+8
switch_term	switch_term _12,fail,_34	1/2	4/7
trust	trust _1234	1	2/3
trust_me_else	trust_me_else fail[4]	1	1
try	try 8,_1234	1	3/4
try_me_else	try_me_else 8,_1234	1	3/4
unify_constant	unify_constant -44	2	5
unify_local_value_x	unify_local_value_x X1	1	2
unify_local_value_y	unify_local_value_y Y1	1	2
unify_nil	unify_nil	1	1
unify_value_x	unify_value_x X1	1	2
unify_value_y	unify_value_y Y1	1	2
unify_variable_x	unify_variable_x X1	1	2
unify_variable_y	unify_variable_y Y1	1	2
unify_void	unify_void 8	1	2

Table B-1: Lcode Instruction Set Formats - *continued*

opcode	% instr	data bytes	instr bytes	% weight
add	0.026	0.00	3	0.01
add_constant	0.014	0.00	6	0.01
allocate	3.491	16.00	2	5.27
call	3.347	0.00	3	0.84
comp_x	0.151	1.35	3	0.05
comp_y	0.114	6.04	4	0.12
cond_x	1.104	1.10	2	0.23
cond_y	0.416	7.20	3	0.29
cut	0.859	14.88	1	1.18
cutd	0.247	12.53	2	0.30
cut_strong	0.628	6.84	1	0.43
deallocate	1.670	8.00	1	1.26
decrement	0.047	0.00	2	0.01
divide_constant	0.026	0.00	6	0.01
escape[1]	1.119	23.62	2	2.60
execute	3.037	0.00	3	0.76
failure[2]	6.009	44.59	0	22.49
get_atom[3]	1.823	4.40	6	1.49
get_integer[3]	0.223	4.52	6	0.18
get_list	5.117	2.64	2	1.88
get_nil	0.500	3.20	2	0.20
get_structure	6.437	5.83	6	6.52
get_value_x	1.953	11.17	2	2.13
get_value_y	0.187	13.21	3	0.25
get_variable_x	0.560	0.00	2	0.09
get_variable_y	6.051	4.00	3	3.56
increment	0.234	0.00	2	0.04
jump	0.359	0.00	2	0.06
proceed	2.447	0.00	1	0.21
put_atom	0.254	0.00	6	0.13
put_integer	0.107	0.00	6	0.05
put_list	0.531	0.00	2	0.09
put_nil	0.049	0.00	2	0.01

Table B-2: Lcode Instruction Reference Characteristics (notes 1-7 in text)

type	% instr	data bytes	instr bytes	% weight
put_value_x	2.647	0.00	2	0.44
put_value_y	6.878	4.00	3	4.04
put_structure	0.383	4.00	6	0.32
put_unsafe_integer_x	0.277	0.40	2	0.06
put_unsafe_integer_y	0.096	3.04	2	0.05
put_unsafe_value_y	1.617	8.61	3	1.57
put_variable_x	0.372	4.00	2	0.19
put_variable_y	2.475	4.00	3	1.45
retry	0.768	4.00	2	0.39
retry_me_else	2.133	4.00	2	1.07
switch_constant	0.867	0.61	10	0.75
switch_structure	0.914	4.72	10	1.12
switch_term	3.657	0.51	4	1.36
trust	0.267	7.93	2	0.22
trust_me_else	2.842	8.00	1	2.15
try	0.330	44.17	3	1.34
try_me_else	4.414	42.64	3	16.69
unify_atom	0.890	5.12	5	0.71
unify_integer	0.092	4.20	5	0.07
unify_nil	0.051	3.37	1	0.03
unify_value_x[4]	0.905	26.86	2	2.11
unify_value_y	0.042	6.74	2	0.05
unify_variable_x	6.257	4.00	2	3.15
unify_variable_y	2.627	8.00	2	2.20
unify_void	3.099	0.00	2	0.52
copy_atom[5]	0.396	4.00	5	0.30
copy_integer	0.270	4.00	5	0.20
copy_local_value_x[6]	0.230	6.33	2	0.18
copy_local_value_y	0.103	11.89	2	0.11
copy_nil	0.398	4.00	1	0.17
copy_value_x[7]	1.928	5.90	2	1.26
copy_value_y	0.912	10.65	2	0.94
copy_variable_x	1.794	4.00	2	0.90
copy_variable_y	1.110	8.00	2	0.93
copy_void	0.302	5.24	2	0.19

Table B-2: Lcode Instruction Reference Characteristics - *continued*

type	% instr	data bytes	instr bytes	% weight
procedure control	12.59	14.18	1.80	24.31
failure	6.36	38.24		21.32
head matching	20.94	6.75	3.44	13.91
structure matching	19.97	6.01	2.44	12.83
clause control	14.11	4.80	2.20	9.35
goal matching	14.15	2.45	3.25	8.77
unification	3.11	14.36		3.54
escape	1.49	16.66	2.00	3.00
indexing	7.55	3.78	2.75	2.89
arithmetic	0.39	0.00	3.80	0.09

Table B-3:   Lcode Characteristics by Type

Appendix C

Local Memory Management Algorithms

In this appendix, the management algorithms for the choice point buffer, copyback stack buffer, and copyback environment stack (E-stack) buffer are presented. Note that the algorithms are written for clarity, not optimality. Buffer management must often be performed *within* normal instruction semantics. For instance, in Figure C-2, **allocate** resets **E** and **TOS**, manages the buffer, and then writes the new environment. This last portion of the instruction semantics is not included in the algorithm and can be found in Tick [84].

```
action is
        reference i(B):
                if (valid and BufferSize≤i)
                        access buffer[i];
                else
                        access memory[B+i];
        try n:
        try_me_else n:
                if (valid)
                        memory[B..B+m] = buffer[0..m];
                else    valid = 1;
                if (n > BufferSize)
                        m = BufferSize;
                else    m = n;
        cut:
        trust:
        trust_me_else:
                valid = 0;
```

Figure C-1: Choice Point Buffer Management

---

action is
    reference to a:
        if (valid and Z≤a and a≤A)
            access buffer[a];
            if (write) dirty[a] = 1;
        else
            access memory[a];

deallocate:
    CP = CP(E);
    E = E(E);
    reset( );

cut:
    B = B(E);
    if nondeterminate B = B(B);
    HB = HB(B);
    reset( );

trust:
trust_me_else:
    B = B(B);
    HB = HB(B);
    reset( );

allocate n:
    E = TOS += n+4;
    set(n+4);

try n:
try_me_else n:
    B = TOS += n+4;
    set(n+4);

Figure C-2:   Stack Buffer Management

```
set(n):
     if (n>BufferSize)
           if valid
                 valid = 0;
                 copyback(A-Z+4);
     else
           if (valid)
                 InUse = A-Z+4;
                 LeftOver = BufferSize - InUse;
                 d = n - LeftOver;
                 if (d>0)
                       copyback(d);
                       Z += d;
                 A = TOS;
           else
                 valid = 1;
                 A = TOS;
                 Z = A-n;

reset( ):
     if (E>B)
           TOS = E;
     else
           TOS = B;
     valid = TOS≥Z;
     if (valid)
           dirty[Z..Z-TOS+A+4] = 0;
           A = TOS;
     else
           dirty[Z..A+4] = 0;

copyback(d):
     for (i=Z;i<Z+d;i+=4)
           if (dirty[i])
                 dirty[i] = 0;
                 memory[i] = buffer[i];
```

Figure C-3: Stack Buffer Management Support

```
action is
      reference to a:
            if (valid and Z≤a and a≤A)
                  access buffer[a];
                  if (write) dirty[a] = 1;
            else
                  access memory[a];
      deallocate:
            CP = CP(E);
            E = E(E);
            reset();
      cut:
            B = B(E);
            if nondeterminate B = B(B);
            HB = HB(B);
            reset();
      trust:
      trust_me_else:
            B̄ = B̄(B);
            HB = HB(B);
            reset();
      allocate n:
            E = TOS += n+4;
            set(n+4);
```

```
reset():
      if (E>C)
            TOS = E;
      else
            TOS = C;
      valid = TOS≥Z;
      if (valid)
            dirty[Z..Z-TOS+A+4] = 0;
            A = TOS;
      else
            dirty[Z..A+4] = 0;
```

Figure C-4: E-Stack Buffer Management

References

1. S. Abe, T. Bandoh, S. Yamaguchi, K. Kurosawa, K. Kiriyama. High Performance Integrated Prolog Processor IPP. 14th Annual International Symposium on Computer Architecture, IEEE Computer Society, June, 1987, pp. 100-107.

2. D. B. Alpert. *Memory Hierarchies for Directly Executed Language Microprocessors*. Ph.D. Th., Stanford University, June 1984. also available as Technical Report CSL-TR-84-260.

3. J. Archibald. High Performance Cache Coherence Protocols For Shared-Bus Multiprocessors. Technical Report 86-06-02, University of Washington, Seattle, WA 98195, June, 1986.

4. Y. Asakawa, H. Komatsu, T. Kurokawa, N. Tamura. A Very Fast Prolog Compiler on Multiple Architectures. Fall Joint Computer Conference, ACM and IEEE Computer Society, November, 1986.

5. C. Barney. "This New Design Outruns Vectorizing Minisupers". *Electronics* (April 30 1987), 65.

6. P. Bitar and A. M. Despain. Multiprocessor Cache Synchronization. 13th Annual International Symposium on Computer Architecture, IEEE Computer Society, June, 1986, pp. 424-433.

7. P. Bitar. personal communication. December 1986.

8. G. Borriello, A. Cherenson, P. B. Danzig, and M. Nelson. RISCs or CISCs for Prolog: A Case Study. Second International Conference on Architectural Support for Programming Languages and Operating Systems (ASPLOS II), IEEE Computer Society, October, 1987.

9. D. L. Bowen, L. M. Byrd and W. F. Clocksin. A Portable Prolog Compiler. Logic Programming Workshop '83, Universidade Nova de Lisboa, June, 1983, pp. 74-83.

10. D. L. Bowen. NIP: New Implementation of Prolog. Dept. of Artificial Intelligence, University of Edinburgh, May, 1984. unpublished.

11. R. Butler, E. L. Lusk, R. Olson, and R. A. Overbeek. ANLWAM: A Parallel Implementation of the Warren Abstract Machine. Argonne National Laboratory, Argonne, IL 60439, 1986.

12. L. Byrd, F. C. N. Pereira, and D. H. D. Warren. A Guide to Version 3 of DEC-10 PROLOG. 19, Dept. of Artificial Intelligence, University of Edinburgh, July, 1980.

13. L. Byrd. personal communication. 1985.

14. M. Carlsson. Compilation for Tricia and its Abstract Machine. Technical Report 35, UPMAIL, Uppsala University, September, 1986.

15. L. M. Censier and P. Feautrier. "A New Solution to Coherence Problems in Multicache Systems". *IEEE Transactions on Computers C-27*, 12 (December 1978), 1112-1118.

16. K. L. Clark and S. Gregory. "Notes on the Implementation of PARLOG". *Journal of Logic Programming 2*, 1 (April 1985).

17. S. K. Debray. Efficient Register Allocation for Temporary Variables in the Warren Prolog Engine. Research Paper 85/10, Department of Computer Science, SUNY at Stony Brook, April, 1985.

18. D. DeGroot. Restricted And-Parallelism. International Conference on Fifth Generation Computer Systems, November, 1984, pp. 471-478.

19. D. R. Ditzel and H. R. McLellan. Register Allocation for Free: The C Machine Stack Cache. Symposium on Architectural Support for Programming Languages and Operating Systems, March, 1982, pp. 48-56.

20. T. P. Dobry, Y. N. Patt, and A. M. Despain. Design Decisions Influencing the Microarchitecture for a Prolog Machine. The Seventeenth Annual Microprogramming Workshop, IEEE Computer Society, October, 1984, pp. 217-231.

21. T. P. Dobry, A. M. Despain, and Y. N. Patt. Performance Studies of a Prolog Machine Architecture. 12th Annual International Symposium on Computer Architecture, IEEE Computer Society, December, 1985, pp. 180-190.

22. T. P. Dobry. A Coprocessor for AI: LISP, Prolog and Data Bases. Proceedings of Spring Compcon '87, IEEE Computer Society, February, 1987, pp. 396-402.

23. T. P. Dobry. *A High Performance Architecture for Prolog*. Kluwer Academic Publishers, Norwell, MA 02061, 1988.

24. B. Fagin and T. P. Dobry. The Berkeley PLM Instruction Set: An Instruction Set for Prolog. Research Report UCB/CSD 86/257, Computer Science Division, University of California at Berkeley, September, 1985.

25. Introduction to the CLIPPER Architecture. Fairchild Camera and Instrument Corp., Palo Alto CA 94304.

26. M. J. Flynn and L. W. Hoevel. A Theory of Interpretive Architectures: Ideal Language Machines. Research Paper 170, Stanford Electronics Laboratory, Stanford University, Stanford, CA 94305, 1979.

27. M. J. Flynn and L. W. Hoevel. "Measures of Ideal Execution Architectures". *IBM Journal of Research and Development 28*, 4 (July 1984), 356-369.

28. M. J. Flynn with G. E. Rossmann and A. J. Smith. *Studies in Processor Design.* , 1987. in preparation.

29. R. P. Gabriel. *Performance and Evaluation of Lisp Systems.* MIT Press, Cambridge MA, 1985. also available from Stanford University Computer Science Dept. as Research Paper 111.

30. J. Gabriel, T. G. Lindholm, E. L. Lusk, and R. A. Overbeek. A Tutorial on the Warren Abstract Machine for Computational Logic. Research Paper ANL-84-84, Argonne National Laboratory, Argonne, IL 60439, June, 1985.

31. J. Gee, S. W. Melvin, Y. N. Patt. Advantages of Implementing Prolog by Microprogramming a Host General Purpose Computer. Fourth International Conference on Logic Programming, University of Melborne, May, 1987.

32. D. H. Gibson. Considerations in Block-Oriented Systems Design. AFIPS Conference Proceedings, Spring Joint Computer Conference, April, 1967, pp. 75-80.

33. A. Gupta, C. Forgy, A. Newell, and R. Wedig. Parallel Algorithms and Architectures for Rule-Based Systems. 13th Annual International Symposium on Computer Architecture, IEEE Computer Society, June, 1986, pp. 28-37.

34. M. V. Hermenegildo. An Abstract Machine for the Restricted AND-Parallel Execution of Logic Programs. Third International Conference on Logic Programming, Imperial College, July, 1986, pp. 25-39.

35. M. V. Hermenegildo. *Restricted AND-Parallel Prolog and its Architecture.* Kluwer Academic Publishers, Norwell, MA 02061, 1987.

36. M. V. Hermenegildo and E. Tick. Performance Evaluation of the RAP-WAM Restricted AND-Parallel Architecture on Shared Memory Multiprocessors. Technical Report PP-085-87, Microelectronics and Computer Technology Corporation (MCC), Austin, TX 78759, March, 1987.

37. M. V. Hermenegildo. Relating Goal Scheduling, Precedence, and Memory Management in AND-Parallel Execution of Logic Programs. Proceedings of the Fourth International Conference on Logic Programming, May, 1987.

38. M. D. Hill and A. J. Smith. Experimental Evaluation of On-Chip Microprocessor Cache Memories. 11th Annual International Symposium on Computer Architecture, IEEE Computer Society, 1984, pp. 158-166.

39. J. C. Huck. *Comparative Analysis of Computer Architectures.* Ph.D. Th., Stanford University, March 1983. also available as Technical Report CSL-TR-83-243.

40. S. C. Johnson. YACC - Yet Another Compiler Compiler. Unix Programmer's Manual.

41. Y. Kaneda. Sequential PROLOG Machine PEK Architecture and Software System. International Workshop on High-Level Computer Architecture, The University of Maryland, May, 1984, pp. 4.1-4.6.

42. M. G. H. Katevenis. *Reduced Instruction Set Computer Architectures for VLSI.* Ph.D. Th., Computer Science Division (EECS), University of California Berkeley, October 1983.

43. L. Kleinrock. *Queueing Systems, Volume 1: Theory.* John Wiley & Sons, 1975.

44. R. A. Kowalski. Predicate Logic as a Programming Language. Information Processing 74, IFIP Congress, August, 1974, pp. 569-574.

45. R. A. Kowalski. *Logic for Problem Solving.* North Holland, 1979.

46. P. Kursawe. How To Invent A Prolog Machine. Third International Conference on Logic Programming, Imperial College, July, 1986, pp. 134-148.

47. M. E. Lesk and E. Schmidt. LEX - Lexical Analyzer Generator. Unix Programmer's Manual.

48. J. W. Lloyd. *Logic Programming.* Springer-Verlag, 1984.

49. V. W. K. Mak. A Survey of Concurrent Architectures. Technical Report CSL-TR-86-307, Computer Systems Laboratory, Stanford University, Stanford, CA 94305, September, 1986.

50. H. Matsumoto. "A Static Analysis of Prolog Programs". *SIGPLAN Notices 20,* 10 (October 1985), 48-59.

51. J. McCarthy. *Lisp 1.5 Programmer's Manual.* MIT Press, Cambridge MA., 1965.

52. C. S. Mellish. An Alternative to Structure-Sharing In the Implementation of a Prolog Interpreter. In *Logic Programming,* K. L. Clark and S.-A. Tarnlund, Ed., Academic Press, 1982, pp. 99-106.

53. C. L. Mitchell. *Processor Architecture and Cache Performance.* Ph.D. Th., Stanford University, June 1986. also available as Technical Report CSL-TR-86-296.

54. J. M. Mulder and E. Tick. A Performance Comparison Between PLM and an MC68020 Prolog Processor. Fourth International Conference on Logic Programming, University of Melborne, May, 1987.

55. J. M. Mulder. *Tradeoffs in Processor-Architecture and Data-Buffer Design.* Ph.D. Th., Stanford University, 1987.

56. H. Nakashima and K. Nakajima. Hardware Architecture of the Sequential Inference Machine: PSI-II. 1987 International Symposium on Logic Programming, IEEE Computer Society, August, 1987.

57. R. Nakazaki, et. al. Design of a High-speed Prolog Machine (HPM). 12th Annual International Symposium on Computer Architecture, IEEE Computer Society, June, 1985, pp. 191-197.

58. H. Nishikawa, M. Yokota, A Yamamoto, K. Taki, S. Uchida. The Personal Sequential Inference Machine (PSI): Its Design Philosophy and Machine Architecture. Logic Programming Workshop '83, Universidade Nova de Lisboa, June, 1983, pp. 53-73.

59. R. A. O'Keefe. "Prolog Compared With Lisp?". *SIGPLAN Notices 18*, 5 (May 1983), 46-56. Also available from Edinburgh as Research Report 180.

60. R. Onai, H. Shimuzu, K. Masuda, and M. Aso. "Analysis of Sequential Prolog Programs". *Journal of Logic Programming 3*, 2 (July 1986), 119-141.

61. D. A. Patterson and C. H. Sequin. RISC I: A Reduced Instruction Set VLSI Computer. 8th Annual International Symposium on Computer Architecture, IEEE Computer Society, May, 1981, pp. 443-458.

62. . Quintus Prolog User's Guide and Reference Manual - Version 6. Quintus Computer Systems Inc., Mountain View CA 94041.

63. G. Radin. "The 801 Minicomputer". *IBM Journal of Research and Development 27* (May 1983), 237-246.

64. M. Ratcliffe and P. Robert. The Static Analysis of Prolog Programs. CA-11, ECRC, October, 1985.

65. R. Rau. Sequential Prefetch Strategies For Instructions and Data. Research Paper 131, Digital Systems Laboratory, Stanford University, Stanford, CA 94305, 1977.

66. J. A. Robinson. "A Machine-Oriented Logic Based on the Resolution Principle". *Journal of the ACM 12* (1965), 23-41.

67. J. A. Robinson. *Logic: Form and Function.* North-Holland, 1979.

68. M. L. Ross and A. G. McMahon. Memory Behaviour of a Sequential Prolog Interpreter. Research Paper 84/6, Dept of Computing, Royal Melbourne Institute of Technology, 1984.

69. M. L. Ross and K. Ramamohanarao. Paging Strategy for Prolog Based on Dynamic Virtual Memory. Technical Report 86/8, Dept of Computing, Royal Melbourne Institute of Technology, 1986.

70. P. Roussel. Prolog: Manuel de Reference et d'Utilisation. University d'Aix-Marseille, Groupe de IA, Marseille, France, 1975.

71. K. Seo and T. Yokota. Pegasus: A RISC Processor For High-Performance Execution of Prolog Programs. International Conference on Very Large Scale Integration, IFIP Congress, August, 1987. submitted for publication.

72. E. Y. Shapiro. A Subset of Concurrent Prolog and Its Interpreter. TR-003, ICOT, Minato-ku Tokyo 108, Japan, January, 1983.

73. K. Shen. An Investigation of the Argonne Model of OR-Parallel Prolog. Master Th., University of Manchester,November 1986.

74. A. J. Smith. "A Comparative Study of Set Associative Memory Mapping Algorithms and Their Use for Cache and Main Memory". *IEEE Transactions on Software Engineering SE-4*, 2 (March 1978), 121-130.

75. A. J. Smith. "Cache Memories". *Computing Surveys* (September 1982), 473-530.

76. J. E. Smith and J. R. Goodman. A Study of Instruction Cache Organizations and Replacement Policies. 10th Annual International Symposium on Computer Architecture, IEEE Computer Society, June, 1983, pp. 132-137.

77. G. L. Steele Jr.. *Common Lisp*. Digital Press, 1984.

78. L. Sterling and E. Shapiro. *The Art of Prolog*. The MIT Press, 1986.

79. W. D. Strecker. Cache memories for PDP-11 Family Computers. 3rd Annual International Symposium on Computer Architecture, IEEE Computer Society, January, 1976, pp. 155-158.

80. Symbolics 3600 Technical Summary. Symbolics Inc., Cambridge, MA.

81. G. S. Taylor, P. N. Hilfinger, J. R. Larus, D. A. Patterson, and B. G. Zorn. Evaluation of the SPUR Lisp Architecture. 13th Annual International Symposium on Computer Architecture, IEEE Computer Society, June, 1986, pp. 444-452.

82. E. Tick. Prolog Memory-Referencing Behavior. Technical Report CSL-TR-85-281, Computer Systems Laboratory, Stanford University, Stanford, CA 94305, September, 1985.

83. E. Tick. Memory Performance of Lisp and Prolog Programs. Third International Conference on Logic Programming, Imperial College, July, 1986, pp. 642-649. also available as Stanford University Technical Report CSL-TR-86-291.

84. E. Tick. A Prolog Emulator. Technical Note CSL-TN-87-324, Computer Systems Laboratory, Stanford University, Stanford, CA 94305, May, 1987.

85. E. Tick. A Comparison Between the WAM and DEC-10 Prolog Architectures. Technical Note CSL-TN-87-323, Computer Systems Laboratory, Stanford University, Stanford, CA 94305, May, 1987.

86. H. Touati and A. Despain. An Empirical Study of the Warren Abstract Machine. 1987 International Symposium on Logic Programming, IEEE Computer Society, August, 1987.

87. A. K. Turk. Compiler Optimizations for the WAM. Third International Conference on Logic Programming, Imperial College, July, 1986, pp. 657-662.

88. K. Ueda. Guarded Horn Clauses. Technical Report TR-103, ICOT, Minato-ku Tokyo 108, Japan, June, 1985.

89. P. Van Roy. A Prolog Compiler for the PLM. Master Th., University of California at Berkeley,August 1984. also available as Technical Report UCB/CSD 84/203.

90. P. Van Roy and B. Demoen. Improving the Execution Speed of Compiled Prolog with Modes, Clause Selection, and Determinism. TAPSOFT '87: Joint Conference on Theory and Practice of Software Development, March, 1987.

91. S. Wakefield. *Studies in Execution Architectures*. Ph.D. Th., Stanford University, December 1982. also available as Technical Report CSL-TR-83-237.

92. D. H. D. Warren and L. M. Pereira. Prolog - The Language and its Implementation Compared with Lisp. Symposium on AI and Programming Languages, ACM, August, 1977, pp. .

93. D. H. D. Warren. *Applied Logic — Its Use and Implementation as Programming Tool*. Ph.D. Th., University of Edinburgh, 1977. also available as SRI Technical Note 290.

94. D. H. D. Warren. An Improved Prolog Implementation which Optimises Tail Recursion. Research Paper 156, Dept. of Artificial Intelligence, University of Edinburgh, 1980.

95. D. H. D. Warren and F. C. N. Pereira. An Efficient, Easily Adaptable System For Interpreting Natural Language Queries. Research Paper 155, Dept. of Artificial Intelligence, University of Edinburgh, February, 1981.

96. D. H. D. Warren. An Abstract Prolog Instruction Set. Technical Report 309, Artificial Intelligence Center, SRI International, 1983.

97. D. H. D. Warren. Prolog Engine. Artificial Intelligence Center, SRI International, April, 1983. unpublished draft.

98. P. F. Wilk. Prolog Benchmarking. Research Paper 111, Dept. of Artificial Intelligence, University of Edinburgh, December, 1983.

99. A. Wolfe and B. Cole. "The World's Fastest Microprocessor". *Electronics* (March 19 1987), 61.

100. D. Znidarsic. personal communication. March 1987.

Index